GENESIS–RUTH

Morning Conversations

on the Creation of a People and Place

Days 1–236 of your
devotional journey through
the Old Testament with

JON R. ROEBUCK

© 2021

Published in the United States by Nurturing Faith, Macon, GA.
Nurturing Faith is a book imprint of Good Faith Media (goodfaithmedia.org).
Library of Congress Cataloging-in-Publication Data is available.

ISBN: 978-1-63528-163-7

All rights reserved. Printed in the United States of America.

Scripture quotations taken from the (NASB®) New American Standard Bible®, Copyright © 1960, 1971, 1977, 1995, 2020 by The Lockman Foundation. Used by permission. All rights reserved. www.lockman.org

Scripture quotations marked (NLT) are taken from the Holy Bible, New Living Translation, copyright ©1996, 2004, 2015 by Tyndale House Foundation. Used by permission of Tyndale House Publishers, Carol Stream, Illinois 60188. All rights reserved.

Scripture quotations marked (NIV) are taken from the Holy Bible, New International Version®, NIV®. Copyright © 1973, 1978, 1984, 2011 by Biblica, Inc.™ Used by permission of Zondervan. All rights reserved worldwide. www.zondervan.com The "NIV" and "New International Version" are trademarks registered in the United States Patent and Trademark Office by Biblica, Inc.™

Dedication

This book is dedicated to my parents, Floyd and Ann Roebuck, whose prayerful support, gentle encouragement, and unwavering love have offered me a lifetime of strength, wisdom, and boundless joy.

Contents

Preface 1

Genesis 3
    Days 1 through 50

Exodus 53
    Days 51 through 90

Leviticus 93
    Days 91 through 117

Numbers 120
    Days 118 through 153

Joshua 190
    Days 188 through 211

Judges 214
    Days 212 through 232

Ruth 235
    Days 233 through 236

Preface

In 2013, I published a devotional book titled, *Morning Conversations*. The book contains a brief devotional thought drawn from every chapter of the New Testament... 260 in all. It was written in response to a congregant who once called to ask for a recommendation on some devotional reading material. I informed him that I was practicing a discipline of writing a devotional thought from a New Testament chapter each morning. When asked if he was interested in reading it, he replied, "That sounds great, I'd love to read what you have written." So, I began to e-mail my thoughts to him each morning. With my permission, he started passing it along to others... first to his father and then to several other friends. The feedback was very positive. The thought occurred to me that members of my own family, friends, and a few church members might enjoy reading these devotionals as well. Word spread and soon, I found myself sending my morning devotional thoughts to more than 200 people each day. After I wrote my way through the Gospels, I kept right on writing. I finally decided to keep going until I covered the entire New Testament. Eventually, the collected thoughts made their way into book form.

A few years later the thought occurred to me, "What if I could write a devotional thought from every chapter of the Old Testament?" The thought was daunting, overwhelming, and exhausting. It was also exciting to imagine. There are 929 chapters in the Old Testament. To write a thought from each chapter would literally take years... and it did. What you now hold in your hand is the result of more than 3½ years of work. I decided to write a chapter every weekday, starting sometime in the summer of 2016. Just before Christmas of 2019, I typed my final thoughts from the book of Malachi. It was quite a journey to take... all the way from the days of creation to the post-exilic period. I walked with characters like Jacob, Moses, David, Jeremiah, and Ezekiel. I learned from prophets, politicians, and poets. I wandered in the wilderness and crossed the Jordan too many times to count. I read, reflected, and wrote. The journey was well worth the effort, and I hope that some of my thoughts will help you along your journey as well.

In any such undertaking, those of us who write, do so armed with wisdom, commentary, and insights gleaned from a lifetime of study and influence. On occasion as I wrote these devotions, to remind myself of past events and stories, I referenced articles drawn from Google searches and other internet inquiries. Such references, if quoted directly, are cited within the text. Other background material on various books, passages, and characters has been drawn from multiple sources, even including old Seminary notes! I am indebted to several sources that prompted my memory, aided in my research, and inspired my thinking. In particular, I want to commend the work contained in three important works, *The Broadman Bible Commentary* (Allen, Clifton J. 1969. Nashville, Tennessee: Broadman Press Vol. 1-8), *The Nelson Study Bible* (1997 Nashville, Tennessee: Thomas Nelson Publishers), and *Moody Bible Commentary* (Rydelnik, Michael & Vanlaningham, Michael 2014. Chicago, Illinois: Moody Publishers). I referred to these sources often for both clarity and historical insight. But as you will discover, most of what is presented in each day's devotion is simply my personal reflection on the text, hopefully inspired through the work of the Spirit, and my musings on how to best apply the wisdom of God's word to daily life.

Morning Conversations on the Creation of a People and Place is the first volume of a set that follows the natural order of the Old Testament canon, and spans the Biblical narrative from the opening chapter of Genesis to the end of the book of Ruth.

Morning Conversations on the Rise and Fall of Kings and Kingdoms continues the orderly progression, spanning the books of 1 Samuel through Esther.

Morning Conversations on the Wisdom of the Ages covers all five books of wisdom literature from Job to the Song of Solomon.

Morning Conversations on the Prophetic Word wraps up the Old Testament with a look at the books of prophecy, covering both the Major and Minor prophets, Isaiah through Malachi.

Additionally, the previously published collection of devotional thoughts from the New Testament, *Morning Conversations*, will be reformatted and renamed *Morning Conversations on the New Testament*, the final volume of this collection.

As you read through these volumes, my hope is that you will take the time, not to simply read what I have written, but to reflect with me on what the ancients have written. Let me challenge you each morning to take a moment to read the suggested focus chapter from a trusted translation before you dive into my words. Read and reflect. As you make your way through this book, and those that will follow, you will discover a lot of my life story written into these pages. But more importantly, I hope you will discover a lot about God's story… the one carefully crafted and persevered for you. For in hearing God's story, you will hear the echoing refrain of God's desire to know you, to love you, and to redeem you. Welcome to the conversation.

Day 1 — Genesis 1: The Image of God

> "God created man in His own image, in the image of God He created him; male and female He created them." Genesis 1:27 (NASB)

Observation
There is a lot going on in this single verse. First, you have Creator God bringing order to what was once a "formless void." At the height of this creative work, God brings humankind into existence, made in God's own likeness. The power of God is demonstrated throughout the chapter as God simply "speaks" all things into being. Second, God chooses to make humankind in God's image. Something about who we are, how we think, and perhaps even how we look, somehow reflects the image of our Father. Third, notice the instantaneous creation of both male and female. From the beginning, the image of God is placed in both sexes. There is no second-class citizenship given, but rather an equality of creation.

Application
What does it mean to be made in the image of God? First, there is a sense that we possess certain qualities that God possesses. We can think, reason, exercise limited dominion, experience relationship, communicate, love, and re-create. God has given us the ability to be like God in many ways, though certainly never equal. God is Creator, we are still the creations. But here's a second thought. In the ancient Hebrew texts, the verse could be translated as… "God created man as His image" rather than using the word, "in His image." That's different. Of all things created, humankind alone is called upon to bear the image of God before the nations. Think about it. What the world must know of God, it should begin to learn from each of us. What a challenge… Are we like our Father? Do we love unselfishly, share abundantly, forgive extravagantly, treat others patiently? When people see us, do they see God? Is God's image clearly stamped on each of us? Like a coin minted with the image of one of our founding fathers, the image of God should be deeply imprinted on us. Everything about us should display a little of what God is like. I may not like the pressure of thinking that someone's only impression of God is tied to their impression of me, but it is a responsibility that I must shoulder. How well will you bear God's image today? It's something to think about.

Prayer
God, may I begin to reflect your image more clearly to all those that you bring into my world. Amen.

Day 2 — Genesis 2: The importance of Sabbath

> "Then God blessed the seventh day and sanctified it, because in it He rested from all His work which God had created and made." Genesis 2:3 (NASB)

Observation
At the end of the first creation account, God "sanctifies" the seventh day, or "sets it apart" as a day for rest and reflection. Why did God need to rest? Does God get tired? Was God exhausted by all that creative effort? Does God gets worn out like we do? Such questions fly in the face of our view of an all-powerful God "who neither slumbers nor sleeps" (Psalm 121:4 NIV). I think the problem is one of a basic Biblical understanding of this verse. It is not that God needs to rest, but that God takes the time to enjoy what has been created. God "pauses" long enough revel in the joy that creation has brought. Another key point to note is the setting aside of such a day for the purpose of rest, reflection, and interaction with creator God.

Application
Maybe our view of Sunday should be a bit different from how it often is. On our best days, we think of Sunday as a day of rest, but we seldom rest. We think of Sunday as being a special day, but we seldom treat it as such. In fact, once we get church out of the way, we usually use the day just like any other day of the week. How should we view this seventh day of our week? God blessed it and set it aside. Yes, something about the day should be really different from all the other days of our week. God intends for it to be a day of reflection, of rest, of different living so that God is honored.

This verse is particularly challenging in our day and age where a third of the working population goes to work on Sunday. Sunday is no longer the Sabbath day of rest that it once was. In fact, for many businesses it's the biggest retail day of the week. Let's steer away from legalism for a moment. Sabbath observance does not have to be on Sunday… but it is to be observed as a part of our weekly routine. Whether it is Sunday or some other day, we need to observe a Sabbath. Can we slow down long enough to reflect on God's grace? Can we set aside some time to enter God's presence? Can we alter the pace so that we can find refreshment each week? If we are not careful, our endless toil will rob of us of discovering the importance of connecting with God. We need a day to rest, reflect, and interact with God. It will not happen by accident. Sabbath rest must be an intentional act on our part.

Prayer
Thank you, God, for creating a day of rest and reflection. May I pause long enough today to sit with you to enjoy your creation. Amen.

Day 3 — Genesis 3: "Houston, We Have a Problem..."

> "Then the eyes of both of them were opened, and they knew that they were naked; and they sewed fig leaves together and made themselves loin coverings." Genesis 3:7 (NASB)

Observation

Chapter 3 of Genesis is one of the most defining chapters in all of scripture. This chapter describes the "Fall" of humanity. It is in this chapter that sinful disobedience first appears and begins to take its toll. The serpent... the shrewdest of all creatures... begins to offer his deceitful words to Eve. He begins to twist the words of God in her mind. He introduces the idea that it's okay to disobey God. He gets her to play with the possibilities. "You surely will not die! For God knows that on the day you eat from it your eyes will be opened, and you will become like God, knowing good and evil" (Genesis 3:4-5 NASB) And having listened to his deceitful words, she and Adam take a bite of the forbidden fruit and everything changes... the relationship with Holy God is forever redefined. It will not be until the "Second Adam" appears, even Jesus our Lord, that sin's divide is spanned once again.

Application

The text indicates that at the moment they ate the forbidden fruit, "their eyes were opened, and they knew they were naked." The problem was not that they suddenly saw each other's nakedness, but what they began to see *in* each other. They began to see each other differently. They saw in one another, not the beauty of God's intention for their lives, but the ugliness caused by sin. What they attempted to cover up was not just physical attribute, but what they no longer loved about each other.

There is a timeless lesson in their story. It is the "cause and effect" of disobedience. Somewhere along the way, a small voice begins to whisper in our ear, "You don't really have to take God seriously. You don't have to obey God's commands. God is just trying to limit your life and steal your joy." We begin to play with the possibilities of disobeying God. At such a moment we begin to look at ourselves differently. Rather than see ourselves as beautiful and innocent children of God, we see guilt, and shame, and brokenness. We long for some "fig leaf" to hide our "naked shame" from both God and ourselves. We no longer like the image reflected in our own mirror.

But there is hope. We no longer have to hide from God behind the branches of our remorse. God offers the cleansing, healing, forgiving grace of Jesus Christ who takes away the sins of the world. Through the lens of Christ's love, God sees us differently. We are beloved, washed, and welcomed in God's presence.

Prayer

Thank you, God, for grace that restores, heals, and redeems. Amen.

Day 4 — Genesis 4: My Brother's Keeper

> "Then the LORD said to Cain, "Where is Abel your brother?" And he said, "I do not know. Am I my brother's keeper?" Genesis 4:9 (NASB)

Observation

Genesis 4 tells the story of the first two sons of Adam and Eve. Their names were Cain and Abel. In the course of time, as both present offerings before the Lord, Abel's offering is accepted by God while Cain's is not. It leads to bitter jealousy and Cain murders his brother. God questions Cain about what he has done, and Cain tries to hide his sin and cover his guilt by saying that he doesn't know. He claims that he is not his brother's keeper. The passage has much to say about the power of jealousy to end relationships and even lives. It also speaks to the problem of trying to hide our sins before God. We only add to our sinfulness when we attempt to deceive the God who cannot be deceived.

Application

Allow me to chase a slightly different thought this morning. This thought of being my brother's keeper. Cain, in his sinfulness, asked the Lord in a rather impudent fashion if he was responsible for his brother's whereabouts. The truth is that he was, as we our for ours. Something about the Christian life must move us beyond selfish thinking. Our lives must be focused on more than just ourselves or our needs. As the people of God, we really are responsible for others. God has given us the responsibility to bear God's image, which forces us to act in ways that honor God. We must see the stranger in our midst. We must care for the poor. We must encourage the defeated. We must forgive the sinner. We must ease suffering when we discover it. What if we cared for our brother with the same passion with which we care for ourselves? Would not our faith have greater depth? Was it not our Lord who said, "Love your neighbor as much as you love yourself?"

What does being your brother's keeper resemble in your life this morning? Something about our faith must bind us to one another. We must care that people are victimized because of race. We must care that the poor are exploited. We must care that basic human needs are not met because of political disagreement. God expects us to be involved with the world around us. We cannot view the world as though we cannot see, close our ears as though we are deaf, or stand still as though our feet can't move. We are our brother's keeper.

Prayer

Teach me to care for my brother. Teach me to "act as Christ" to all those I may encounter today.

Day 5 — Genesis 5: Fade to Gray

> "Enoch walked with God; and he was not, for God took him."
> Genesis 5:24 (NASB)

Observation

The writer of this chapter, believed by most to be Moses, takes the time to fill in the generations from Adam to Noah. The thing that is remarkable as you read through the chapter is the extreme length of days that men of that time period lived. Most whose names are recorded lived more than 900 years! (I have a friend whose mother is now 112 and we think she's old!) In this listing of Adam's descendants, there are a few verses dedicated to a man named Enoch. Enoch only lived to around the age of 300, because, as our focus verse states, "He walked with God and he was not, for God took him." There is not a lot of detail, but it is apparent that in some special way, Enoch simply disappeared. That's quite an image of his death, is it not, that he simply walked with God into the glory of heaven.

Application

Most of us can probably imagine what a Hollywood movie producer would do with this scene: God's arm around Enoch's shoulders as the two walk off into the distance and simply fade away until they are no longer seen.

I am reminded of a funeral service I once officiated. A gentleman who had been enlisted to play taps was positioned on a nearby hill. With our heads bowed and our eyes closed, he began playing. But after only a few notes, the music came to an abrupt stop. I peeked up and looked in his direction. He was gone! He had vanished! Then I discovered that he had stumbled over backwards and rolled down the hill!

For most of us, the experience of death is not so dramatic or mysterious as the experience of Enoch, but the imagery may still be valid. When Jesus is Savior and Lord, the fear of death is diminished. We walk a life of faith here on earth and when the moment comes, God ushers us into that newness of life. Though our earthly bodies may not disappear in some miraculous way like that of Enoch, it is with the Father's arm draped around our shoulders that we walk from this life to the next. The assurance of God's word is that "nothing can ever separate us from the love of God which is in Christ Jesus," not even death. I challenge you to walk this life with faith secure in Christ, so that when the times comes, you can walk boldly into the next being held secure in the strong arms of your Father.

Prayer

Thank you, O God, that your love and provision for our lives transcends even life here on earth. Amen.

Day 6 — Genesis 6: Proven Faith

> "Thus Noah did; according to all that God had commanded him, so he did." Genesis 6:22 (NASB)

Observation
The story of Noah begins in this chapter. Because Noah was blameless before the Lord, unique among all the men of his generation, God chose him to play a critical role in the drama of saving all the animals during the flood. God revealed to Noah all that was to come and how God would bring to Noah all the animals for safe keeping. God told Noah about the flood waters and about the huge boat that he was to build so that his family and the animals can survive. Despite what must have been the constant jeers and taunts of his neighbors, Noah painstakingly built the ark and prepared for the flood. He never wavered in doing all that God had commanded.

Application
Sometimes the ways of God seem absurd to the minds of men. Sometimes God asks us to step out and do things for the sake of the kingdom that just don't make sense to the world. Ever hear of a successful businessman called away from his career to go to the mission field? Ever hear of the parent of a murdered child extend forgiveness and grace to the man who murdered that child? Ever hear of a wealthy entrepreneur who turns over his entire fortune to aid the needs of the poor? Ever hear of a bright scholar, who can explain the intricacies of human DNA, admit that well beyond the science stands a purposeful Creator God? You get the point... God still commands us to do extraordinary things and the faithful are careful to do all that God commands. What has God required of you? What task is God asking you to complete? What sacrifice is God asking you to make? You will discover no greater joy than that of doing those things that God asks of you to do, even the things that are difficult.

Another point to make about Noah is that of his faith-step. Before the first raindrop falls, he is called to build the boat. He steps out in faith, and in the face of uncertainty and opposition, Noah stands resolute. God commanded him to build a boat and he starts putting the planks together. What is God asking you to do during this season of your life? The boat you are asked to build might carry your children into a better world view. It might carry your community into greater tolerance and acceptance of those who are different. It might carry your heart out of a dark place and let you find rest in the greater things that God intends for your life. If in faith, God is calling you to build a boat, why are you not headed to the lumber yard?

Prayer
Give me the heart of Noah, that I might be faithful to do the things that you command me to do this day.

Day 7 — Genesis 7: What Is Your Job?

> Then the LORD said to Noah, "Enter the ark, you and all your household,
> for you alone I have seen to be righteous before Me in this time."
> Genesis 7:1 (NASB)

Observation
The great flood is described in detail in this chapter. Nothing on the earth outside of the ark would survive as the flood waters remained on the earth for more than 150 days. In a very real way, God was "re-booting" the earth. God's intention for humanity had not been lived out. The men of earth had chosen disobedience, enmity, and strife. Sin marred the intention of God's creation. There were none who were found to be righteous, except Noah. And because of Noah's faithfulness in a faithless world, God singled him out as a special servant for a very special task.

Application
Among the lessons to draw from the experience is that of the difference one man can make. God literally changed the world through Noah. Using his talents for ship building, logistics, and family peace keeping, coupled with his extreme faithfulness, God was able to re-create the world in a way that would provide for newness of life among both the people and the animals. Sometimes, it is the faith of one person that makes all the difference. Sometimes, there are very specific tasks to be accomplished and it is only through you—yes you—that God wants to work. When we choose to live a life of obedience, surrendering all that we are under the authority of God, we place ourselves in a position to be used in ways we might never dream possible. Our offering of self becomes a tool in the hand of God to accomplish God's work.

Ever wonder about your life purpose? Ever wonder what God may ask you to do with your walk on this planet? Those are big questions to ponder. But make it simpler this morning: What do you think God wants you to do with your life today? Who do you need to call to offer a word of encouragement? What charity needs your check? What rift needs your attempt at reconciliation? What relationship needs a little mending? If not you, then who? If not now, then when? If not here, then where?

Prayer
Dear God, help me to see this day, the very thing that you want me to accomplish. Set my feet and my heart to that task. Amen.

Day 8 — Genesis 8: That Was Easy.

> "Then God spoke to Noah, saying, 'Go out of the ark, you and your wife and your sons and your sons' wives with you.'" Genesis 8:15-16 (NASB)

Observation
At the end of the great flood, after 40 days and nights of rain and then, after 150 days of floating around, the ark finally came to rest on Mt. Ararat. Noah and his family, along with the animals, were finally able to step off the ark and onto solid ground. What a sense of freedom and relief that day must have brought! After being cooped up for months, it must have been really nice to walk out onto the ground and breathe a breath of fresh air. No doubt Noah was left with a great sense of satisfaction, knowing that he had completed the task that God had brought his way.

Application
I recently took on the task of building a swing-set for the grand kids in the backyard. It was not a simple task. I went to Home Depot and bought the lumber, the wood screws, the chain, etc. Then I spent a long, hot afternoon putting it all together. It took longer than I thought. It was harder than I thought. It was heavier than I thought. But when it was all in place, I sat back with a very contented feeling. And each time I push a grandchild in the swing, I get that same feeling of contentment.

Some commandments of God are easier to follow than others. Building the ark was no small task. Gathering provisions for man and beast was no small task. Managing the boat and all its inhabitants for months was no small task. Obeying God's instruction to "step off..." Now that was easy! It illustrates the fact that not all of God's commandments are arduous, nor hard to bear. In fact, because God wants to bless us with abundant and meaningful life, many of God's ways will be pleasant for us and will bring us immense joy. We need not think that serving God is some horrible curse that limits our lives and steals our happiness. It's not that way. When we find ourselves in the center of God's plan for our lives, we will know no greater joy or satisfaction, and yes... Sometimes the instructions are the very thing we want most to do.

Prayer
Dear God, knowing that you desire only what is best for our lives, teach us to be obedient in all things that you lead us to do. Amen.

Day 9 — Genesis 9: A Gentle Reminder

> "It shall come about, when I bring a cloud over the earth, that the bow will be seen in the cloud, and I will remember My covenant, which is between Me and you and every living creature of all flesh; and never again shall the water become a flood to destroy all flesh." Genesis 9:14-15 (NASB)

Observation
When the time of the flood had come to an end, God established a new covenant with Noah and his family. God promised would never again destroy the earth by water again nor wipe out mankind in like manner. God established a sign, the rainbow, and fixed it in the sky as a reminder of that covenant. Notice this detail as you read the chapter: not only was the rainbow set as a sign to remind humankind of God's promise, but it was also placed in the sky to remind God of the covenant with humanity. Interesting. Why would an all-powerful, all-knowing, all-present God need a reminder of promises made? Was there a chance God would forget?

Application
Sometimes our memories need a little help. We write on a post-it note or set an alarm on our phone to help us remember. We are easily distracted and need a little something to pull our focus back in line. That's because we are human. Our memories can fade. But it's not that way with God. Rest assured that God's memory is fine. The only thing God forgets are forgotten intentionally, like our sins. Check out Isaiah 43:25: "I, even I, am the one who wipes out your transgressions for My own sake, and I will not remember your sins" (NASB). God forgives and forgets our sin, but never does God forget us. We are way too important to God to ever be forgotten.

So back to the rainbow... Why use a reminder? Maybe it's to be a reminder to God, not about rain, but about God's love that will continue to transcend our sin and disobedience. God established a covenant with humankind, knowing that the things that brought about the flood would continue to be a part of the human equation. The reminder was to love creation despite the disappointments of such a relationship. It seems that God desires to keep our needs ever in attention and thus a sign of God's grace is offered amid our sins. I will leave you with this... If it is important for God to be reminded of God's grace that must be offered to us, how much more important that we remember such love? And as we experience such grace, how can we not offer it to others?

Prayer
Thank you, O God, for your willingness to enter a permanent relationship with each of us. Amen.

Day 10   Genesis 10: What's in a Name?

> "Now these are the records of the generations of Shem, Ham, and Japheth, the sons of Noah; and sons were born to them after the flood."
> Genesis 10:1 (NASB)

Observation

This chapter is filled with the various genealogies of the three sons of Noah. It is probably not the most exciting chapter to read in the Bible. There is no great story line to follow, no profound word of wisdom to reflect upon, no big demonstration of God's power. Just names. And yet, this chapter has been just as carefully preserved by God as any other chapter in the Bible. Makes you wonder why. Certainly, the establishment of bloodlines is always an important discipline in the days of tracing ancestry. But maybe there is something more. Maybe the names are preserved by God because people are important to God. What might seem like some funny sounding name from a very distant past to us, represents a very important person to God.

Application

Recently I had the opportunity to spend a morning walking around a cemetery in Mobile, Alabama. I was joined by my wife and mother-in-law as we looked for the gravesites of several relatives. As I wandered about, I read dozens and dozens of various headstones. Most simply offered the name and the dates of each person's life. I thought about how each life has a story, but how that life story will slip away with each new generation. What a person once did, how he/she spent their lives, or even what contribution they made to their families will soon fade to grey. In the great passage of time, we may record the names, but the stories will dissipate. But the names are important... both to God and to us.

God does care about names because God cares about us. There are no unimportant people, no insignificant names, no life stories that aren't of great value to God. Sometimes it is easy for any of us to question the relative importance of our lives. We all have a way of feeling a bit insignificant in light of the billions of others who share the planet with us. We can always look at others whose stories are more important and whose lives are much more exciting. But it's not that way with God. To God, every life has a really good story. Because God has created us, God cares about even the smallest detail. Chances are that your name will never be written in the pages of God's word, but rest assured your story is written onto the pages of God's heart. Your life matters to God, always has... always will.

Prayer

Thank you, God, that all of us are important in your sight. Thank you for helping to orchestrate our life stories. Amen.

Day 11 — Genesis 11: Who's Calling the Shots?

> "They said, 'Come, let us build for ourselves a city, and a tower whose top will reach into heaven, and let us make for ourselves a name, otherwise we will be scattered abroad over the face of the whole earth.'"
> Genesis 11:4 (NASB)

Observation
After the time of the flood when the world began to populate once again, one of mankind's oldest sins began to resurface. Just look at the pronouns in our focus verse this morning and you will begin to see the problem. "Let us build... Let us make for ourselves a name." It was the old problem of giving up God-dependency for the sake of self-sufficiency. The people of earth began to think too highly of themselves. They began to think that life was theirs to control, that it was possible to make themselves great... maybe even greater than their creator. There was a mentality that stated, "We can do whatever we want to do. No one, not even God, can tell us what to do."

Application
I have a friend who flies jets for Northwest Airlines... the really big jets... the fly-across-the-ocean kind of jets. Because I have an interest in flying, I pick his brain from time to time and recently we discussed the protocol of communication between the pilot and co-pilot. There are very specific instructions in place when the authority for flying the plane is transferred from one pilot to the other. For the safety of all concerned, there can be no doubt about who is in control. It's the same in our relationship with God. It's never about us.

It is always a slippery slope when we begin thinking too highly of ourselves. When we begin to build our lives around our own sense of morality, our own sense of judgement, and our own sense of authority, we will find ourselves plunging headlong into the abyss of destruction. If we are not careful, we will soon forget that this is not our world to control, and not our place to act as though it is. New Testament writer James tells us how foolish it is for us to say, "today or tomorrow we will go to such and such a place, engage in a business, and earn a profit. You do not know what your life will be like tomorrow. You are but a vapor... Instead, we ought to say, 'if the Lord wills...'" (James 4:13-14 NASB). It's this simple. We must recapture a sense of God's ultimate authority over our lives and God's right to control our lives. We must remain dependent upon God. Let us look to God, and not to ourselves, to make our plans, set our paths, and decide our choices.

Prayer
Teach me, God, that it is foolish for me to think that I have the right to take even one step in life apart from your leadership and authority.

Day 12 — Genesis 12: Steps of Faith

> "Now the LORD said to Abram, 'Go forth from your country, and from your relatives and from your father's house, to the land which I will show you.'" Genesis 12:1 (NASB)

Observation

Chapter 12 of Genesis marks the beginning of the story of Abraham. Up to this point in the book of Genesis, the Biblical narrative has focused on God's dealing with all of humanity. Now the narrative shifts to focus specifically on how God will establish a covenant with the descendants of Abraham. It all begins with this verse. God calls Abram (whose name will later be changed to Abraham) to go forth from his country, leaving behind all that is familiar and comfortable, to go to the place God has ordained for him to inherit. Journeys of faith are often like that. We are called to leave, to risk, to step out… to claim all that God has in store for us. Abram left home, his family, his house, and his past, to claim God's promise.

Application

You've seen the old Tarzan cartoons where Tarzan makes his way across the jungle by swinging from one vine to the next. There seems to be an endless number of vines… at least in the cartoons. There is a point of transition that is critical as he navigates his way from tree to tree. To grab the next vine, he has to release his grip on the one that currently supports him. It's called risk. It happens at the precise moment we are willing to let go of one life, in order to embrace the new one… the one we chase in pursuit of God's calling for our lives.

So, what's keeping you from living the life that God has planned for you to live? What are you afraid of let go? What will following God's direction in your life cause you to forfeit or leave behind? Sometimes faith demands that we take steps of faith. Sometimes we have to risk. Sometimes we have to boldly step out into the uncertainty of a new direction with only the promise that God will be with us along the journey. Abraham could have stayed in Haran for the rest of his life. He could have died an old man, warm in his bed, at the end of a long and boring life. And yes, he would have missed it. He would have missed the adventure, the joy, and the excitement of walking each day with his God. Not to follow God would have lessened his life. So, I've got to ask… Are you living the life God wants you to live? Are you living your life to fullest? Have you ever dared to boldly go where God calls you to journey?

Prayer

Remind us this morning, O God, that our best life and brightest future will only be found when we dare to step forward in faith to the places you call us to go.

Day 13 — Genesis 13: A Promise Keeper

> "I will make your descendants as the dust of the earth, so that if anyone can number the dust of the earth, then your descendants can also be numbered." Genesis 13:16 (NASB)

Observation

In this chapter of Genesis, Abram and his nephew, Lot, return from their sojourn in Egypt and enter the land of Canaan. Lot and his family settle to the east in the Jordan River valley and Abram in the west. It is at this point in the narrative that God renews the covenant with Abram. God promises that Abram and his descendants will inherit forever, the land on which they are now walking. God also promises that Abram's descendants will be as plentiful as the dust of the earth. It's a quite a promise to make to an old man and his barren wife. But as is always the case, God keeps promises. Soon a son, Isaac, will be born and the line of descendants will start.

Application

Anyone can make a promise… it's the keeping of the promise that defines our character and reveals our nature. Honoring a commitment takes resolve, dedication, and fidelity to the vision of being trustworthy. Like you, I have made a lot of promises in my lifetime. Some have been easy to keep while others have taken a lot of effort. For example, when I took on the challenge of pastoring my previous church, I made the promise that every Sunday when I stood in the pulpit, I would bring a fresh, new word from the Lord that was the result of dedicated labor and careful study. What a joy it was to leave that 17-year pastorate, knowing that I had fulfilled that pledge. It took effort. Keeping promises demands that of us.

Our God is very much a promise keeper. Any covenant God has made, any promise God has offered, has, is, and will be kept. That should bring us a lot of hope, for God's promises to us come in abundance. Through Christ, God has promised us God's abiding presence. Through Christ, we are promised the indwelling of God's Spirit. Through Christ, God has promised us forgiveness of sin. Through Christ, God has promised us eternal life. Such promises will never be broken. The same God who once made a nearly impossible promise to Abram come true, will surely keep a promise word to us. Take the time to make a mental list of what God has promised you through God's word. Claim the promises. They WILL be kept.

Prayer

Thank you, O God, for your faithfulness to each and every generation. Thank you for the bright promises that always find fulfillment. Amen.

Day 14 — Genesis 14: What We Will Do for Family...

> "When Abram heard that his relative had been taken captive, he led out his trained men, born in his house, three hundred and eighteen, and went in pursuit as far as Dan." Genesis 14:14 (NASB)

Observation

This chapter tells the story of nine different kings who go to battle against each other. The various kings form alliances so that five of the kings fight against the other four. In the process, the King of Sodom is caught up in the fray and his kingdom is overrun. Lot, Abram's nephew, is captured and enslaved. When Abram hears this, he organizes his men and goes in pursuit of those who have taken Lot and his family. Lot's captors are defeated, and Lot is rescued and returned to Sodom. Though we do not often connect Abram to stories of battle, he was certainly willing to heed the call when members of his extended family needed his help.

Application

Linda and I raised three amazing children who now have families of their own. I'd like to think that they made it to adulthood, not in spite of us, but, in part, because of us. I'd like to think that our counsel, insight, discipline, and wisdom helped them to succeed. It's what we do as family. We protect, we push, we prod. Because of the love we share, we take care of our own.

So, here's my thought this morning: are we willing to go to battle for our families? There are a lot of enemies out there, you know. Are we willing to fight for the families that God has placed in our care? Do we defend our children and our spouse against the evil influences that swirl around them each day? Do we rise up against the threats to their safety, their morality, and their health? Do we offer ourselves sacrificially to "stand in the gap?" I remember when the kids were young, we owned a very sweet-natured dog who never acted aggressively towards anyone... unless one of the kids was treated in some way. I remember watching in amazement one day when a stranger walked into our yard. Instinctively, our dog put herself between the stranger and kids and started to growl as if to say, "You are not about to get close to these children!"

I would hope that we have that same instinct when it comes to our kids... and not just to the kids that share our last name. I hope that we carry a compassion and burden for all the children within our sphere of influence. We will fail the next generation if we are unwilling to safeguard them from the dangers of this world. Let me encourage you to be a defender of children and their rights. They need our help.

Prayer

Thank you, O God, for the families entrusted into our care. May we have the strength and wisdom to defend them against all foes. Amen.

Day 15 — Genesis 15: Faith that Gains Favor

> "And He took him outside and said, "Now look toward the heavens, and count the stars, if you are able to count them." And He said to him, "So shall your descendants be." Then he believed in the LORD; and He reckoned it to him as righteousness." Genesis 15:5-6 (NASB)

Observation

These verses represent a renewal of the covenant between God and Abram. God speaks to Abram in a vision and tells him to go outside and count the stars. God promises that Abram's descendants will one day be as great in number. "Then he believed in the Lord; and He reckoned it to him as righteousness." Notice what it is that makes Abram righteous in the eyes of God. It is not because Abram had done a bunch of good and noble deeds. It was not because Abram had earned God's favor with tithes and offerings and good works. It was simply a matter of faith. Abram chose to believe in God. It was because of his faith, that he found favor in the eyes of the Lord. Also, note this phrase, "reckoned it to him as righteousness." The image is taken from the world of accounting. To "reckon" in this case means to "be counted toward" or "added to his account." Each time that Abram expressed faith in God, God added to the blessings in his life.

Application

God rejoices when we express our faith. Our acceptability in the eyes of God is not the result of good works. Who among us could ever do enough good deeds to merit God's favor? Instead, our acceptability is based in our faith. What God requires of us is a simple belief and trust in both God's existence and in God's daily interaction with us. Whenever we express our faith, God is pleased. Whenever we live out our faith, God is excited. Whenever we rely on our faith, God is satisfied. And, as in the case of Abram, there is blessing through our belief. The more we are open to God's leadership, the more we will enjoy the blessings that come each day by trusting in God. So, how will you live your life today?

Faith is always contested by the realities of life here on earth. Faith demands that we believe beyond what we can see, that we accept beyond what we can reason, that we claim the assurance of things not yet revealed, and that we expect beyond simple comprehension. It is to acknowledge absolute trust in the unseen God. Faith requires steps—steps of belief, steps of risk, and steps of obedience. Will your faith please the Father today?

Prayer

O God, may I have a faith that pleases you and one that blesses my life this day. May I know the joy of trusting fully in you. Amen.

Day 16 — Genesis 16: Stick with the Plan

> "So Sarai said to Abram, 'Now behold, the Lord has prevented me from bearing children. Please go in to my maid; perhaps I will obtain children through her.' And Abram listened to the voice of Sarai."
> Genesis 16:2 (NASB)

Observation

Sometimes we have difficulty trusting the Lord to fulfill promises. Just a few verses ago in the Biblical narrative, God promised Abram that his descendants would number as many as the stars. Sarai, his wife, is barren and growing older by the minute. She suggests that Abram sleep with her maid and maybe he can obtain a son through their relationship. Abram listens to Sarai, sleeps with Hagar, and has a son named Ismael. As soon as he is born, Sarai becomes jealous of how her maid had given Abram that which she cannot and therefore, she treats her harshly. The real underlining problem is this… Both Abram and Sarai's lack of trust in God's promise, cause them to act sinfully. They usurp the plans of God and substitute those of their own.

Application

Ever get into one of those do-it-yourself jobs to install something new at your home and the directions that come in the box clearly state in big, bold letters, "READ THIS FIRST?" But we don't… we quickly scan the instructions and attempt to start the task all on our own. We don't always pay attention to the instructions… we think we know better. Things don't always work like they should. (I always get worried about those one or two bolts that are left over.)

How often do we attempt to manipulate God's plans? Sometimes, when answers seem slow in coming, or when we just don't agree with those plans, we push aside God's direction for our lives to impose our own self-will. The results are never good. How many times have we found ourselves dealing, sometimes for years, with the consequences of a poor choice? How often do we suffer because we have chosen to act in our own initiative rather than seek the council of God? Never forget that God longs to be revealed to each of us. James says if we "lack wisdom, we should ask of God, who gives to all men generously." We don't have to stumble through life with uncertainty and poor choice. Instead, we can seek God's counsel each day by simply asking God to reveal God's will to us, and then ask for the courage to act on what we discover. Chasing God's plans may mean we head off in a direction long before knowing the destination, but the journey of Godly pursuit will bring success and blessing all along the way.

Prayer

Teach me today, O God, that my greatest success in life will come when I follow your plan for my life and not the whims of my own understanding. Amen.

Day 17 — Genesis 17: The God Who Speaks

> "Abram fell on his face, and God talked with him, saying, 'As for Me, behold, My covenant is with you, And you will be the father of a multitude of nations. 'No longer shall your name be called Abram, but your name shall be Abraham; For I have made you the father of a multitude of nations.'" Genesis 17:3-5 (NASB)

Observation
Several remarkable things take place in this chapter. First, notice in our focus passage that God talks to Abram. It is not that Abram talks to God through prayer… God clearly speaks to Abram, reminding him again of the covenant relationship the two of them will share. Second, this chapter also reveals the "changing of the names" of both Abram and Sarai. Abram, which means "exalted father," is forever changed to Abraham, which means "Father of a Multitude." Sarai, meaning "noble woman," is changed to Sarah, meaning "princess." The changing of the names was significant. They were no longer to be known by their old names… the relationship with God would change both their names and their destinies. The third important component in this chapter is the declaration of circumcision as the sign of the covenant for all the Hebrew males.

Application
A few years ago, my wife and I had the honor of attending a gala event in Sevier County, Tennessee for the opening of a celebrity theatre in Pigeon Forge. A large group of people swarmed Peyton Manning when he stepped into the reception. We took the opportunity the diversion afforded us to head to the shrimp table. We were not the only ones… Suddenly, we found ourselves standing face-to-face with George and Barbara Bush! We shook hands and made brief introductions. Then it got a little awkward. What do you say to a former president?

Notice the conversation recorded in Genesis 17. Abram and God have a conversation filled with promise, blessing, and instruction. What would we say in such a moment? Would our tongues be tied and our words confused? Notice that it's God who does the talking. Abram doesn't have to carry the weight of the conversation. Abram is not the first or the last with whom God speaks. We share the same experience. It may not be an audible voice booming from the sky, or words inscribed on tablets of stone. But make no mistake, God longs to speak to us all the time. God speaks through scripture, the Holy Spirit, creation, and yes, even through God's servants. Perhaps today we should simply ask for the wisdom to listen.

Prayer
Father God, speak to us this day. Help us to listen. Amen.

Day 18   Genesis 18: A Privileged Conversation

> "And Abraham replied, 'Now behold, I have ventured to speak to the Lord, although I am but dust and ashes.'" Genesis 18:27 (NASB)

Observation
A lot happens in this chapter of Genesis, including the appearance of three men who deliver God's promise of a son to Abraham within the next year. Sarah laughs at the thought of it all and so the child is to be named "Isaac," which means "laughter." The three messengers depart from the presence of Abraham on their way to Sodom and Gomorrah, where they will bring about destruction because of the wickedness of those cities. Abraham is very much concerned because his nephew, Lot, lives there, and he is fearful that Lot and his family could get swept away in the destruction. A dialogue ensues between God and Abraham over the destruction of the city. Abraham actually bargains with God and talks God into relenting from destruction if there are only 10 righteous people left in the city. It is a bold move on his part to speak to the Lord with such brashness.

Application
Recently, I had the opportunity to speak with the CEO of a large corporation here in Nashville. It took several weeks to get on his calendar. His office was impressive and well-guarded. After identifying myself with a photo ID, I was allowed into the building. I was met by a receptionist who told me to wait. Another receptionist soon came to greet me and led me to the CEO's office. Finally, I was allowed into the inner office. The receptionist reminded me that I had only 30 minutes with the CEO and asked that I be conscious of his time. I couldn't decide if I should have been impressed, humbled, or put-off by the conversation.

At least Abraham understood that it was no small thing to stand and speak in the presence of Almighty God. Though he was but "dust and ashes," he ventured to dialogue with The Almighty. I wonder if we have any appreciation at all for the incredible privilege and honor that is ours to speak with Almighty God. Who do we think that we are to even come into God's presence and speak of our needs and wants? We can do so because we are invited into God's presence. God longs to hear from us and dialogue with us. But even though we are there at God's bidding, let us never treat that time flippantly as though it is not of great importance. We should pray alertly, consciously, humbly, thoughtfully, and gladly. Let us never treat moments with God as some casual conversation.

Prayer
Thank you, O God, for the privilege of prayer. May I enter your presence with both thanksgiving and humility. Amen.

Day 19 — Genesis 19: Led by God

> "But he hesitated. So the men seized his hand and the hand of his wife and the hands of his two daughters, for the compassion of the LORD was upon him; and they brought him out, and put him outside the city."
> Genesis 19:16 (NASB)

Observation
This verse is within the story of the destruction of Sodom and Gomorrah. Two angels have visited Lot and warned him of the impending destruction of the city. Lot has been told to flee from the city with his wife and his daughters. Lot hesitates at the moment of destruction. Either paralyzed by fear or by the grief of what is about to unfold, he stands frozen for a moment. The angel of the Lord himself, takes Lot, his wife, and his daughters by the hand and physically leads them out of the city. The "compassion of the Lord" was upon them and so their lives were spared. Sometimes there are moments when the will of God is accomplished in spite of man's reluctance.

Application
This is an interesting scene. The angel of the Lord physically leads Lot and his family by the hand in order for them to escape destruction. It is a reminder that when God chooses, God's ultimate and complete will is accomplished. A theologian named Leslie Weatherhead once wrote a book titled, *The Will of God* (Abingdon Press, 1999). In that book he described God's will in three ways. He spoke of the *intentional* will of God... Moments in time when God deliberately acts in our lives, altering events, conversations, etc. Weatherhead also spoke of the *allowed* will of God... Moments when God seemingly allows things to happen in our lives, sometimes good and bad. And then he wrote of the *ultimate* will of God... When God brings to completion God's ultimate plans for the judgment of the world and the redemption of God's children.

Though we at times have the ability to thwart the plans of God for our lives with disobedience and poor choice, the ultimate will of God will indeed come to pass. We are powerless to hold it off. God's kingdom will come and the righteous will be rewarded. No power on earth, no will of man, no intervention of evil will keep that from occurring. The good news is that through Christ, we are included in God's compassion. God will take us by the hand and lead us into glory. We are and will forever remain in God's grip. Though we begin this day without the knowledge of when the kingdom will come in its fullness... we also begin this day with the powerful assurance than when the day unfolds, God will take our hand and lead us forward.

Prayer
Thank you, God, for your saving grace in Christ, that takes away our fears and leads us into ultimate victory. Amen.

Day 20 — Genesis 20: Forcing Our Way Through Life

> "Abraham said of Sarah his wife, 'She is my sister.' So Abimelech king of Gerar sent and took Sarah." Genesis 20:2 (NASB)

Observation

When Abraham and Sarah began to settle in the land of Canaan, Abraham feared that, because of her beauty, Sarah would catch the attention of foreign dignitaries. The fear was that Abraham might be killed so that his wife could be taken into the household of another man. So, Abraham developed a scheme to protect himself. He and Sarah agreed that they would tell anyone who asked that Sarah was his sister and not his wife. When a moment presented itself, Abraham lied, and Sarah was taken away by Abimelech. Later, God revealed to Abimelech what he had done, and out of fear for his life, Abimelech returned Sarah to Abraham.

Application

Allow me to recall a moment of American history. When President Ronald Reagan was shot on March 30, 1981, chaos ensued behind the scenes at the White House. With no real protocol in place for such a situation, everyone involved had to improvise and hope that everything would turn out right. In an attempt to keep everyone calm, Al Haig, Reagan's Secretary of State, committed a PR *faux pas*—and showed a glaring lapse in basic knowledge of the Constitution—by telling the press that he was in charge while the President was in surgery. He tried to take matters into his own hands.

This incident recorded in Genesis 20 was not one of Abraham's better moments. Though he may have believed in the promises that God had made to him, he didn't fully trust God to protect him as he sojourned in a strange land. And so, Abraham took matters into his own hands and developed his elaborate scheme. Is this not the same sin that we often commit? Rather than wait on the plan and protection of God, we often try to impose our own plans, thinking that we know what is best for our lives. We don't trust God fully enough to answer our prayers, lead our journey, and direct our paths and so we take matters into our own hands. We impose self-will and push the plans of God to the side. How short-sighted can we be? How faithless can we walk? If God is great enough to create our lives, offer us salvation, and continually dwell within us, then surely God is great enough to guide our steps and protect our days. As we learn to trust God fully, we will discover a better life that is free of stress, worry, and painful lessons.

Prayer

Teach me, O Lord, to allow you to guide my daily steps. May I learn to walk according to your will and not my own foolish thoughts. Amen.

Day 21 — Genesis 21: Plenty of Joy to Go Around...

> "Sarah said, "God has made laughter for me; everyone who hears will laugh with me." Genesis 21:6 (NASB)

Observation

This verse is taken from the experience of Sarah giving birth to Isaac. As you may recall, Isaac was born when Abraham and Sarah were quite advanced in age... 100 and 90 respectively. His name was Isaac (laughter) because of Sarah's response to the improbability of it all. The angel reminded her that nothing is impossible with God. Sarah finds great joy in the experience. In this verse, she expresses the emotion of her heart. The verse literally means, "God has created joy for me, and those who hear will share in my joy" (translation mine). It is the idea that Sarah's joy would be contagiously shared by those who knew her, and who knew of her long wait for a child.

Application

My wife and I enjoy watching several television comedies. Many of the shows are reruns and we know them so well that we can quote nearly every line. They make us laugh. But what really makes us laugh are "outtakes" that you sometimes catch on-line in which the various actors get tickled. Their laughter causes another actor to lose focus and soon everybody is laughing hysterically. You can't watch those outtakes without joining in the fun.

Joy is one of the greatest gifts of God to each of us. It is in fact a contagious commodity. When we see others experience joy, our spirits are lifted, a smile comes across our faces, and we share in the exuberance. At least that's the way it ought to be... Sometimes, however, we can become "joy-stealers." Rather than revel in the joy of someone else's success, we jealously resent their enthusiasm. We quickly take the joy of the moment and dampen it with our negativity. Would it kill us to share in their zeal for a moment? Would it really cost us a lot to help others experience a brief moment of exuberance? The truth is that we often miss a moment of joy that could be ours because we become too jaded by the problems of our own lives. Let's be like the friends of Sarah. Let's learn the value of sharing in the joy of others' successes. Let's learn the value of encouragement as we celebrate with others.

Prayer

Teach me, O God, that part of being a true friend is learning how to share the joy of another's good fortune. Amen.

Day 22 — Genesis 22: Tempted and Tried...

> "Now it came about after these things, that God tested Abraham, and said to him, 'Abraham!' And he said, 'Here I am.'" Genesis 22:1 (NASB)

Observation

In one of the more dramatic scenes in all the Bible, God tells Abraham to go to Mount Moriah and offer his son, Isaac, as a burnt offering to the Lord. Abraham does as God commands, taking his son to the mountain, fully intending to slay him. But the Lord stops him at the last moment and the child's life is spared. The key to the whole story is found in the first verse... "God tested Abraham." It is important to understand the fundamental difference between tempting and testing. Tempting has Satan as its author and its intent is to *destroy* our relationship with God. Testing, on the other hand, has God as its author and the intent is to *strengthen* our relationship with God. New Testament writer James adds clarity, "Let no one say when he is tempted, 'I am being tempted by God'; for God cannot be tempted by evil, and He Himself does not tempt anyone" (James 1:13 NASB). Abraham was "tested" by God in order to prove the strength of his faith.

Application

I love the little story that my dad used to tell occasionally in his sermons. It goes like this... A little boy was standing near the door of the old general store. A large barrel of apples was close by. He picked one up and carefully held it, pacing back and forth near the door. The store owner, who had been watching for a while, finally looked over his glasses and asked, "Little boy... are you trying to steal that apple?" The little boy replied, "No, sir, I'm trying not to." That's the way of temptation. It tries to force us into poor decisions. Testing, on the other hand, tries to prod us into greater obedience.

Let's give credit where it is due. The temptations that come our way have the potential of "tripping up" our walk with God. Temptation's goal is to make us less than God longs for us to be. It is never God who tempts us. Never say that you are being tempted by God. Testing, however, IS God's way of building strength and character in our faith. Admittedly, some moments of testing are rather severe. Our tests can be hard to endure. But again, as James states, "the testing of your faith produces endurance" (James 1:3 NASB). So take a moment to consider what life is currently throwing your way. Are you being tempted to do evil, or are you being tested to prove the strength of your faith? Run from the temptations. Embrace the tests. Remember that it is God's will for you to be strengthened.

Prayer

Thank you, God, for the testing of my faith. May my faith prove strong enough to overcome the temptations that come my way. Amen.

Day 23 — Genesis 23: Honesty

> "And he spoke with them, saying, 'If it is your wish for me to bury my dead out of my sight, hear me, and approach Ephron the son of Zohar for me, that he may give me the cave of Machpelah which he owns, which is at the end of his field; for the full price let him give it to me in your presence for a burial site.'" Genesis 23:8-9 (NASB)

Observation

In this passage, Sarah, Abraham's wife has died at the age of 127. He looks for a proper place to bury her but, owning no land, he must go to the Canaanites to negotiate a land purchase. He wants to pay the full price for the land he needs. Ephron is more than happy to deed Abraham a piece of land. In fact, Ephron wants to simply give him the land, but Abraham refuses the gift and insists on paying the full price. The deed is drawn up and Abraham pays the full price of the land in silver.

Application

Years ago, I noticed a strange event that unfolded at a local restaurant. Patrons would leave a tip on the table. The busboy would clean the table but leave the tip for the waitress to collect. After all, it was the waitress who had earned the expression of gratitude. But here's what he did. He would keep a carefully folded dollar bill concealed in his hand. When no one was looking, he would drop the dollar onto the table and take the tip money, which was always more. His deception made it look as though a tip had been left, just not a large one. I reported him to the manager. He was punished for his actions. It just made me think about his level of trustworthiness. If he was willing to steal a small amount, how far would he go in the other areas of his life?

Somewhere in this story of Abraham is a lesson on Godly ethics. Abraham has a need, negotiates a price, and pays for the field. There was no attempt to be deceitful, no attempt to play the "servant of God" card, no attempt to be unfair in any way. He is honest and forthright in his dealings with Ephron. There is something to be said for such an approach to life. Honesty really is the best policy. We honor God when we show integrity in all our dealings. We honor God when our words are honest and our actions are up-front. It speaks to our trustworthiness. If people can trust our actions in even the smallest of our dealings, then they will be able to trust our words when we speak of our faith. Let us resolve to never compromise our witness because we have acted less than honestly in even the small things of our lives.

Prayer

Teach me, O God, that to being faithful in even the small things will give me the ability to be heard when I speak of kingdom things. Amen.

Day 24 — Genesis 24: Following God's Leadership

> "Then Laban and Bethuel replied, 'The matter comes from the LORD; so we cannot speak to you bad or good.'" Genesis 24:50 (NASB)

Observation

In this passage, Abraham sends a servant back to his homeland to find a bride for his son Isaac. Abraham does not want Isaac to marry a Canaanite woman and so the servant is dispatched to find a suitable bride from Abraham's relatives. As the servant travels, he offers a prayer to God asking for God's will to be revealed. While stopping to water his camels, he meets Rebekah, who offers to provide water for the camels. The servant sees in the event a sign from God. Rebekah is the daughter of Bethuel and is the sister of Laban. When the servant goes to Bethuel and his wife to explain his intentions to take Rebekah back to Isaac, they reply that the matter is out of their hands... That it comes from the Lord. And so Rebekah leaves her home and becomes the bride of Isaac.

Application

My wife and I once lived in a small town in middle Kentucky that was supported by a volunteer fire department. Those who had been trained to drive the engine, stretch the hoses, and put out the flames were common, ordinary citizens. They were farmers, bankers, and gas station workers. But they understood the importance of their charge. If the alarm ever shattered the quiet, peaceful mood of the community, these volunteers would drop everything they were doing and rush to firehouse. Their obedience, without hesitation, had the potential of saving both lives and property.

What is remarkable to me in our focus passage, is the trust that Laban and Bethuel place in the will of God for their sister and daughter. Certainly, it was no small thing to give away Rebekah to a man whom they had never met. And yet, perceiving that it was the purpose of God to do so, they offer their blessing. I wonder how willing we are to blindly follow the will of God for our lives. To be honest, most of us want a little reassurance now and then. We want God to answer and answer and answer, multiple times, before we "give in." But what if our walk with God was close enough, steady enough, and faithful enough, that we were able to build a level of trust between God and ourselves? What if, when God prompted us to do something, that we simply followed? In other words, what if obedience, not delay or hesitation, was our first response? Surely God has great things in store for each of our lives. Let us pray to discern God's leadership and then courageously follow God's voice.

Prayer

Call us, O God, to an attitude of obedience that will allow us to move at your bidding. Amen.

Day 25 — Genesis 25: The Danger of Quick Decisions

> "Esau said, 'Behold, I am about to die; so of what use then is the birthright to me?'" Genesis 25:32 (NASB)

Observation
A lot happens in this chapter. Abraham dies at the age of 175. Isaac's wife, Rebekah, is barren and unable to give him a son. Isaac prays for his wife and God responds. Rebekah conceives and twins, Jacob and Esau, are born. Esau enjoys the benefits of being the firstborn. He has both a birthright and a blessing to claim from his father. Jacob, however, is loved by his mother Rebekah, who will help him to escape the wrath of his brother. In this portion of the narrative, Esau comes home one afternoon, famished after a day of hunting. Jacob has been cooking a delicious stew all day. Esau longs to eat the savory soup. But first Jacob offers a deal. He will give Esau the stew if Esau will promise the birthright. In a foolish moment, Esau trades the lasting for the temporary. He is willing to trade away his birthright for a bowl of stew.

Application
Those of you who know me well, know that I am a "car nut." (I come by it honestly.) I like cars. I like to buy them and drive them and trade them. In fact, you would be shocked to know how many cars I have swapped around in my lifetime. There is an expression called, "buyer remorse." Ever experienced it? It's when you make a purchase on the spur of the moment only to regret it a few days later as you realize the strings attached to your purchase. For example, I traded my previous car… a beautiful Mini Cooper Clubman S for a Hyundai Sonata because the crimson color of the Sonata caught my attention. I still miss the Mini. It happens. We make foolish choices because we fail to think about the consequences.

We look at the story of Esau and think, "How foolish can you be?" Who in their right mind would trade the pleasure of one day in exchange for things that last a lifetime? The truth is that most of us make that same foolish choice at key moments in our lives. We sometimes fail to count the costs of a quickly made decision. We willingly exchange our reputation, our peace of mind, and our self-esteem, for a quick moment of pleasure or a fleeting moment of popularity or notoriety. We just don't always count the costs. We trade away our blessings in moments of stupidity. Like, Solomon, we should pray daily for wisdom. We should seek the rewards of common sense and not a moment's fleeting pleasure. What are you willing to trade away in exchange for your reputation or character? I pray that nothing is worth such a loss.

Prayer
Teach us, O God, the simple lesson of weighing the choices in our lives. May we choose those that honor you and benefit us. Amen.

Day 26 — Genesis 26: Blessing Your Children

> "I will multiply your descendants as the stars of heaven, and will give your descendants all these lands; and by your descendants all the nations of the earth shall be blessed; because Abraham obeyed Me and kept My charge, My commandments, My statutes and My laws." Genesis 26:4-5 (NASB)

Observation

In this passage, God renews the covenant once made with Abraham with Abraham's son Isaac. Isaac was sojourning in the land of the Philistines to escape the famine that had occurred in the land of Canaan. During this time, God greatly blessed Isaac with bountiful crops, much livestock, and many servants. The renewal of the covenant was another sign of God's faithfulness to him. But notice why the covenant is offered to Isaac… "Because Abraham obeyed Me and kept My charge, My commandments, My statutes and My laws." It was because of the faithfulness of his father that Isaac received the continued blessings of God.

Application

Interesting… Our faithfulness, our obedience, our fidelity to God, will always impact future generations. Our children will be blessed by our attentiveness to our faith and to our faith disciplines. As we live out our faith, we will model for our children the life that God desires for us to live. Because our children will have the opportunity to be raised in households where the love of God is demonstrated and the ways of God are taught, they will know blessings in their lives that will extend throughout their lives and even to the lives of their children. I see in this passage a mandate to live a Godly life in the presence of our children. Our relationship with God will bless their lives… Our lack of faith will impoverish them. Are you living fully a life of obedient faith that will one day bless your children?

All of us have hopes and dreams for the things we long to pass down to the next generation. We want to leave them with a good education, financial stability, and life tools to help them navigate their walk through life. But above and beyond all that we hope to instill deeply within them, must be the faith that will guide their journey and seal their salvation. There is no greater legacy to leave than a life of faith obediently lived and doggedly pursued. This morning, be conscious of the ways you long to bless your children. Make sure that the living out of your faith is at the top of the list.

Prayer

Dear Father, remind us that each faithful life has rippling effects to all those who encounter it. May my life be one of them. Amen.

Day 27   Genesis 27: When You Feel a Little Left Out...

> "Esau said to his father, 'Do you have only one blessing, my father? Bless me, even me also, O my father.' So Esau lifted his voice and wept."
> Genesis 27:38 (NASB)

Observation

These verses portray one of the saddest moments in scripture between a father and his beloved son. It is the climactic moment of the story of Jacob and Esau, just after Jacob has deceitfully taken away his brother's blessing. Isaac has been tricked and gives his final blessing to Jacob and not to its intended recipient, Esau. In this verse we can read and feel the anguish of Esau's heart as he begins to understand that there is no further blessing to give. All that he had hoped to receive from his father has now been taken. Esau is left with a sense of loss, betrayal, and anger.

Application

A few years ago, I had the privilege of being on mission to the impoverished nation of Haiti. My team led a medical clinic in a very small and remote area. One of my assignments that week involved food distribution. Many of those who came to the clinic were extremely malnourished and we were able to give them a supply of rice and beans. Others, assessed by the doctors not to be as critically in need, were sent away empty-handed. Though our desire would have been to give food to all who came to the clinic, there were simply not enough supplies to go around. It was very difficult to send some away empty-handed.

    Esau felt left out, cheated, betrayed, and short-changed. He had lived much of his life with the anticipation that his father would one day offer the final blessing. Esau knew that there would be justice and that he would claim a greater blessing than his brother. And yet, with Jacob's deceitful act, it was torn from his hands. What a sad moment to realize that another blessing could not be offered... That there was simply not another blessing that could be given by his father. Ever feel like Esau? Ever felt as though life hasn't given you everything that you thought it should? Ever felt slighted, as though you have missed out on some promised gift? The truth is that life is seldom fair and quite honestly, you may have missed out on a few things that you rightfully deserved. But the good news is that unlike those of Isaac, God's blessings are not extinguishable. There is plenty to go around. You will receive all that God longs for you to have. Take heart... You may not ever get all you deserve here on earth, but a day is coming when you will know the Father's blessings in abundance.

Prayer

Father, remind me today that your grace is inexhaustible and that your love is unfailing. Amen.

Day 28 — Genesis 28: What Claim Have We?

> "Behold, I am with you and will keep you wherever you go, and will bring you back to this land; for I will not leave you until I have done what I have promised you." Genesis 28:15 (NASB)

Observation

Notice this covenant between God and Jacob, given the night that Jacob flees from the presence of Esau. This verse is a part of the dream experience that Jacob has in which he sees a ladder extending into the heavens with angels ascending and descending. Perhaps more remarkable than his dream is the covenant that God establishes with Jacob. Though he had dealt deceitfully with both his brother and his father, still he received the promises of God. God affirmed in his life the same promises that God had once made to Abraham. God is a promise-keeper and here God promises to watch over Jacob and bring him back to this land. It's not what Jacob expected from God.

Application

There is such joy in the unexpected blessings that come our way. Special moments when we become the recipients of a "grace gift" tend to lift the spirit, brighten the countenance, and gladden the heart. On a recent morning commute to work I stopped by McDonald's to grab a biscuit from the dollar menu. A little prompting of the Spirit told me to buy a second one… not for me, but for someone I would encounter. Often on the drive to work I pass homeless individuals who sell newspapers at the red lights in Nashville. I rolled down the window and motioned the paper-seller to my car. "I don't need a paper today, but how about a sausage biscuit?" His eyes lit up and offered me a very sincere word of gratitude. The blessing flowed to both of our lives. Unexpected blessings can do that.

Back to Jacob's situation. Sometimes God gives us what we don't deserve. Jacob should have received a rebuke. He should have received punishment. He should have received judgment. But instead, he received the promise of God's watch care and God's blessing. It's called grace. There is not a thing we can ever do to deserve the favor of God. In fact, we do everything within our power not to deserve it. And yet sometimes it just comes to us… God's love, God's patience, God's hope, God's grace. Maybe Paul says it best when he writes, "But God demonstrates His own love toward us, in that while we were still sinners, Christ died for us" (Romans 5:8 NASB). I can't explain why God chooses to love those whom who should instead be punished… Neither can you. I can only receive God's grace with thankfulness and somehow let God's gift transform my life.

Prayer

Father, thank you for your grace, your love, and your mercy. It is undeserved, but certainly welcomed. Amen.

Day 29 — Genesis 29: Crazy Love

> "So Jacob served seven years for Rachel and they seemed to him but a few days because of his love for her." Genesis 29:20 (NASB)

Observation
Jacob has met and fallen deeply in love with his Uncle Laban's daughter, Rachel. Seeing the opportunity to gain a strong, healthy, worker, Laban agrees for Jacob to marry his daughter, but only after seven years of labor. Our focus verse speaks of Jacob's love for Rachel. He gladly serves seven years in order the claim the love of his life. In fact, the sacrifice of time and energy seems small in comparison to what he will gain. The seven years seem to him, "but a few days because of his love for her." Of course, if you read the rest of the narrative, you will discover that Jacob is tricked into marrying the older sister, Leah. He must agree to seven more years of enslavement to have the privilege of being wed to Rachel.

Application
In 1967, Marvin Gaye and Tammi Terrell broke onto the pop music charts with the hit, "Ain't No Mountain High Enough." (It was later recorded by the Temptations and the Supremes.) The song insists there's no mountain too high, no valley too low, no river too wide to keep the crooner from their love. Remember the song? Even now the melody is probably starting to reverberate in your head. It was a love song describing a love so intense and a desire so strong that no barrier was going to separate the lovers from one other. For Jacob the barrier was seven years and seemed to him but a few days.

Let's talk about the power of love this morning. I want you to think about the love of God for your life. There is no barrier high enough, low enough, or wide enough to keep God's love from finding your heart. In fact, God will gladly sacrifice in order to claim you as the "love of His life." Just so that God can claim you and welcome you into the family, God was willing to watch Jesus suffer and die in order to atone for your sins. God was willing to pay whatever price was demanded to claim you. You have never been loved like that in your whole life. It's hard to even imagine the depth of God's commitment towards each of us. But it's true and it's powerful. So as we start a new day, let's take a moment to remember the one who has loved us supremely, devotedly, and sacrificially.

Prayer
Father, thank you for your love that drives you to do outlandish things on our behalf. Amen.

Day 30 — Genesis 30: Remembered by God

> "Then God remembered Rachel, and God gave heed to her and opened her womb. So she conceived and bore a son and said, 'God has taken away my reproach.'" Genesis 30:22-23 (NASB)

Observation

In the on-going saga between Rachel and Leah, matters are made worse for Rachel because of her barrenness. In the meantime, Leah gives Jacob six sons and a daughter. In jealousy, Rachel gives her maid to Jacob, and the maid bears sons for Jacob. In response, Leah gives *her* maid to Jacob, and she bears sons! Everyone is able to do what Rachel cannot. According to our focus verse, God remembered Rachel, opened her womb, and finally she was able to conceive and bear a son whose name was Joseph. (This is the eleventh son born to Jacob.) Rachel said about the birth of her son, "God has taken away my reproach."

Application

Here's what we need to notice... God was able to meet the greatest need and desire in Rachel's life. Though once barren, she was able to produce a son. Though once ashamed of her plight, she was now able to rejoice because of God's intervention. Because we are loved by God, God longs to meet our needs and even many of our "wants." God is faithful to God's children, providing for us by meeting our biggest needs. In fact, through Christ, God provides for our eternal life and through the Holy Spirit, God provides for our daily needs by giving us God's daily presence and comfort. It is important to understand that God knows our needs, from the greatest to the smallest. And like Rachel, God remembers us and gives us what we need.

So, what are your biggest needs today, your biggest fears, your biggest worries? I invite you to talk honestly with God about them and watch how God responds to your prayers. It is always important to know that God never forgets about us or the circumstances that swirl around our lives. In fact, when we think that God has forgotten us, we are the ones with the bad memory. We have forgotten who God is. God is the one who loves us with intensity and grace. Though we may wonder at times about the timing of God's answers and provision in our lives, we should never wonder about God's character. God hears your thoughts this day. God sees your needs, feels your anxious heart, and responds to your concerns.

Prayer

Father, thank you for knowing about the needs in my life and for caring enough to respond to them. Amen.

Day 31 — Genesis 31: Offer Your Blessing

> "Laban said, 'This heap is a witness between you and me this day.' Therefore it was named Galeed, and Mizpah, for he said, 'May the LORD watch between you and me when we are absent one from the other.'"
> Genesis 31:48-49 (NASB)

Observation

In a very strange and angry scene, Jacob and his father-in-law, Laban, part company. After 20 years of serving Laban, Jacob flees in the night with his wives, his children, and his livestock. After a week of pursuit, Laban catches up with him and confronts him about his secret departure. The two have somewhat of an angry exchange and finally agree to part company. They set up a pile of stones, called Mizpah, and swear out an oath to each other, stating that neither will pass by the stones to do harm towards the other. Our focus verse is the essence of the oath, "May the Lord watch between you and me when we are absent from the other."

Application

Though these words were first spoken with a hint of "you'd better watch out or else," I think it is appropriate to use the same words with a better intention. Rather than offer a threat toward others, what if we offered words of blessing? Could we not use the words of Jacob as a blessing to offer friends and loved ones whenever we are absent from them? "May the Lord watch between us..."

Here's my thought. We need to do more blessing than cursing. We need to offer more goodwill to those around us than anger or bitterness. We need to offer more hope than mean-spiritedness. We need to think about the ways in which we can part as friends and not as enemies seeking revenge. Is it not one of the defining qualities of the Christian faith that we "love one another?" I don't know how many bridges you have burned that need to be rebuilt. I don't know how many broken relationships you have left in your wake. I don't know how many poorly chosen words have poured through your lips. But I do know we all need the heart of Christ that will teach us to bless more and curse less. Mend your fences. Extend your grace. Live in peace. May the Lord watch over all of us when we are absent from one another.

Prayer

Father, teach us that the one of the ways we find peace with you is by finding peace with others. Amen.

Day 32 — Genesis 32: Angels

> "Now as Jacob went on his way, the angels of God met him."
> Genesis 32:1 (NASB)

Observation

Chapter 32 is an extremely important chapter in the Jacob and Esau narrative. At the close of this chapter Jacob wrestles with God during a long soul-searching night. At the end of the wrestling match God gives Jacob a new name, Israel. (The name means, "One who finds victory as he wrestles with God.") This opening verse sets the tone for what will follow in the narrative. As Jacob goes on his way, attempting to return home and make peace with his brother, the "angels of God met him." What a comfort it must have been to Jacob to know that his journey would be walked in the presence of God's angels.

Application

Can we talk about this whole "angel thing" for a moment? Most of us approach the subject with a little curiosity and uncertainty. We'd like to believe in the reality of angels, but most of us have never seen one, at least not that we know. Their presence, however, is certainly well-documented in the pages of both the Old and the New Testaments. I think it would be foolish of us to assume that they don't exist. In Matthew 18:10, Jesus speaks of children whose angels watch over them from heaven. The writer of Hebrews states, "Do not neglect hospitality, because through it some have entertained angels without knowing it" (Hebrews 13:2 NASB). Who knows... Maybe there are angels that are watching over you as you make your way out into the world this morning. That's a comforting thought, is it not, that the divine messengers of God are carefully watching over your steps? The older I become, the more I am convinced of their existence.

The word angel really means, "messenger." Typically, angels served as the mouthpieces of God. As in the story of Mary, the angel Gabriel relayed to Mary all that God wanted to do in her life. It was sometimes the role of angels to take the words and intentions of God and share them with people.

To be sure, most of us don't look like angels, nor do we have wings, nor are we able to float back and forth to the heavens. But here's what we can do... We can act like angels by sharing the words of God with others. In fact, God is counting on us to do just that. It just may well be that before this day is done, God will use you as representative.

Prayer

Thank you, O God, that you give us the task of speaking on your behalf. May we be "as angels" delivering your words to your people. Amen.

Day 33 — Genesis 33: Let Others See Jesus in You

> "Jacob said, 'No, please, if now I have found favor in your sight, then take my present from my hand, for I see your face as one sees the face of God, and you have received me favorably.'" Genesis 33:10 (NASB)

Observation

This chapter tells the story of the reunion between Jacob and Esau after 20 years of separation. When they were last together, Esau had sworn to kill his brother for his trickery in taking from Esau both his birth rite and his father's blessing. But time and distance had healed the wound and Esau received him back in a warm and gracious way. In our focus verse, Jacob is offering a number of gifts to his brother as a reconciliation offering. He said of his brother, "I see your face as one sees the face of God." Jacob had obviously seen grace, forgiveness, and acceptance in the face of his brother. Jacob knew that such favor could only be a result of God's work in Esau's heart.

Application

Sometimes our faces convey an entirely different message from the words that flow out of our mouths. Those who know us well can see emotion in our eyes or read the countenance written on our faces. Often, our faces tell our true emotions. And maybe more than some storm of emotion, people can see a gentle peace within because of our consistent walk with Christ.

What do people see as they look to us this day? What can they discern from our spirit, our demeanor, our countenance? Can they tell that we have spent time with the Father? Will they know that we live under the authority and influence of the Lord Jesus Christ? They should. Because we have spent time with God, our lives should change. There should be a spirit of patience, forgiveness, acceptance, compassion, and love. In fact, Paul reminds us "But the fruit of the Spirit is love, joy, peace, patience, kindness, goodness, faithfulness, gentleness, and self-control" (Galatians 5:22 NASB).

In very tangible ways, we, the people of God, must stand counter to our culture. The way we receive others, the way we react to disappointment, the way we extend care, the way we deal with anger, the way we build relationships—all should reflect our allegiance to God. I challenge you to be "as salt and light" today as you live your life. I hope it even shows in your face.

Prayer

Teach us today, O God, that we reflect you in every dealing with others. May you be glorified through us and not dishonored by our actions. Amen.

Day 34 — Genesis 34: The Wrong of Revenge

> "Then Jacob said to Simeon and Levi, 'You have brought trouble on me by making me odious among the inhabitants of the land, among the Canaanites and the Perizzites; and my men being few in number, they will gather together against me and attack me and I will be destroyed, I and my household.'" Genesis 34:30 (NASB)

Observation
This chapter tells a horrible story of rape and revenge. The daughter of Jacob and Leah is attacked and raped while visiting friends. After several twists and turns in the story, two sons of Jacob, Simeon and Levi, seek revenge. They trick the evildoers and slay all of them by the sword. They also pillage the homes and property of the men who are slain. When the news gets back to Jacob about all that they have done, they are chided by their father for the escalation of violence their revenge will cause.

Application
Revenge is one of the darkest human desires. That's why the Bible and Christ, in particular, go to such great lengths to warn us against it. We are to "turn the other cheek, love our enemies, and pray for those who persecute us." We are to avoid revenge at all costs. The problem with revenge is the escalating anger and destruction it causes. One bad action leads to payback. The payback leads to further action and soon damage is done and lives are destroyed. When the book of Exodus prescribes the "eye for an eye," the law was intended to allow only a retribution equal to the original infraction. (See Exodus 21:24.) The Jesus ethic goes further. He claims rather than offer any retribution at all, we are to turn the other cheek. (See Matthew 5:38-39.) When we practice revenge, we ultimately hurt ourselves. We introduce ourselves to a life of anger, hatred, and chaos.

Have you been wronged by someone lately? Are you plotting a little revenge? Are you thinking about taking matters into your own hands? Guess whose life you destroy when you give in to such thoughts? Be better. Be stronger. Be more Christ-like and work to heal, not harm. Theologian Frederick Buechner wrote, "Of the Seven Deadly Sins, revenge is possibly the most fun. To lick your wounds, to smack your lips over grievances long past, to roll over your tongue the prospect of bitter confrontations still to come, to savor to the last toothsome morsel both the pain you are given and the pain you are giving back—in many ways it is a feast fit for a king. The chief drawback is that what you are wolfing down is yourself. The skeleton at the feast is you" [*Wishful Thinking: A Seeker's ABC* (HarperOne: New York, 1993) 2].

Prayer
Teach us today, O God, that we do not have the right to extend revenge, nor can we control its result when unleashed. Amen.

Day 35 — Genesis 35: Honoring God

> "So Jacob said to his household and to all who were with him, 'Put away the foreign gods which are among you, and purify yourselves and change your garments; and let us arise and go up to Bethel, and I will make an altar there to God, who answered me in the day of my distress and has been with me wherever I have gone.'" Genesis 35:2-3 (NASB)

Observation
This chapter tells of the birth of Benjamin, Jacob's last son, and the death of Jacob's beloved wife, Rachel, during his birth. It describes the renewal of God's covenant with Jacob. God uses the same words spoken to Abraham and Isaac. God tells Jacob to move to Bethel and create an altar to God in response to God's deliverance. In preparing for the move and as a way to honor God, Jacob insists that all who are with him put away any hint of foreign gods once served, that they purify themselves, and that they change their garments. It is to be a new day lived in a different way before God.

Application
Things were a little different back in the day. I remember how we had to "clean-up" before we went to the dentist or doctor's office. Mom insisted that we represent the family well whenever we journeyed to an important place. We typically took off our "play clothes" and put on our best school clothes. Changing our garments was part of the routine.

I wonder if we don't need to do the same thing from time to time in response to our faith in the God who leads our path. Surely there need to be moments of renewal. Like a spring cleaning that causes us to remove all the clutter and dirt from our homes, maybe there needs to be a cleansing of life that allows us to renew our relationship with God. We tend to collect a few foreign gods along the way. We let possessions, involvements, and even our schedules become the objects of our worship. Maybe today is a good day to surrender those things before God. Maybe we need to purify ourselves.

When was the last time you really took the time to pour out your heart before God in confession? If we are not careful the plaque of our sins can quickly encrust our hearts. Maybe today we need to move to a new place, not physically, but in relationship with God. Maybe today we need to set some new goals, determine some new resolve, and travel to a better place of spiritual discipline. Today, let's honor God, maybe not with clean clothes, but with a cleansed life.

Prayer
Thank you, God, for being the guide of our lives. May we honor you today with a renewed sense of discipleship. Amen.

Day 36 — Genesis 36: Family Ties

> "Then Esau took his wives and his sons and his daughters and all his household, and his livestock and all his cattle and all his goods which he had acquired in the land of Canaan, and went to another land away from his brother Jacob. For their property had become too great for them to live together, and the land where they sojourned could not sustain them because of their livestock." Genesis 36:6-7 (NASB)

Observation
This chapter in Genesis goes into great detail about the descendants of Esau, Isaac's firstborn. The verses carefully trace all the lines of his descendants. Even though he lost both his birthright and his blessing to his brother's trickery, it is evident that God continued to bless him and gave him many children and possessions. Our focus verse speaks to blessings of God that came to both Jacob and Esau. In fact, so great were their blessings that the land could not sustain them both. Esau moves to the land of Seir where his family becomes known as the Edomites.

Application
Sometimes families separate and move out to new places. Most of us have experienced that to some degree. When I was young, I knew my cousins well. There were four of us boys, all about the same age. We lived within an hour of one another and seemed to spend nearly every holiday together. Now we live in four different states. It has been years since the four of us have connected in some significant way. I guess the last time we were physically together was at our grandmother's funeral. This is not unique to our family. It probably has happened in yours as well.

Long gone are the days when families all grow up in the same town, work the same jobs, and attend the same church. Society has become much more mobile. In our pursuit of education, career, and opportunity, families quickly spread across the nation and sometimes even to the other side of the ocean. That's not necessarily a bad thing, but it can prohibit families from being physically together. Most of us have to work at maintaining family lines. Tools like social media, e-mail, and video calling have certainly helped keep families connected. But still, it takes some deliberate effort. Families are important. The family ties need to stay intact. I hope you will take the time to connect with yours as often as you can. Maybe even this morning you need send your sibling a text.

Prayer
Thank you, God, for families. Thank you for the heritage they provide and for the support they offer. Amen.

Day 37 — Genesis 37: Do the Right Thing

> "Reuben further said to them, 'Shed no blood. Throw him into this pit that is in the wilderness, but do not lay hands on him'—that he might rescue him out of their hands, to restore him to his father." Genesis 37:22 (NASB)

Observation

Genesis 37 tells the story of Joseph and his coat of many colors, given to him by his father as a sign of his favored status. Through the years, the other brothers became increasingly jealous of Joseph and sought to harm him. They got their chance once as Joseph traveled to check on them as they were pasturing the flocks in a distant place. At first, the brothers planned to kill Joseph, but cooler heads prevailed and he was thrown into a pit until other plans could be made. It is the older brother, Reuben, who attempts to do the right thing. He prevents the others from taking his life but is later unable to stop them from selling their brother into slavery.

Application

Years ago, I had the joy of serving as pastor of the First Baptist Church of Gatlinburg, Tennessee. The church had made a strategic decision a few years before I arrived to sell the downtown property and build a new building a little further out from town. It was a good decision, and the new building was glorious. Those who were there when the decision was made to move like to tell the story of the business meeting in which that choice was made. At the end of the meeting, the moderator asked, "Is there anything else to come before the church?" Not expecting anyone one to have anything to say, he was shocked when one of the senior adult ladies, a matriarch in the church, stood up and made a motion to sell and move. No one had seen it coming. The church discussed the motion for about 10 minutes and voted to move!

Never underestimate the power of one. In the Biblical narrative, the noble actions and wise counsel of the oldest brother saved Joseph from death. His willingness to stand up to the others prevented a very tragic event from unfolding. It is not always easy to do the right thing. Peer-pressure, financial pressure, temptation, and fear have a way of preventing us from doing the right and noble thing. It comes down to character. Are we willing to stand up for our beliefs, defend our faith, and show allegiance to God's word? When those who know the right and just decisions to make but fail to make those decisions, evil triumphs. God has not called us to an easy life, but to a life that honors God. Don't be afraid to do the right thing. Be honest. Be fair. Be visionary. Be Christ-like.

Prayer

Teach us this day to never compromise, nor bend to the suggestive words of evil. May we stand firm and honor you with the choices we make. Amen.

Day 38 — Genesis 38: It Only Gets Worse...

> "Then Judah said to his daughter-in-law Tamar, 'Remain a widow in your father's house until my son Shelah grows up'; for he thought, 'I am afraid that he too may die like his brothers.' So Tamar went and lived in her father's house." Genesis 38:11 (NASB)

Observation
The story line in this chapter takes a lot of twists and turns and has enough sexuality to make a Sunday School teacher blush. Judah, one of the sons of Jacob, leaves his brothers to marry a Canaanite woman. She bears Judah three sons. The oldest son takes a wife named Tamar. Unfortunately, the oldest son does evil in the eyes of the Lord and so the Lord "takes his life." (See Genesis 38:7b NASB.) Tamar is left as a young widow. Judah gives his second born to her in the hope of producing offspring, but he too is evil and God also "takes his life." She is left with the promise that when the third son is old enough, she will be given to him in marriage. It is an empty promise on Judah's part. He is afraid that he too may die like his brothers. Then Judah himself is later tricked into sleeping with his former daughter-in-law. (Told you that it got a little twisted.)

Application
The real problem in the story was caused by Judah's lack of integrity. He made a vow to Tamar that he really had no intention of keeping. Rather than deal with an issue, he put it off for years, hoping that the issue would somehow resolve on its own. Sound familiar? Sometimes we handle our problems the same way. Rather than confront an issue, deal with it swiftly and carefully, we move the resolution off to some distant point in the future. We don't want a confrontation. We don't enjoy an awkward conversation. We don't like the stress and so we take the path of least resistance hoping that time or someone else will solve our problems for us. It's the old idea that if we ignore a problem, surely it will go away. Rarely does such a strategy work. Problems tend to fester and grow over time. What may have once been manageable quickly grows out of control. Ephesians 4:26-27 states, "Do not let the sun go down on your anger, and do not give the devil an opportunity" (NASB). Why let small problems grow into huge headaches? Isn't it better to deal with an uncomfortable conversation today rather than stressing over it for weeks... knowing that the conversation still must occur? Today, work on making peace. Pray for courage and for a civil dialogue. You might just solve a problem and save a lot of stress.

Prayer
Dear God, teach us today that procrastination is one of our strongest enemies. May we seek today, to live in peace with others as we actively engage in restorative conversation. Amen.

Day 39 — Genesis 39: Influencing Others

> "It came about that from the time he made him overseer in his house and over all that he owned, the LORD blessed the Egyptian's house on account of Joseph; thus the LORD's blessing was upon all that he owned, in the house and in the field." Genesis 39:5 (NASB)

Observation

Taken to Egypt by some Ishmaelite traders, Joseph soon found himself in the possession of a government official named Potiphar. Joseph performed well and soon was put in charge of all of Potiphar's house. The only hiccup in the story comes as Potiphar's wife continues to pursue Joseph with sexual advances. When he refuses her, she gets revenge by accusing him of attempted rape and he is thrown into prison. The focus verse tells us that the house of the Egyptian is blessed because of Joseph's presence. Because of Joseph's connection to God, those around him are blessed.

Application

An old expression says, "When you raise the level of the bay, all the boats float." Sometimes the success in one life leads to blessings in the lives of others. I read recently about a former University of Alabama player who is now playing in the NFL. Because of his athletic ability, he signed a huge contract and makes a good living. He's now worth millions of dollars. The members of his family have benefited from his blessings. His mother got a new house. A brother got a new job. Others in the family have had debts paid or cars purchased. His success has led to an economic ripple effect in the life of his family.

Go back and read the focus verse again. The message is clear... The people of God can bring about the blessings of God in the lives of others. Whenever we live out our faith with authenticity and faithfulness, we begin to influence the lives of those around us. Our witness, our daily attention to matters of faith, can have rippling effects in the lives of others. God can influence others, speak to others, and work in the lives of others, all through our lived-out faith. How many of us came to faith through the faith of our parents? How many others among us came to faith through the testimony of close friends? We can make a difference. As we strive to live out the Christian faith, day in and day out, others take notice and kingdom grows as they begin to experience faith through our witness. Your corner of the world can be blessed by your faith. Are you willing to take on that responsibility?

Prayer

O God, may each of us live our faith so authentically before the world, that others around us can feel the warmth of our relationship with you. Amen.

Day 40 — Genesis 40: The Mysteries of God at Work

> "Then they said to him, 'We have had a dream and there is no one to interpret it.' Then Joseph said to them, 'Do not interpretations belong to God? Tell it to me, please.'" Genesis 40:8 (NASB)

Observation
Joseph had been placed in jail because of the false accusations by Potiphar's wife. In the course of time, Pharaoh's chief baker and cup bearer are placed in jail because they have displeased the King. Both men have strange dreams on the same night. Joseph, of course, has the ability to interpret such dreams. He listens carefully and shares with each man the meaning behind his dream. Eventually, the cup bearer remembers Joseph's ability and Joseph is released from jail.

Application
God had carefully arranged all the events in Joseph's life to place him in just the right spot, at just the right time, with just the right people, so that God's ultimate purpose could be accomplished. It would be his ability to interpret dreams that would eventually place him before Pharaoh and would further put him in a position to save the nation from famine, including his own brothers. I believe that God does that kind of thing all the time: carefully arranging the people, places, and events of our lives to move us according to God's plan. Though we may not always see God's movement as we work through the day-to-day events of our lives, there will be those moments when we retrospectively look back and see how God was at work. Right now, you are being prepared by God to be used for God's purpose. Though it may seem like just another ordinary day, God is up to something. Be thankful now for what God is preparing you to do later.

Sometimes moments when we seem to be languishing in neutral and not really moving toward any goal are referred to as "wilderness" moments. But if you read the biblical record carefully, you will discover that just after any of God's people experienced wilderness moments, great events unfolded. Moses stumbled around in the wilderness tending sheep before God called. Joseph stayed in prison for two years. Paul traveled for three years before starting his ministry after his conversion. Elijah hid in a cave. Jesus battled temptation for 40 days. You get the point… what may seem like a time of idleness, can in fact, be an important time of Godly preparation. So even if your life seems stuck on hold this morning, be reminded that God is constantly at work. Great events are just ahead. Be ready.

Prayer
O God, remind us today that you are constantly at work preparing us for your plan.

Day 41 — Genesis 41: Common Respect

> "Then Pharaoh sent and called for Joseph, and they hurriedly brought him out of the dungeon; and when he had shaved himself and changed his clothes, he came to Pharaoh." Genesis 41:14 (NASB)

Observation
When Pharaoh had a recurring dream that could not be interpreted by his court officials, one servant, the cup bearer, remembered Joseph and how he had once interpreted dreams while in prison. Pharaoh quickly had him brought into his presence in the hope that Joseph could interpret his strange dreams. Joseph does in fact interpret accurately the dreams of Pharaoh and as a result, Egypt and the surrounding nations are able to survive a great famine. Notice in our focus verse that before Joseph could stand in the presence of Pharaoh, he first shaved and put on clean clothes.

Application
Most of us would have done the same. If we had been living in a dark and dank prison for two years and were suddenly set free to stand in front of the most powerful ruler on the earth, wouldn't we too take a moment to tidy up a bit? Joseph removed the stubble from his face and the dirty clothing from his body. The idea was to make himself a little more presentable.

There is a lesson here about how we approach our God. Most of us have experienced what it is to live in the captivity of our sins and our poor choices. We languish in the shame of our guilt and remorse… sometimes for years. And then the day comes, when God calls for us and sets us free from the past that once enslaved us. We are invited to stand in the presence of the ruler of the universe. Doesn't it make sense that we would attempt to tidy up a bit? It's never about our filthy clothes, the unkempt hair, or the dust on our feet. It's about the purity of our hearts and the attitudes of our lives. How can we be anything but thankful?

So, let's clean up our act. Let's pray for forgiveness from our sins. Let's ask for our transgressions to be wiped clean. Let's express a willingness to be obedient. In other words, let us realize in whose presence we stand and let's attempt to offer God our best. Repentance is the key. We offer to God our resolve to live differently, to live faithfully, to live joyfully. We were not created to live in a prison of darkness, but in a kingdom of light.

Prayer
Father, forgive the mess of our lives. Thank you for your acceptance and for your invitation to live a life of freedom and joy. May we live out our gratitude before you. Amen.

Day 42   Genesis 42: Get Busy

> "Now Jacob saw that there was grain in Egypt, and Jacob said to his sons, 'Why are you staring at one another?' He said, 'Behold, I have heard that there is grain in Egypt; go down there and buy some for us from that place, so that we may live and not die.'" Genesis 42:1-2 (NASB)

Observation
This chapter tells the story of Joseph's reunion with his brothers. Years earlier, they had sold him into slavery and had long assumed he was dead and gone. Now, because of famine in the land, the brothers are sent by their father, Jacob, to Egypt to buy grain so that they will not perish. It is in the buying of grain that the family will eventually be reunited. It is a story of God's provision and protection. It is also an explanation of why the sons of Israel had relocated to Egypt, where their ancestors will eventually become enslaved until the Exodus experience.

Application
One of the key phrases that catches my attention in this narrative is the question asked of the brothers by their father, "Why are you staring at one another?" The implication was clear. "Stop your delay and move to action. Go to Egypt and buy the grain that will save our lives." It is a call to action.

I think there are times when the Spirit of God must surely confront us with the same question. "Why are you staring at one another?" In other words, "Why are you not doing the things that God expects of you?" Think about it. We have been commissioned, trained, equipped, and gifted to help move the kingdom forward. God has put us in the right places, at the right moments, and with the right resources that we might act on God's behalf. There are lives to change, situations to alter, and communities to impact. Maybe we have stared at each other long enough. Maybe it's time for us to risk a conversation, or support a local ministry, or invest our time in a mission opportunity. There is work to be done. Perhaps one of our greatest sins is the sin of inactivity. We know there are needs. We know we are called. We know we are equipped and empowered by God. So why do we find ourselves just standing in the mire of lethargy, when there is work to be done? Go volunteer. Go invest. Go lead. Go work.

Prayer
Father, thank you for allowing us to share in the joy of building your kingdom. Give each of us a vision of how we are to fit into that plan this day. Amen.

Day 43 — Genesis 43: Need a Moment?

> "Joseph hurried out for he was deeply stirred over his brother, and he sought a place to weep; and he entered his chamber and wept there."
> Genesis 43:30 (NASB)

Observation

In this long story of Joseph reuniting with his brothers, the moment comes when Joseph stands face to face with his youngest brother, Benjamin. Surely the last time that he had seen him, Benjamin was very young. Overcome with a mixture of agonizing grief over time lost, joined with the exuberance of reunion, Joseph is brought to tears. Because he does not yet want to reveal his identity, he quickly leaves the presence of his brothers to find a place to weep. He goes to a private spot to surrender to the flood of emotion that overcomes him.

Application

I once knew an African-American pastor who taught me a lesson about "living water." He told me that sometimes on his long drive home from work he would take the time to reflect on all his blessings. He said that at times it became overwhelming to the point that he would have to pull his car over to the side of the road and let a little "living water" flow from his eyes. I have always liked that image of tears as the "living water" of joy that God sometimes brings to our lives. I also like the idea of pausing long enough to be overwhelmed by the goodness of God in our lives.

Joseph feels the need to find a private spot where he can release the joy, frustration, and grief of the moment. To join the situation to a more modern expression, Joseph simply needs a little "down time." Most of us do. We live at such a hectic pace, with so overcrowded schedules that if we are not careful, we forget to take the time needed to reflect, to wonder, and to grow. Sometimes, like Joseph, we have to be very deliberate in finding the places where that can happen. We need the quiet moments, the reflective moments, those moments that feed our souls with contemplative thought. I want to challenge you today, in the midst of your very busy life, to find five minutes of "down time." Get away to a place of solitude where you can breathe for a moment, maybe hear the sounds of creation around you, and maybe listen to whisper of God in your ear. You may need to weep, to laugh, or to simply relax for a moment. God offers us a welcomed peace and rest each day if we will take a moment to find it.

Prayer

Dear Father, thank you for the gift of this life that we live. May we maintain enough perspective to enjoy it. Amen.

Day 44 — Genesis 44: Learning from Mistakes

> "For how shall I go up to my father if the lad is not with me—for fear that I see the evil that would overtake my father?" Genesis 44:34 (NASB)

Observation
This is a very intense and interesting scene. As these words are spoken, it has just been discovered that a very valuable silver cup has been found in Benjamin's possession. (The cup, of course, was planted there by Joseph to see how the brothers would react.) In this verse, Judah, who had made a sacred vow to his father, Jacob, that he would not return without his brother, is pleading for Benjamin's release. He asks, "For how can I go up to my father if the lad is not with me?" Judah knew that would break his father's heart and that his father would die because of that heartbreak. It is Judah's remorse that will cause Joseph to reveal his identity.

Application
What's the dumbest mistake you have ever made? Did you learn from that mistake? For years, while serving as a pastor, visitors to my office would often confess some great mistake in their life while describing the guilt still carried on their shoulders. I would often remind people that making mistakes is part of being human. None of us are perfect. The real tragedy is if we fail to learn from our mistakes.

Over the course of time, Judah and his brothers have grown a bit. They have matured in emotion and spirit. Years earlier they had quickly sold their brother, Joseph, into slavery. They were too immature to know the grief that it would cause their father. They were too blinded to understand the guilt and remorse that they would carry for years. They were too thoughtless to know the years of agony that their actions would cause their brother. In this scene, they give evidence of a deeper conscious, a more mature outlook, and a greater concern for others. Life had offered some lessons and they were wise enough to have learned from the experiences.

If the truth be told, we will all make a few mistakes. We will make some bad decisions, deal thoughtlessly with others, and act with immaturity and selfishness. The fool is not the one who makes mistakes, but the one who refuses to learn from them. In our prayers to the Father we should ask for at least two things. One, forgiveness for the dumb and insensitive things we have done. And two, wisdom to learn and grow from those mistakes. May God grant that the longer we live the more wisdom we gain.

Prayer
Father, forgive our selfish, insensitive, and foolish actions. May such lessons be learned only once. Amen.

Day 45 — Genesis 45: The Joy of Grace

> "Weeping with joy, he embraced Benjamin, and Benjamin did the same. Then Joseph kissed each of his brothers and wept over them, and after that they began talking freely with him." Genesis 45:14-15 (NLT)

Observation

This chapter reveals the climactic moment when Joseph finally reveals himself to his 11 brothers. All the grief, anguish, thoughts of revenge, and anger are released as Joseph cries from the depth of his soul, so loudly that even the Egyptians living nearby hear his wailing. He lets it all go and with overwhelming joy he reconnects with his brothers. He tells them not to fear or to feel remorse over what they had done. Joseph sees the unfolding events of his life as the result of God's plan. Verse 7 says, "God has sent me ahead of you to keep you and your families alive and to preserve many survivors" (NLT). The brothers are amazed to be standing the presence of Joseph whom they once had sold into slavery. As our focus verse indicates, they wept tears of joy at this moment of glad reunion.

Application

I think that theologian Philip Yancey is right when he once stated that grace is "the last best word of the church." He insists that the word still holds much of its original meaning and power still today. Even as we say "grace" before our meals, we continue to claim that what is set before us is something unearned and undeserved. Define it however you will but grace is always that special gift of God in our lives that forgives, heals, redeems, and welcomes us into God's presence. It is a gift, and we are the glad recipients.

In the narrative of Joseph and his brothers, the extension of grace changes the lives of 11 men and their families. Joseph's willingness to love beyond pain, to forgive beyond hurt, and to embrace beyond rejection opens the door to full reconciliation and to a better life. Grace has done the same for us. When God extends grace to us, inviting us to feel the full embrace of the kingdom, everything changes. Guilt and shame are completely erased. Rejection is never mentioned again. Broken hearts are mended. Thoughts of being worthless evaporate as we realize we are warmly embraced by a loving Father. We weep with joy as our hearts dance with gladness.

And... lest we forget, the grace extended to us is also intended to flow through us to others. We are human. We can cling to anger for a long time. We can harbor thoughts of revenge. We can grow accustomed to brokenness. Or... we can choose grace. Which is the better way to live?

Prayer

Father, for grace that heals, forgives, and challenges us to be better, we offer you our praise. Amen.

Day 46 — Genesis 46: The Desires of Our Hearts

> "I will go with you down to Egypt, and I will bring you back again. You will die in Egypt, but Joseph will be with you to close your eyes."
> Genesis 46:4 (NLT)

Observation
As Joseph travels, he has a dream in which God reveals to him again both his promise and protection. The traveling party has many of members. According to verse 27, once they all arrive there will be 70 members of his family living in Egypt. All the descendants, servants, and livestock make the trek. Our focus verse reveals that God clearly tells Joseph that this will be his last journey. He will die in Egypt. But rather than cause a moment of panic, God gives him the assurance that he will be in the presence of his beloved son when he dies. So willfully and joyfully he begins the journey to be with his son and find a place of survival.

Application
Though he lived long before King David wrote the words of Psalm 37, Jacob surely understood the sentiment of David's heart when David wrote, "Delight yourself in the Lord, and He will give you the desires of your heart" (Psalm 37:4 NASB). Jacob learned by experience the truth of that verse. It had been a long faith-journey for Jacob. He had tricked his brother, fled for his life, married two sisters, and welcomed 12 sons into the world. The journey had a lot of twists and turns. But his spirit was broken and his heart torn apart when his beloved son was presumably killed by wild animals, as evidenced by a torn and bloodied coat of many colors.

But this day was different. He had been told by God that he would see his son again and that when the time came for him to die, Joseph would be with him. God had given him the desire of his heart. It's fair question to ask if God *gives us the desires of our heart* when we trust in God, or if our desires *change through knowing* God. Either way, we are promised that God has a way of bringing ultimate fulfillment to our lives. For some, the sense of peace, joy, and satisfaction may come in the course of this present life. For others, one's heart's desire may only come in the fulfillment of God's kingdom. But rest assured, God does not ignore the longings of our hearts. So, my challenge for you this day is the call to a faithful life in which you learn to trust God between the peaks and valleys. Knowing God and trusting God's provision for your life will bring a delight that you can't even imagine.

Prayer
Father, thank you for your presence, provision, and future blessings. Amen.

Day 47 — Genesis 47: God's Watch Care

> "Jacob lived in the land of Egypt seventeen years; so the length of Jacob's life was one hundred and forty-seven years." Genesis 47:28 (NASB)

Observation

Who would have thought that Jacob would live the last 17 years of his life in Egypt, away from the land of Israel? Because of the severity and length of a famine, Jacob and all his sons had moved to Egypt to live with Jacob's son, Joseph. Because Joseph had predicted the severity of the famine and had prepared the nation adequately for it, both the Egyptians and the Israelites survived it. More than survive it, the sons of Israel prospered. They acquired land, status, and livestock. At the moment of Jacob's death, his sons were becoming a young, but strong nation.

Application

Jacob had tricked his brother out of birthright and blessing. He had fled to Haran where he himself was tricked by Laban into marrying two daughters. He would have 12 sons by his two wives and their two maids. His beloved son Joseph would disappear for years only to reappear as a prince in Egypt. Jacob's journey was not always easy, but certainly lived out in eyes of God. God protected Jacob, blessed him beyond what he deserved, and gave him the joy of seeing his sons prosper.

Something of our lives is reflected in his story. Our journey through life may not always be easy, but it will be lived out before the eyes of God. We too will be protected and blessed beyond measure. We too will have the ability to look back at where we have been and see the continual guidance of God. The key for living such a life is bound up in one word... faithfulness. When we settle the issue of clinging to God as the guardian of our days and the Savior of our lives, we will walk continually in God's presence, and we will find joy, even in arduous moments. Let's not pretend that all of life is easy and smooth. We all live with the challenges of each day. Storms blow into our lives. Disruptions are frequent. Moments of confusion and perplexity sometimes invade our pursuit of God. And yet nothing about the trials we face mean that God has chosen to distance from us. In fact, just the opposite is true. In the midst of a very chaotic and challenging world, the one constant to which we can cling is the goodness of our God who watches over us, never sleeping. Even this day, God will watch over you, offering you grace, protection, and direction. You may not be exactly where you thought you would be at this point in your life, but never forget that God abides with you always. God is with you today.

Prayer

Father, give to each of us a patient, enduring faith so that we will know your guidance. Amen.

Day 48 — Genesis 48: Legacy Living

> "The angel who has redeemed me from all evil, Bless the lads; And may my name live on in them, And the names of my fathers Abraham and Isaac; And may they grow into a multitude in the midst of the earth."
> Genesis 48:16 (NASB)

Observation

This chapter tells the story of Jacob's final blessing to his son, Joseph. By this point in the story, Jacob is very old, his eyesight is weak, and he will soon die. When Joseph is called to his side, he brings with him his two young sons, Ephraim and Manasseh. Our focus verse this morning is the blessing that Jacob gives to his grandsons. He prays for God to bless them and that his own name would live on in them as well as the names of Abraham and Isaac.

Application

What are you leaving behind for the next generations? That's an important question. We sometimes earmark items in our wills to leave to certain individuals. One child gets the old clock, another receives the good china, or another gets the oil painting. But maybe we need to think about leaving behind things of even greater value. What tools do you leave in their hands to help them cope with life? What skills do you pass along? What wisdom do you impart? What reputation do you pass along?

Jacob prays for his grandsons what we would all pray for our children and grandchildren, that we would live on in them and that God would pour out blessings on them. Who wouldn't want to leave that type of legacy? Who wouldn't want to be remembered well in the lives of future generations? Leaving a legacy, however, is more than offering a quick prayer in the final moments of one's life. Leaving a legacy is the result of living consistently, authentically, and obediently before God. To leave a legacy means that we must *live* a legacy. We must love the Lord our God so devotedly that our children see that love expressed in a thousand different ways—in our words, our deeds, our interaction with others, our compassion. We must act with such grace that they inherit a knowledge of forgiveness. We should strive to be kind so that a gentle heart will develop in them as well. What an important gift we offer, this gift of legacy to future generations. May you live out your faith well so that when the generations which follow mention your name, they will speak of your faith, your commitment to Christ, and your compassion for your fellow man.

Prayer

Father, call us to live a legacy that we may offer to our children and the generations that follow, a testimony to your grace and love. Amen.

Day 49 — Genesis 49: Choosing a Blessing

> "Then Jacob summoned his sons and said, 'Assemble yourselves that I may tell you what will befall you in the days to come.'" Genesis 49:1 (NASB)

Observation
This chapter opens with Jacob gathering his sons to his side that he might pronounce his final blessing on each of them before he dies. The final verse of the chapter describes his death. These "blessings" given to each son are more of a prediction of the future for each of them. Some receive warm words from their father while others receive a stern rebuke for the things they have done over the course of their lives. It is a rather honest look at what these men have brought upon themselves by the choices they have made.

Application
Who among us would not want to receive some great blessing in our lives? We would all desire to receive favor, honor, riches, and respect. Such things, however, do not come from some great heavenly spin of the "Wheel of Fortune" prize-wheel that happens to point to us. Our lives are not blessed by sheer luck or happenstance, but by the choices that we make. In many ways, we choose our own destiny. We choose peace or anger, joy or heartache, greed or generosity, friendship or strife. In other words, we often bring upon ourselves the eventual outcomes for our lives. There are choices to be made that shape who we are and how we view life. The critical choice is that of obedience before God. Whenever we begin to align our lives according to the God's principles, we find hope, prosperity, and peace. God outlines the choices to be made for a life of contentment and grace. As we follow God, we find a joy that cannot be erased by the pressures and problems of everyday living.

And maybe there are some among us who need to rethink what it means to be blessed by God. Let's don't assume that the only way to be blessed is to have plenty of cash in the bank. There are greater blessings to enjoy like love, joy, peace, patience, and contentment with who we are in Christ. It is better to find a peace with God and with ourselves than to know the temporary comfort of treasure that "moth and rust destroy." The blessings we truly crave are a result of the obedience we live out before God. It's a daily choice to follow God. Choose well. You are in fact choosing your blessings.

Prayer
Father, teach me today the simple law of cause and result. Teach me that if I choose a consistent life of obedience, I will discover a consistent life of blessing. Amen.

Day 50   Genesis 50: Slow Walk to Joy

> "As for you, you meant evil against me, but God meant it for good in order to bring about this present result, to preserve many people alive."
> Genesis 50:20 (NASB)

Observation
The book of Genesis closes with the death of Jacob. His sons fulfill the promise they had made and return to Canaan to bury his body. As they return to Egypt, the sons fear that now that their father is dead Joseph may finally take revenge on them. But instead, they find only peace and continued reconciliation. Joseph offers the important words of our focus verse... "You meant evil against me, but God meant it for good." Joseph saw that God was able to bring great and powerful things from their evil actions.

Application
If you make your way to the middle of the small, Southern town of Enterprise, Alabama, you will discover the only memorial in the world honoring an insect... the boll weevil. In the early part of the 20th century, this voracious insect ate its way across the deep south, decimating cotton fields and destroying the economy. Farmers were forced to heed the advice of agricultural scientists like George Washington Carver and diversify their planting with peanuts, sweet potatoes, and soy beans. Soon, things began to turn around. The region around Enterprise rebounded economically with the largest peanut harvest in the nation in 1917. What had been a terrible blight, in fact, became one of the great economic engines of the deep south.

It can be difficult to see God's plan. We live in the present and see with limited vision. We feel the pain, the heartache, and the sufferings of the present time and we wonder how such things can be used by God for God's glory. And then time gives us a different perspective. We look back through the lens of our faith and see how God was at work, arranging the moments of our lives. What may have been a very difficult season or painful moment, turns out to be a blessing. God brings order from the chaos of our lives, joy from moments of despair, victory from troubling days. Paul writes, "And we know that God causes all things to work together for good, for those who love God, to those who are called according to His purpose" (Romans 8:28 NASB). Living in the meantime is just that... It is sometimes very mean. However, difficult days are not a sign that God is absent. Rather, be reminded that even in those moments, God is moving toward victory.

Prayer
Father, though we may not welcome the difficult moments of life, remind us that even then you are present and working to bring Glory to your name. Amen.

Day 51 — Exodus 1: Priority Living

> "But the midwives feared God, and did not do as the king of Egypt had commanded them, but let the boys live." Exodus 1:17 (NASB)

Observation
The great story of the Exodus is birthed out of fear and loyalty. A new Pharaoh came to power who knew nothing of the story of Joseph or how his wisdom had protected Egypt during the famine. All he knew was that the minority population was growing, and he feared their influence and rise to power. Pharaoh reasoned that the best way to curb the population would be to kill all Hebrew baby boys at birth. He asked the midwives to kill the boys born to the Hebrew women they assisted with delivery. But driven by a holy fear and respect for God, in defiance of Pharaoh, these women refused to obey Pharaoh and chose an allegiance to God instead.

Application
Did you notice the courageous act of these midwives? Even with the threat of death hanging over their own heads, they chose obedience to God above all else. In a world of pressures and paranoia, they chose to do the right thing and give their loyalty to God. I wonder if we have such courage. For most of us, the problem is not a failure of knowing and understanding the ways of God. Most of us have a pretty good sense of right and wrong. We know the "moral compass" always points toward the will of God revealed through scripture. No, for us, the problem is obedience. We are forced each day to choose between the pressures of the world and demands of Godly obedience. How easy it is to follow the crowd, to join in the mob mentality, and to let peer pressure force us into making choices not governed by the word of God. We let greed overrule grace. We let lust overrule love. We let selfishness overrule service. We let our allegiance to the kings of this world overrule our allegiance to Almighty God. I wish we had the courage of an Israeli mid-wife. I wish we had the boldness to do the right thing even though it might cost us popularity, position, and power.

Where is your ultimate allegiance? Under whose authority have you placed your life? This might frighten you a bit… but you will be tested today. Count on it. You will be faced with the choice of courage or capitulation. You will be called upon to speak hope, grace, and truth in the face of society's fickle voice. Will you be obedient? There are enough half-hearted, pseudo-Christians out there. Why not be a believer who makes a difference?

Prayer
Father, teach us that you desire obedience above all else. May we have the courage to live boldly our Christian faith in the midst of the pressures of this world. Amen.

Day 52 — Exodus 2: What It Takes to Raise a Child...

> "The child grew, and she brought him to Pharaoh's daughter and he became her son. And she named him Moses, and said, 'Because I drew him out of the water.'" Exodus 2:10 (NASB)

Observation
In this chapter, the story of Moses begins. In an attempt to lessen the Hebrew population, Pharaoh had ordered every baby boy to be thrown into the Nile. Moses' mother refuses for three months and when she finally complies, she "places" him in the Nile in a basket, rather than tossing him in, with the hope that somehow, some way her child might be spared a watery grave. You know the story. Pharaoh's daughter discovers the basket, takes pity on the child, and decides to raise him as her own. He is returned to his mother in order to be nursed and brought from infancy to childhood. Our focus verse tells of the moment when Moses' mother surrenders him over to the care of Pharaoh's daughter.

Application
I've often thought of this moment of surrender. How difficult it must have been for Moses' mother to give up her son into someone else's care. Would she ever see him again? Would he remember her when he was older? Would he remember those early days spent in the sheltering love of his mother's arms? So, what would motivate a mother to give up her son? Was it not the overwhelmingly powerful love of a mother who was willing to sacrifice for the sake of her child? Though she might not ever see him again, she surely loosens her grip with the hope that he will make the journey to a better life, one that she cannot offer to him.

It's the image of a mother who sacrifices much in order to offer her child the hope of a better life. It's what good parents always do. We sacrifice much to provide the best life we can for our children... Not an indulgent life, but one with opportunity and promise and potential. The best parents I know are those who put aside self-interests, lavish lifestyles, and career-path successes for the sake of investing time and energy into the lives of their children. We only get one shot at this thing called parenthood. What makes a difference at the end of the day is not the money we can throw at our kids, or the prestigious educations that we can grant, or the great toys we can buy, but instead, the time we spend being a part of their lives. What is it about your life that you are willing to sacrifice to have the time to invest in your children? You won't regret your choices.

Prayer
Father, thank you for giving us the responsibility of parenthood. May we be willing to make the sacrifices needed to know success. Amen.

Day 53 — Exodus 3: A Holy God

> "Then He said, 'Do not come near here; remove your sandals from your feet, for the place on which you are standing is holy ground.'"
> Exodus 3:5 (NASB)

Observation
God speaks to Moses from the burning bush, calling him to become the liberator of Israel. As soon as Moses "turned aside" to see the burning bush, God began to speak to him. As he drew close, God commanded Moses to remove his sandals out of respect and reverence for God. Moses would not be allowed to step on sacred ground with sandals caked with mud. Even in that solitary spot, God demanded a sense of holiness.

Application
Two thoughts this morning from this verse... First, we need to catch a renewed sense of the holiness of God. I wonder if we sometimes treat God and the things of God a little too lightly. Could it be that we approach God with a flippant attitude, a causal spirit, and a distracted heart too often? When I consider the ways we throw God's name around in our conversations, without a thought, have we lost a sense of reverence? When we gauge our worship experience by the quality of the choral piece or the eloquence of the pastor's sermon, or by the number of people in the pews, haven't we lost sight of the fact that we stand in the presence of the Almighty who calls us to worship and not critique the experience? When we quickly dismiss the principles that undergird the 10 Commandments, have we not lessened our respect for God? It's very easy for us to skip into God's presence with the mud of our humanity on our feet, never considering that to be in God's presence should call us to a different standard.

Second, even in solitude, we should offer God our best sense of reverence and worship. Moses stood on the mountain alone. Even there, God would not allow a casual worship and attitude. The sandals on Moses' feet were the product of his own hand. They spoke of self-reliance. Covered with the dust and dirt of his journey, the sandals told the story of the places where Moses had once walked. God asked him to remove his sandals and, in essence, to take off his former life. There was a new direction and destiny for Moses to embrace. Moses needed to be reminded that he served a Holy God who demanded both reverence and respect. It was a sacred moment. It should be the same for us. Even in the moments of our daily routine, when we turn aside long enough to have a minute of interaction with God, there should be a sense of awe and reverence. Let us treat each moment with God as truly sacred.

Prayer
Father, who are we that we should even dare to stand in your presence? Teach us that when you call us into fellowship, we are to offer our best selves. Amen.

Day 54 — Exodus 4: What's in Your Hand?

> "You shall take in your hand this staff, with which you shall perform the signs." Exodus 4:17 (NASB)

Observation
As Moses receives final instruction from God concerning his call to return to Egypt and free the Hebrews from oppression, God provides Moses with a tool to do the miraculous signs. He is to take use his staff to turn the Nile to blood, part the Red Sea, and draw water from a rock. His staff will truly become the "instrument of God" in his hands. (A staff is a long, wooden pole with a shepherd's crook at the end.) God used the wooden staff that Moses had used for years—the one that fit his hand so well from years of use—and transformed it into a powerful tool with which Moses would do the work of God.

Application
So, what do you hold in your hand? What is the thing that you have used for so long in your ordinary life that God can now transform and use? I heard about a lady who clipped coupons for years. Now she is teaching others to do the same so that local food bank ministries can be filled with nutritional foods. I know a guy who is a pretty good "shade tree" mechanic. It finally dawned on him that he could start a ministry to provide car care for recently-widowed ladies who know very little about automobile maintenance and up-keep. I know a woman who figured out that local bread places throw away a lot of "day-old" bread. She faithfully goes to those places to collect the leftovers and delivers them to local homeless shelters. Her ministry tool is simply her car that she uses to haul the bagels and bread from one place to another.

Here's the point: God is willing to transform the simple things that you have been doing for years—clipping coupons, changing the oil, driving a car—to change lives and make a difference. What God needs is your willingness to be used. So, what's in your hand? What's your hobby or talent and how can God use it to do ministry? Often, we fail to see how God equips us. We miss the point that the simple, every-day skills we have developed have great ministry potential. We just need to do the things we do, "as unto the Lord." Again, what's in your hand? A needle and thread? A hammer and saw? Hair-cutting scissors? A bag of flower and a baking pan? A pen and paper? A telephone? A set of hand tools? A lawnmower? A rake? A spreadsheet? Look at what you hold in your hand and then ask the simple question, "How could I minister to someone with this tool?"

Prayer
Father, thank you for equipping us. Use the tools in our hands for ministry. Amen.

Day 55   Exodus 5: The Frustration of Unanswered Prayer

> "Ever since I came to Pharaoh to speak in Your name, he has done harm to this people, and You have not delivered Your people at all."
> Exodus 5:23 (NASB)

Observation
Moses and Aaron have gone to Pharaoh to seek the release of the Hebrew slaves. Pharaoh, of course, is unwilling to offer freedom and in anger even increases their workload by making the Hebrews gather straw to be used in making bricks. (Up to this point, the Egyptians had supplied the straw.) When the Hebrews become unable to meet their daily quotas, many of the Hebrew supervisors are beaten. The Hebrews become angry at Moses for having made matters worse. Moses then becomes frustrated with God and offers the harsh words of our focus verse.

Application
Moses was frustrated and angry with God because God had not responded to his prayers in the way that Moses wanted. After all, God had called him to perform this "liberation" task. Why would God respond differently than how Moses expected? Don't we at times feel the same frustration? We wonder why God does not always answer our prayers in the way we think they should be answered. We get frustrated when God's timetable and answer are different from our timetable and our hoped-for answers. In other words, we don't always get the answer to our prayers when we want and how we want. Does that mean that God doesn't care or that God is unable to do the great and mighty things that we want? Not at all. It simply means that God's wisdom is vastly superior to our own and God is at work in ways we have yet to perceive. Just because we don't see God at work doesn't mean that God is not actively involved in our lives.

Our vision is dim at best. God, on the other hand, sees with the clarity of perfect wisdom and through the lens of transcendent time. The solution is not for us to stop praying, but perhaps to pray with even greater intensity. When we do that consistently, the interaction with God will shape our hearts, define our spirits, and change our lives. Adversity and frustration are not a call to cease from praying, but rather a challenge to pray with even greater consistency knowing that God is at work and that as we pray, we connect our hearts to God's.

Prayer
Father, thank you for allowing us to come into your presence with our daily petitions. May we discover both your will and your heart as we spend moments with you each day.

Day 56 — Exodus 6: Telling the Story

> "So Moses spoke thus to the sons of Israel, but they did not listen to Moses on account of their despondency and cruel bondage." Exodus 6:9 (NASB)

Observation
As the story of Exodus begins, God tells Moses to go tell the Israelites that God has heard their cries and that God is going to free them from the bondage of oppression. (This is before Moses goes to Pharaoh and begins the series of plagues that will eventually culminate with the Passover event.) The Israelites are so "beaten down" in their spirits and so despondent over their plight that Moses' words fall on deaf ears. Their lack of belief is borne out of the depth of the many years of their oppression. Their hope was drained.

Application
A couple of faith lessons... First, whenever we dare to share the message of Christ's hope, grace, and forgiveness to those around us who have been "beaten down" by life, we need not be surprised if our message seems to fall on deaf ears. There are many who view themselves with such low self-esteem, such guilt, and such failure, that the Gospel really does seem "too good to be true." Though the Gospel really does have the power to lift spirits, change lives, and heal wounds, for many a single dose of testimony is not enough to convince them to embrace all that a relationship with Christ can mean. So, don't become discouraged if they don't listen. It is their despondency and cruel bondage that makes it hard for them to even hear. So, tell them again... and again... and again. Be consistent and patient as you offer hope.

Second, sometimes people have a hard time believing in the changes the Gospel can bring because the ones talking about the Gospel seem to have been unchanged by it themselves. It is quite a calling and responsibility to be an ambassador of the Good News. Who will believe our testimony if our lives remain filled with hatred, anger, grudges, and unkind attitudes? Who will listen to our words if our actions betray them? Maybe the problem with doubters believing the message of Christ is not with the message, but with the messenger. Our goal is to be so filled with the story of Jesus that it radically changes our lives. It is the *lived-out* testimony of our faith that will bear the strongest message. So, when the Lord puts a despondent person in your path, start telling them the story of Jesus. Be consistent in your testimony and consistent with your witness.

Prayer
Father, give us a passion for telling others the story of Jesus and give to us a consistency of lifestyle so that our message becomes plausible. Amen.

Day 57 — Exodus 7: Bold Steps

> "The Egyptians shall know that I am the LORD, when I stretch out My hand on Egypt and bring out the sons of Israel from their midst."
> Exodus 7:5 (NASB)

Observation

As Moses and Aaron prepare to go before Pharaoh to begin the series of 10 plagues that will bring the eventual freedom of the Israelites, they do so with the words of our focus verse resonating in their minds. God promises them that God will be revealed before the nation of Egypt. God's power, strength, and authority will become evident. "The Egyptians shall know that I am the Lord..." As this chapter unfolds the first two miracles are recorded. Aaron's staff turns into a snake and the water of the Nile turns to blood. Though Pharaoh's mind is unchanged by the events, God's revealing before the Egyptians begins.

Application

When I was a kid, my father introduced my brother and me to the yard-mowing business. He taught us how to use a mower, how to take care of the engine, and how close to cut the grass. He sent us out into the neighborhood to seek our fortune. But he also did something else: He bought us a mower to use and a gas can to fill. He didn't just push us out of the door and said, "Give it your best shot." He taught us, trained us, and equipped us. He set us up for success.

Whenever God calls us to do a task, we should go forth with boldness knowing that God's power and might go with us. Wherever and whenever God calls us to do something to accomplish God's purposes, we are not sent with no tools, abilities, nor power. In fact, long before we take our steps of faith, the Holy Spirit has been at work preparing hearts and arranging situations. In other words, God ordains the moments in which we are called to serve. It could be through a compassionate act, or a spoken word of witness, or even through a sacrificial gift. Through the eyes of faith, we see God at work. What a privilege is ours to know that our lives can be used by God. Truthfully, at times we all feel a little inadequate. We fear that we won't have the right words to say, or the right prayer to pray, or the right talent that will make a difference. Rest assured God is always involved. God has not called you to do something that you are not equipped you to handle. The old expression states, "God does not want your abilities, but your availability." I challenge you to offer God a willing heart and see where God may lead you today.

Prayer

Father, give us a bold faith that will prod and push us into areas of ministry. Remind us that we never go forth apart from your presence. Amen.

Day 58 — Exodus 8: Stubborn as a Pharaoh

> "Then the magicians said to Pharaoh, 'This is the finger of God.' But Pharaoh's heart was hardened, and he did not listen to them, as the LORD had said." Exodus 8:19 (NASB)

Observation
Talk about stubborn... Even the magicians of Egypt tried to explain to Pharaoh that he was up against something really big. Read through this chapter carefully and you will see how the land of Egypt had to endure a number of really nasty things. First there were frogs that appeared everywhere. Then there was a pestilence of gnats followed by a pestilence of flies. And still nothing. Pharaoh refused to budge. With each plague, his heart and resolve only hardened. The more stubborn he became, the more his people had to suffer.

Application
My wife and I recently enjoyed a glorious beach weekend when the weather was perfect and the water of the Gulf was crystal clear. We spent a lot of time watching the waves. Sometimes I like to stand ankle-deep in the surf and just take it all in. Have you done that? Have you noticed that the longer you stand still, the deeper you sink into the sand? Stand for several minutes and you become well-anchored.

I hope you have discovered by now that stubbornness really doesn't get you anywhere. A lack of flexibility, an absence of compromise, an insistence on getting your own way... All lead to a difficult life. Now, there are some areas of our lives about which we need to be stubborn. We cannot compromise our Biblical beliefs, nor our Christian ethics, nor our allegiance to God and God alone. That brings resiliency to our faith. It's the other kind of stubbornness that limits our lives.

Sometimes we think that we alone are the harbingers of truth. We think we know all the answers and we refuse to listen to anyone else who might have an idea. Sometimes our stubbornness surfaces in our hoarding of things. We stubbornly cling to our wealth as though it is ours to keep. Rather than share with others and serve humanity, we only tighten the grip. Sometimes our stubbornness closes off our minds to new ideas and even to new ways that God may want to work in our lives. Do you see what happens? We play the part of Pharaoh. We harden our hearts and we hurt others by doing so. Our stubbornness doesn't move the kingdom forward, it does just the opposite, it slows its progress. Take a moment to consider if there are areas of your life about which you are a little stubborn. Are you willing to soften your stance if it means by doing so, God can work more effectively in your life?

Prayer
Father, may our love and grace be stubborn, but may our attitudes be flexible. Amen.

Day 59 — Exodus 9: Waiting on the Lord

> "The LORD set a definite time, saying, 'Tomorrow the LORD will do this thing in the land.'" Exodus 9:5 (NASB)

Observation

In the on-going conversation between Moses and Pharaoh, Moses continues to instruct Pharaoh to let the Israelites go, but Pharaoh's heart is continually hardened, and additional pestilence and plagues are brought to Egypt. Our focus verse this morning contains the words spoken to Moses by God, telling him that on the next day, the pestilence of the livestock will occur. (All the cattle, camels, horses, donkeys, and sheep belonging to the Egyptians would die because of the plague, but none of those belonging to the Israelites would suffer.) Moses was given a very specific timetable by God. God promised that these events would occur the following day.

Application

There are people who like to schedule every event and aspect of their lives to the nth degree and those who don't. The schedulers might plan out their lives several years in advance. The "free spirits" among us tend to go with as little planning as possible. Both groups have their strong points. The planners are probably more productive. The free spirits probably live with less stress. But whether you over-plan or under-plan, timetables are important. Key events must anticipated and plans carried out.

Sometimes we get a little frustrated with God's timetable. We think that God should do certain things, change certain lives, and answer certain prayers all according to our schedules. In our own human wisdom, we think we know what is best. We petition God to do things immediately. We get frustrated and even despondent when our prayers are seemingly unanswered in the time frame in which we think they should be answered. But the simple truth of the matter is that our ways are not God's ways, and our timetables are not always God's. God's knowledge is superior. God's wisdom is infinite. God's love is unfathomable. So why would we ever question the ways in which God works? Count on the fact that God has set a definite time to accomplish all that is to be accomplished. As the writer of Ecclesiastes once mused, "There is an appointed time for everything. And there is a time for every event under heaven" (Ecclesiastes 3:1 NASB). Our role in God's plan is not to attempt the manipulation of God's timetable, but to simply pray and wait. We wait for the moments when God acts, and praise God for those actions. Whenever we develop a sense of frustration with God's schedule, let us turn the frustration into faithful praying. God will hear and, yes, God will respond... in God's time.

Prayer

Father, teach us patience as we wait for your purposes to be accomplished. Amen.

Day 60 — Exodus 10: This Little Light of Mine...

> "Then the LORD said to Moses, 'Stretch out your hand toward the sky, that there may be darkness over the land of Egypt, even a darkness which may be felt.'" Exodus 10:21 (NASB)

Observation
Again, God, through Moses, continues to throw plagues and pestilence toward Pharaoh and the Egyptians. God continues to remind Moses that God's power will be displayed before Egypt. Two plagues are mentioned in this chapter. First is the plague of locusts, which completely cover the land and destroy all the vegetation. Second, is the plague of darkness, which envelops the land for three days. Notice the description... It was a "darkness so deep that it could be felt."

Application
Sometimes you can feel the darkness even in the midst of bright sunlight. Darkness can appear not only at twilight, but also in the hearts and attitudes of men and women. Even though the sun rises each day, there is present among us a troubling darkness. It's the darkness that only evil can produce. It is in greed that pushes away pure motivation and honest dealing. You can feel it in the deceit of a heart that is filled with selfish desire, long shut off from a spirit of care for others. You can feel it rise from the lustful images that fill our screens. You can sense the darkness from the politics of our day that care more for party gain than national service. You can feel the darkness each time a husband turns from his wife to pursue the charms of another woman. You can feel it when the poor are marginalized and needy are ignored. You can feel it when priests molest the very children they are charged with nurturing. You can sense it when even the faithful betray their faith by allowing a compromise of conviction and discipline.

So, what's the answer to darkness? Turn on the light. Jesus said, "You are the light of the world. A city set on a hill cannot be hidden" (Matthew 5:14 NASB). Christ intends for you to be a light-bearer. God has placed you in this world to dispel the darkness. God intends for you to go forth with the message of grace, and peace, and hope, and righteousness that Jesus died to offer. God has not created you to be silent, to be timid, or to be uninvolved. As the people of God, we are set apart to make a difference. Understand, we are not called to some lofty, pious, "I'm-better-than-you" attitude. We are called to shine the light of Christ within us so that the darkness might be dispelled. So how is it with you this day? Are you adding to the darkness, or are you shining the Light?

Prayer
Father, make us different that we might make a difference. Amen.

Day 61 — Exodus 11: The Difference that Faith Makes

> "'Moreover, there shall be a great cry in all the land of Egypt, such as there has not been before and such as shall never be again. But against any of the sons of Israel a dog will not even bark, whether against man or beast, that you may understand how the LORD makes a distinction between Egypt and Israel.'" Exodus 11:6-7 (NASB)

Observation
This is a prelude to the last and great plague, the Passover event, when God will send an angel over the nation of Egypt and all the firstborn of Egypt will die. Notice the descriptive words of turmoil and anguish that will erupt on the part of the Egyptians. "There shall be a great cry... such as there has not been before and such as shall never be again." In contrast, notice the still, calm spirit that will fall on all those who follow the Lord God... absolute peace and quiet. There is a distinction to be drawn between the faithful and those who have not recognized God's authority.

Application
Believers and non-believers have such a difference in life perspective. Those who claim a faith in Jesus Christ live with certain assurances. We live with a peace knowing that our final destiny has been determined. We live with a joy knowing that our sins have been forgiven. We live with a sense of assurance knowing that we are not separated from God, but that God's Spirit abides within us. We live with a contentment knowing that the presence of Jesus is with us each day. We live with the privilege of prayer that allows us to connect with the God of the universe in a personal way at any moment.

Notice the contrast to those who live without a knowledge of God. No peace. No lasting joy. No hope for the future. No removal of guilt. No assurances. No protection from evil. Who would want to live that way? No one. The problem is that so many in our world have simply never really heard the message of the Gospel. Oh, they may have heard the story, or even read a Bible at some point, but the words seem empty and devoid of meaning because no one has "lived-out" such a faith in their presence. The world needs to encounter the Living Lord through the hearts and minds of God's followers. The challenge for those who claim the Christian faith is to live such a faith, authentically, honestly, and consistently. We are given the potential to the world with our lived-out faith. What will you do today to demonstrate the difference that Christ has made in your life? What will you do to offer hope? How will your attitudes demonstrate grace? How will you model compassion?

Prayer
Father, give us such an authentic faith that our very lives will testify to your greatness.

Day 62 — Exodus 12: It's Story Time

> "And when your children say to you, 'What does this rite mean to you?' you shall say, 'It is a Passover sacrifice to the LORD who passed over the houses of the sons of Israel in Egypt when He smote the Egyptians, but spared our homes.' And the people bowed low and worshiped."
> Exodus 12:26-27 (NASB)

Observation
This chapter tells of both the Passover and the institution of the Passover feast. The event was so powerful, so important, and so pivotal to the story of the Exodus that God commanded that all future generations should observe the feast and in so doing, remember God's powerful acts. In telling the story of Passover each Spring, the faithful would continue to teach future generations about God's deliverance from bondage.

Application
I like to think of myself as a good storyteller. I have funeral stories that I love to share because of the humor embedded within them. I have stories about my high school and college days that I love to tell. I often get home in the evening nearly busting at the seams to tell the story of something that happened at work. But I have to ask myself, am I as intentional about telling the stories of faith from the pages of scripture and from my own faith pilgrimage?

The truth is that we have lost some important traditions. We have forgotten how to teach our children the great stories of faith so that they will know the power of the God we serve. Consider Christmas and Easter. Do we take the time to teach the significance of those events to our children? My fear is that we get so bogged down with the trappings of the season that we forget to teach the stories that form the basis of our celebrations. We talk of presents and trees and family meals, but do we really tell the story of Christmas? At Easter, we talk of eggs and new dresses and baskets full of candy, but do our children know of the resurrection?

I believe that there is a growing ignorance among our children in terms of the Biblical narrative. Our kids are losing a connection to the great stories of the Old Testament. Stories that we treasured as children are seldom brought to the attention of the next generation. Even with the New Testament, we seldom take the time to teach our children the parables of Christ, the journeys of Paul, or the miraculous jail escapes from the book of Acts. Let me challenge you to do better. Teach the next generation about the stories of God. If nothing else, buy a Bible story book and read to your kids. Is it not a shame that our children know more about Sponge Bob and Cinderella than they do about Abraham and Joseph?

Prayer
Father, inspire us again to tell the great stories of faith. Amen.

Day 63 — Exodus 13: What's on Your Mind?

> "So it shall serve as a sign on your hand and as phylacteries on your forehead, for with a powerful hand the LORD brought us out of Egypt."
> Exodus 13:16 (NASB)

Observation
Part of the instructions Moses gave to the Israelites about how they were to keep the Passover feast in future generations was to record the story and physically tie it to their hands and foreheads as they prayed during the celebration. A "phylactery" was a small box in which pieces of scripture could be placed. The idea was for the small box to be tied to a person's forehead so that they would remember with great clarity the story of God's deliverance as they prayed. It's the idea that the story of God would be foremost in their minds as they celebrated the Passover.

Application
In a recent meeting with a co-worker, I noticed the window in her office was a bit cloudy. Apparently, the seal has broken between the double panes of glass and there is no way to wipe them clean. It will have to be replaced. Now, every time she looks out the window she has to see through cloudy glass. Let me turn the thought around for a moment. What if, rather than obstructing the view, it gave greater clarity? What if her window was not cloudy but had telescopic properties that allowed her to see the world altogether differently? What if her perspective changed because she looked at life through a different lens?

The story of God and our deliverance should remain at the forefront of our minds. Is it even possible that the story of the Gospel could ever escape our attention? The problem for many of us is the tedium of the day-to-day stuff. If we are not careful, we can lose sight of the greater things of our lives. In other words, we sometimes let life on this earth keep us from our focus on the life that is to come. We do live in a real world, with real problems, and with real needs. We cannot and should not ignore any of that. What we should do however, is to take what our faith teaches us about the ways of God and God's plans for our lives and apply that knowledge to the everyday stuff. We should go out boldly into each new day with the assurances of God's word strapped firmly to the forefront of our minds. I'm not advocating that you walk around with a tiny box strapped to your forehead, but I am suggesting that you walk around with the word of God firmly planted in both heart and mind so that you will remember the story of God and allow it to guide your steps.

Prayer
Father, we ask that you place your word in our hearts and that you keep it at the forefront of our minds each day. Amen.

Day 64 — Exodus 14: Who Fights Your Battles?

> "The sons of Israel went through the midst of the sea on the dry land, and the waters were like a wall to them on their right hand and on their left."
> Exodus 14:22 (NASB)

Observation

Chapter 14 describes the great deliverance of the sons of Israel from the Egyptians as they fled through the midst of the Red Sea. As God instructed, Moses held out his staff over the waters and the sea divided. The Israelites rushed across the dry bed of the sea all through the night. When the morning came and the Egyptians attempted to pursue them, the waters engulfed them, and the victory was complete. By the hand of God, the Israelites were brought safely through, their enemies to be seen never again.

Application

This is one of the great Bible stories that we have imagined since childhood. We see the huge walls of water to the right and to the left. We see the Israelites scurrying along as fast as their feet will take them, walking on the dry ground in the depths of the seabed. Surely it was a wild, frenetic, fearful, fast-paced night. And then we see the waters fold in on top of the pursuing army. Within moments all the charging chariots, fierce warriors, and blood-thirsty soldiers are submerged beneath the water, never to rise again. Surely as the Israelites began to realize the miracle which unfolded before their eyes, they rejoiced with exceeding joy at the providence of God in their lives.

Our God is all about deliverance. It is by God's power that our enemies are defeated and our souls are rescued. What are the biggest enemies you face this morning? What nips at your heels? What robs you of sleep? What fear is eating away at your health? Name your biggest fear. Is it health related? Is it financial stress? Is your enemy some pressure that is driving a wedge into your closest relationship? Is your enemy some addiction? Is it someone at work who just seems to have it in for you? God doesn't want you to live your life cowering under the oppression of fear. If God can defeat an entire army, erasing them from the face of the earth in a single morning, don't you think that God has the power to help you with your enemy? Take a moment to claim your fear and talk to God about the oppression that the enemy brings to your door. Cry out to God and let God's peace and grace wash over your life. Your enemies do not have to define your life... not anymore. The power of God is greater than the power of your enemies. Entrust the battle to God's care and see the salvation of Lord in your life.

Prayer

Father, remind us today of your continual deliverance. Amen.

Day 65 — Exodus 15: An Offering of Song

> "Who is like You among the gods, O LORD?
> Who is like You, majestic in holiness,
> Awesome in praises, working wonders?" Exodus 15:11 (NASB)

Observation
Most of this chapter is a song of praise offered to God for deliverance of Israel from the Egyptian army. The opening verse states that Moses and the sons of Israel sang this song. That's an interesting image of Moses. I usually think of him as a great and powerful warrior and not as a song leader. But on this occasion, even the great liberator breaks out in song over what the Lord has done in their midst. Notice the words themselves. They speak of the majesty of God. They speak of God's greatness and God's uniqueness. It's a rhetorical question, "Who is like You..."

Application
I have never claimed to be a great singer. I can't read music. In our youth group, I was asked to "run the sound equipment" and not sing! But I do like to sing or whistle or hum a tune. I like the way a song can get stuck in my mind early in the morning and stay there all day. Sometimes I even find myself singing the words of one of the great old hymns, finding encouragement as I do.

Let's reflect on the greatness of God reflected in Moses' song. Who is there like our God? Though we sometimes attempt to create our own gods of success, power, and possession, we are forced to confess that our "created gods" are not really gods at all. They are just things we sometimes worship as though they give life and power. There is only One True God, unique in the universe. God is not rivaled in power, nor strength, nor creativity, nor wisdom, nor majesty. Who is like our God?

In our focus verse, Moses and the sons of Israel sing of God's ability to work wonders. That ability to do great and mighty things has in no way diminished through the centuries. The same God Who once parted the sea still works miracles and wonders in our midst. Who among us hasn't experienced an answered prayer? Who among us has not felt God's hand of protection over his/her life? Who among us has not witnessed God's creativity, or felt God's presence in unique ways? Each day, if we are careful to look, we can see God at work. We can feel God's presence. We can revel in God's grace. Maybe we too should break forth with a new song of praise. Who is like our God? Majestic in holiness, awesome in praises, working wonders...

Prayer
Father, this day we praise you with grateful hearts. We celebrate your creativity, your protection, and your presence in our lives. May you be exalted among the nations. Amen.

Day 66 — Exodus 16: Trust Goes a Long Way

> "I have heard the grumblings of the sons of Israel; speak to them, saying, 'At twilight you shall eat meat, and in the morning you shall be filled with bread; and you shall know that I am the LORD your God.'"
> Exodus 16:12 (NASB)

Observation

As the nation of Israel began the trek across the wilderness, they soon began complaining to Moses about the lack of food. They were fearful of starving to death. They asked Moses, "Have you led us out into the wilderness to die?" They forgot for a moment who actually had led them on their deliverance march. They had forgotten that the God who owns the cattle on a thousand hills and who controls the very storehouses of heaven was leading their journey. In our focus passage, God is instructing Moses to tell the people of God's provision of food. They will eat quail at night and manna each morning. God will provide for their needs.

Application

Ever worry that you don't have enough, that you can't make it with the meager resources you have? Every worry that you have too many bills and not enough paycheck? Ever worry that you have too much to do and not enough time? Ever worry that you have too many problems and not enough answers? Welcome to the club.

How much of our anxious worry could be alleviated each day if we remembered God remains in control of our world. We worry and complain about the things that we need as though God is unable to meet those needs. Paul offers these words to the church at Philippi... "And my God shall supply all your needs according to His riches in glory in Christ Jesus" (Philippians 4:19 NASB). Just as the ancient Israelites had to learn the lesson of God dependency, we too must learn to trust God for the needs of our lives. Do we possibly think that the God who gave bread in the wilderness can't help with our hunger? Do we think that the God who led their steps can't provide us with direction? Do we think that the God who heard their cries turns a deaf ear to ours? Do we think that the God who gave them protection from their enemies won't defend us against ours? If God gives you a vision, God will provide the means for its fulfillment. If God gives you a calling, God will provide a way for you to follow. If God gives you a talent, God will provide a place for its use. Rather than worrying about what you don't have, learn to depend on the one who possesses all things. Trust God for both the daily bread and for the supplies to fuel whatever dream God plants in your heart.

Prayer

Father, teach us to learn dependency upon you. Teach us to trust you fully as we embrace the plans you have for our lives. Amen.

Day 67   Exodus 17: I Get by with a Little Help from My Friends

> "But Moses' hands were heavy. Then they took a stone and put it under him, and he sat on it; and Aaron and Hur supported his hands, one on one side and one on the other. Thus his hands were steady until the sun set."
> Exodus 17:12 (NASB)

Observation
Not long after their journey into the wilderness began, Moses and the sons of Israel were attacked by Amalek. Led by God to do battle, Moses stood on the hillside with Aaron and Hur at his side while the Israelites battled the Amalekites in the valley below. As long as Moses stood with his arms in the air, extending the rod of God in his hand, the Israelites prevailed. But when his arms grew tired and he could no longer hold the rod high, the Amalekites prevailed. Aaron and Hur responded to the situation by standing on each side of Moses and holding up his arms. Because of their actions, the Israelites prevailed with an overwhelming victory.

Application
This story is a great lesson about the importance of supporting each other in the battles that matter most in life. Without the help of Aaron and Hur, Moses could not have claimed victory. But with the support of others, the battle was secured. I wonder what battles you face this day and whom you have chosen to help you in the fray. We face a lot of challenges. We struggle to stand strong in our faith. We battle to do the right thing. We fight to raise our kids well and show devotion to our spouses. We battle the enemies of peer pressure, despair, and temptation. We battle financial pressure and job security. We are attacked by many foes. And if the truth be told, when we battle our biggest enemies alone, we tend to falter. We need the help of others. Whom we chose at such moments makes all the difference.

So, who do you have in your corner? Who fights life's battles with you? (I'm not talking this morning about the help you gain through your faith relationship with Christ... I am talking about the flesh and blood people whom you draw to your side.) Who are the dependable people that always push you to do the right thing? Parents? Your spouse? A friend? A spiritual mentor? A teacher? A coach? Take a close look at those with whom you have chosen to surround yourself. Are they a help or a hindrance? Will they hold up your arms during the intense moments or will they abandon you when the pressure mounts? Choose your closest confidants well. They will help you to win the battles.

Prayer
Father, teach us to value our friends and the counsel they offer. May we choose well those in whom we will place our trust. Amen.

Day 68　　　　　　　　　　Exodus 18: We Can't Do It All

> "Furthermore, you shall select out of all the people able men who fear God, men of truth, those who hate dishonest gain; and you shall place these over them as leaders of thousands, of hundreds, of fifties and of tens."
> Exodus 18:21 (NASB)

Observation
Jethro, the father-in-law of Moses, brings Moses' wife and children to the Israelite encampment. He observes the people coming to Moses in great numbers to seek his advice and counsel. People stand in line for hours to speak with Moses. Jethro advises Moses to choose able leaders who can help him in this task, with major disputes still brought before Moses, but smaller cases settled by these chosen leaders.

Application
I have a friend in the ministry who is a little bit of a ... how shall we say it? Control freak. She is a very dedicated disciple of Christ, and she is a very caring and compassionate person but she is way too busy for her own good. She tries to do too much. She sweats every little detail while there are those around her who could help to shoulder the load. I hope she learns the lesson of allowing others to help with various tasks before she suffers from self-destruction.

Moses learned a valuable lesson in time management from his father-in-law. Moses was quickly heading toward burnout. Carrying the weight of all the needs of Israel proved too burdensome for him to manage. Choosing faithful and wise leaders to help with the important tasks would relieve stress for both Moses and those whom he served.

Anybody need to hear that advice this morning? Admittedly, there are a lot of control-freaks among us who feel the need to micro-manage every phase of the work around us. And we wonder why people in every profession tend to burnout so quickly. God surrounds us with people for a reason. Part of that reason is to help carry the load. If you want to lower your stress level and at the same time give others a sense of worth and value, learn to entrust them with responsibility. Off-load a little of the daily grind and find the relaxing peace that can come when you don't attempt to become all things to all people. Sometimes the key in being successful is to discover the things you do really well and focus on doing those things, instead of trying to do all things. In other words, do what you do well and let others do what they do well. Choose capable folks to entrust with some of your tasks, and watch your health and stress level improve.

Prayer
Father, teach us the importance of shared responsibility. May we learn the value of allowing others a place to serve and use their gifts. Amen.

Day 69 — Exodus 19: May I Introduce You?

> "And Moses brought the people out of the camp to meet God, and they stood at the foot of the mountain." Exodus 19:17 (NASB)

Observation

Three months after the Israelites departed from Egypt, God led them to the foot of Mt. Sinai. God told Moses and that God would be revealed to the nation of Israel there on the mountain. They were to consecrate themselves and put on fresh garments on the third day so that God would appear before them. They were not allowed to go up on the mountain, but to stand at the base and see the presence of the Lord. Notice the wording of our focus verse, "And Moses brought the people out of the camp to meet God." That was his task, to bring the nation into the presence of God.

Application

In like fashion, we are charged with bringing people into the presence of God. It is our duty as Christians to help people meet the Father. We are to act as the go-between, the envoy, the ambassador. We take people who live without a knowledge of God, those who live without knowing the love and grace of Jesus, and we make the introduction. We bring them into the presence of the Father. Easier said than done, right? How do we lead others to "meet God?" We never accomplish the work of faith-sharing apart from relationships. In other words, we can't introduce anyone to Christ without building some type of connection to them. It is as we nurture a relationship with a non-believer that the freedom comes to have conversations that focus on spiritual things. We build a bridge of relationship and the Gospel begins to walk across that bridge. So, as we speak to those who are struggling to understand spiritual things, we make the introduction.

Admittedly, many of us struggle with what to say and how to say it. We fear that our Biblical knowledge is insufficient or that our theology lacks all the underpinning that might be needed in the midst of some debate. Good news. You do not have to have all the answers. God's Spirit does and God will guide the conversation. Your job is to get people to the place where the Spirit speaks strongly. God will honor your invitation. As you build the relationship, invite that person to attend church with you. Bring them in your own car or promise to take them to lunch afterward, but do offer a sincere invitation. Encourage them to attend a small group. You might be surprised at how willing your friends are to explore their faith. (As a reminder, this Sunday would be a really good day to bring someone to hear about the love of Christ. Just saying…)

Prayer

Father, teach us ways that we can introduce those who struggle spiritually with your love and saving grace. Amen.

Day 70 — Exodus 20: Just When I Need Him Most...

> "I am the LORD your God, who brought you out of the land of Egypt, out of the house of slavery." Exodus 20:2 (NASB)

Observation

The words of our focus verse serve as sort of a preamble to the 10 Commandments. In the verses that follow, God shares with Moses those foundational principles for worship and living that we call the 10 Commandments. Just before God declares that we are to "have no gods before Him" (20:3 NASB), God reminds Moses, and us, that God is the Lord God: THE God who brought them out of Egypt's enslavement and the God who brings us out of our enslavement of sin. That's God's nature. God hears our cries, God meets our needs, and God offers us grace.

Application

Recently, I was reminded once again of the providential care of God in our lives each day. I was startled awake by a phone call from one of my favorite people. She was obviously in distress. While driving on the interstate in the midst of a thunderstorm, her car hydroplaned and she suddenly found herself spinning out of control. Her car spun across three lanes of traffic and off the road, sliding into a ditch. She was understandably rattled and needed a little support. I was glad to help. Remarkably, and gratefully, she was completely unharmed. Her car had come to rest on top of a downed utility pole and was stuck in some thick mud. Once the tow truck pulled her car out of the ditch, we discovered that it too was still in good shape. I took it for a test drive and gave it the "all clear." My friend was soon back on the road, a little shaken and $80 poorer (tow truck charge), but grateful to be alive and well.

I was reminded again of the God who brings us out of our troubles. Where would we be apart from God's grace? How would we live separated from God's protection? How would we survive without God' love? Just as God reminded the Israelites their redemption from slavery, perhaps we need to be reminded of our redemption from sin. It is God who rescues us from the mess we have made of our lives. It is God who releases us from the enslavement of guilt and shame that sin attempts to bring to our lives. It is by God's power that we are set free to live the life willed for us to enjoy. So, where do you find yourself this morning? Is it possible that you have spun off the road of sane and rational living and find yourself wounded in the ditch, wondering how you will ever make sense of your life? God longs to rescue us from the chains that shackle us to our past lives of mistakes and to bring us out of the "house of slavery" and set us free again. It's time to get out of the ditch and start moving forward again.

Prayer

Father, thank you for your protection, your love, and your forgiving grace. Amen.

Day 71 — Exodus 21: What Sets You Free?

> "And if he knocks out a tooth of his male or female slave, he shall let him go free on account of his tooth." Exodus 21:27 (NASB)

Observation

Chapter 21 of Exodus is a set of ordinances that God tells Moses to "set before the people." In other words, these are guidelines that are to be carefully followed by the Israelites that will bring a sense of peace, fairness, and justice among the people. These guidelines deal with topics like wrongful death, slavery, and revenge. (Admittedly, there are some strange guidelines offered in this chapter.) Our focus verse is an ordinance that offers freedom to a slave if the owner happens to knock out his/her tooth. The slave is to be set free.

Application

That's a little weird for a Bible verse, isn't it? First, that God would allow slavery is a whole different topic for another day, but is it not odd that a slave could be set free by the loss of a tooth? The loss of a tooth could set a man free. What sets you free this morning? All of us have the potential of being enslaved. We are slaves to sin, slaves to guilt, slaves to remorse and shame. We are tethered to our past mistakes, chained to our imperfect pasts, tied to our past poor decisions and choices. What can set us free? What buys our pardon that we might live as free men and women before God? It takes more than the loss of a molar... It takes the giving of a life, not ours, but Christ's.

The whole point of the Gospel story is to remind us that we have been pardoned, redeemed, bought-back, by the sacrifice Jesus Christ made for us on the cross. The cost of our sins was paid, the past mistakes erased, the guilt and shame wiped away. By his wounds we are healed, by his grace we are set free. It's called the doctrine of atonement. In Biblical terms, blood represents life. To reclaim the life that sin has taken from us, we must claim the blood of Jesus Christ offered on the cross. So why live like a slave to that from which Christ has set you free? If Christ sets you free, you are free indeed. As you walk your way through this day, let me encourage you to walk a little differently. Walk with your back a bit straighter, your steps a bit lighter, and your countenance a bit brighter. You have been set free.

Prayer

Father, we thank you for setting us free through the cross of Jesus Christ. May we live this day in the joyful reflection of all that such freedom offers. Amen.

Day 72   Exodus 22: Putting Out the Welcome Mat

> "You shall not wrong a stranger or oppress him, for you were strangers in the land of Egypt." Exodus 22:21 (NASB)

Observation
Like the chapter before it, Chapter 22 is filled with laws and ordinances that deal with a variety of things like property rights, and sundry laws. Our focus verse this morning deals with the treatment of strangers in the midst of Israel. God told the Israelites to remember the time when they lived as strangers (foreigners) in the land of Egypt. Because they knew what it was like to be treated unfairly, they were to treat the strangers in their land better. They were to treat the outsiders in a way that would reflect their own allegiance to God. In other words, God's people should hold themselves to a higher standard of moral and ethical conduct.

Application
Have you ever been on the outside? Have you ever been a newcomer while all those around you ignored your presence? Ever been bullied because your clothes were different, or your accent sounded funny, or your haircut was "stupid?" I would like to think that anyone who has ever been marginalized would have the perspective and courage not to marginalize others.

There is something in this verse that speaks to the idea of Christian hospitality. God commands that the people learn to value others and treat them with simple respect and human dignity. Consider for a moment how we tend to treat the stranger in our midst. You know, the outsider that doesn't speak our language, doesn't know our customs, and doesn't understand our ways. There is a natural tendency to separate "them" from us. Rather than offer them a friendly handshake, a word of kindness, or a helping hand of support, we tend to shun them, lock our doors against them, and even insist that "they" must assimilate fully into our culture and ways. In very real ways we oppress them by not putting our best foot forward.

I wonder what it would do for race relations, long-ingrained bigotry, and prejudicial hatred if the people of God began to act like the people of God? What if we took seriously the role we are to play in extending hospitality? What if we started looking for ways to help the stranger in our midst instead of figuring out new ways of keeping them at arm's length? God expects us to think differently and act courageously toward others. What can you do this day to offer the stranger a little respect and affirmation?

Prayer
Father, we ask that you might show us practical ways of living out our faith before others. May we be known for our inclusive love and our welcoming spirit. Amen.

Day 73 — Exodus 23: What Influences Your Life?

> "They shall not live in your land, because they will make you sin against Me; for if you serve their gods, it will surely be a snare to you."
> Exodus 23:33 (NASB)

Observation
As God finishes giving the law to Moses and the people on Mount Sinai, God tells them about the ways in which they will be lead in their conquest as they enter the promised land. God carefully instructs them on how they are to drive out their enemies from the land. The sons of Israel cannot allow any of them to remain and influence the Israelites to sin against God. God instructs the people to remove those things that lead them to do evil.

Application
This verse raises the subject of influence. God insisted that the current inhabitants be driven from the land so that the threat of negative influence would be removed from the lives of the Israelites. Their influence, culture, and customs would slowly and surely begin to penetrate the hearts and minds of God's people.

I wonder if we are as careful to remove from our lives those people and things that cause us to act in ways that do not honor our Lord? First, are there people in your life that tend to pull you away from God rather than push you towards God? Consider who influences your key decisions, your actions, and your journeys. Have you surrounded yourself with people who desperately seek the heart of God, or have you surrounded yourself with those who care little about spiritual things? Second, take a moment to consider what other "things" influence the way you think and live. What about the music you that plays on your smartphone? What about the radio talk show that you hear each morning? What about the TV programs you watch? What about the books you read? It all speaks to heart and mind. It slowly penetrates and shapes your opinions and thoughts. Third, what about the danger of only listening to our own thoughts? Without the perspective and wisdom of Godly men and women in our lives, we can distort truth and twist theology. We need the insight that others can offer so that our minds won't be limited with selfish perspective. So be careful to monitor all those things that influence your life. Have enough courage to remove those things that lead you in the wrong direction. Embrace those which draw you closer to God.

Prayer
Father, may we have the wisdom to see very clearly the way in which our lives are being shaped by negative influences. Give us the courage to make needed changes. Amen.

Day 74 — Exodus 24: The Face of God

> "Then Moses went up with Aaron, Nadab and Abihu, and seventy of the elders of Israel, and they saw the God of Israel; and under His feet there appeared to be a pavement of sapphire, as clear as the sky itself."
> Exodus 24:9-10 (NASB)

Observation
You may want to read these two verses again. Seventy-four men go up to Mount Sinai and there they "saw the God of Israel." It's not the kind of thing that happens every day. These men, in some magnificent, mysterious, glorious way were able to catch a glimpse of God. They even described the pavement of sapphire on which God walked. (I know what you're thinking... I thought no one could look on God and live. That's usually the case. But God can do as God chooses. And at least on this day, God was seen by the elders of Israel.) Don't you know that this image never left their hearts or minds for as long as they lived. How many times did they tell the story of this day?

Application
Catching a glimpse of Almighty God is a rare thing. I have not seen God's face, nor has anyone else that I know. I do hope to look on God's face one day when Christ introduces me in glory... But that's a different devotional thought for another day. This morning I'm more concerned about seeing the face of God in the everyday lives we live. The truth of the matter is that we CAN see God each day if we know where to look. God inhabits creation. And so, God is revealed to us in tiny glimpses through the faces of people that we encounter. How's that for a thought? A little of God is present in every face we see. If that is true, then God can be seen in the faces of rich and powerful as well as the faces of the poor and powerless. God's present in the face of that homeless guy selling papers on the corner. God's present in the face of that unwed pregnant girl at the shelter. God's present in the face of that troubled teenager you are raising and in the face of the senior adult at the nursing home. And yes, God is even seen in the face that stares back at you from the mirror. What a glorious day it would be today, if you and I really began to see others the way that God does. What if we looked closely enough to even see God's resemblance?

To see God's face, we must look beyond our first-impression judgment of others. We cannot see color, nationality, nor gender if doing so clouds our vision. We must hear beyond language. Our history and experience with an individual cannot be allowed to blind us to the image of God within them.

Prayer
Father, give us the eyes to see your face today in the faces of the people around us. Amen.

Day 75 — Exodus 25: Follow the Blueprint

> "According to all that I am going to show you, as the pattern of the tabernacle and the pattern of all its furniture, just so you shall construct it."
> Exodus 25:9 (NASB)

Observation

Along with the 10 Commandments and other ordinances given on Mount Sinai, God also gave to Moses very specific instructions about the construction of the tabernacle, the Ark of the Covenant, the table of showbread, and the golden lampstand. (These later three items were to be placed in the tabernacle and used as a part of worship.) God would give Moses very exacting measurements for all these items, including dimensions and materials to use. God's "blueprints" were to be followed exactly.

Application

Ask any architect or contractor and they can tell you about the importance of blueprints. Every piece of instruction must be carried out with exact detail if the building is to be sturdy and strong. Not only was God concerned about the details of the tabernacle and its content, but God was, and is, also concerned about the details of our lives. God's instructions are to be carried out with precision if we are to claim the best life possible.

Consider the 10 Commandments for a moment. Rather than view them a rigid set of "dos and don'ts" consider them more of a blueprint for successful living. View them as guidelines to be followed for living the best life possible. For example, when God says, "Do not commit adultery," God is teaching us to honor our marriages. When God says, "Do not kill," God is teaching us to value human life. When God says, "Do not covet," God is teaching us to find contentment in the blessings and provisions we already have from God's hand. Yes, the Commandments are laws, not to be broken, but they should also serve as blueprints to keep our lives "on track." Sometimes we see God as some type of strict disciplinarian. A better viewpoint is that of a loving father that longs to teach us the best ways to live. Just as a parent teaches a child how to be careful and obedient, God longs to instruct us on the ways that provide successful living. Let's pay attention to the blueprint. Let's live according to God's instruction and discover how meaningful life can really be.

Prayer

Father, we thank you for your commandments. May we live as obedient children, not to limit our lives, but to give ourselves the best life possible. Amen.

Day 76 — Exodus 26: Plans & Materials

> "Then you shall erect the tabernacle according to its plan which you have been shown in the mountain." Exodus 26:30 (NASB)

Observation
Each time that I read this passage I am struck with a sense of awe at the precise details that God gave Moses about the tabernacle construction. God didn't just say, "Build me a place of worship." Instead God offered exact dimensions and even instructed the craftsmen how to piece it all together. Every curtain, every pole, every board... all carefully described and measured. This "portable" house of worship would be built according to God's careful instruction.

Application
I recently built a swing set in my backyard for the grand kids to enjoy when they come to visit. (I have to admit that my grand kid's other grandfather owns an entire gymnastics gym and I have to continually step up my game!) To build the swing set, I purchased the lumber and a "kit" from Home Depot. I was impressed with the kit. It was very complete. It contained every bolt, every screw, every brace, and even the chains for the swings. Along with the hardware the box also contained a very complete set of instructions. Though the process was a little time consuming, the swing set came together really well. The kit explained the details.

God cares about the details. Notice that God did not simply envision a place of worship but offered careful direction as to how the tabernacle was to be completed. It's the same with our lives. God doesn't simply say to us, "Go and live a life that honors me." God also gives us detailed plans to get that accomplished. First, God offers the direction of scripture. Reading the Bible is not just a religious discipline. It becomes a source book for how to raise families, how to conduct business, how to honor your spouse, etc. Second, God gives us the church in order that we might learn to worship, serve, and grow in our faith. God doesn't intend for us to struggle our way through life on our own, trying to figure out this whole spiritual aspect. God provides us with people to help us in our journey. God provides people who help us to think, pray, interpret, and reason. Third, God provides us with the Holy Spirit. Embedded deeply within each of us is a source of counsel, wisdom, and direction. God's Spirit continues to lead us daily in our attempt to honor God fully. Let us be grateful this day for the plans God has for each of us and for God's leadership that allows us to build our lives on the principles that bring God glory.

Prayer
Father, we thank you for calling us to a holy life and for giving us the means with which to live it. Amen.

Day 77 — Exodus 27: Keep the Light On

> "In the tent of meeting, outside the veil which is before the testimony, Aaron and his sons shall keep it [Lamp] in order from evening to morning before the LORD; it shall be a perpetual statute throughout their generations for the sons of Israel." Exodus 27:21 (NASB)

Observation

Continuing instructions to the Israelites concerning the tabernacle and the things of the tabernacle, God tells Moses about the lampstand that is to be placed just outside of the veil that separates the Holy of Holies from the rest of the interior space. God gives instructions that Aaron and his sons, whose descendants were selected to be the priestly tribe, are to keep the lamp burning from dusk to dawn every day. They were charged with the task throughout the generations of Israel. In other words, the lamp was to be lit each night and provision made for it to burn continually through the night, every night.

Application

Ever experienced one of those stormy nights when a bolt of lightning flashes and suddenly you are in the complete darkness because the electricity is knocked off-line? It's an eerie sensation. You can almost feel the darkness. It reminds you how much you depend upon and value the small lights in your home that are always lit, that always give you enough illumination to help you keep your bearings. We are scared without the light.

God charged Aaron and his sons with keeping the lamp lit. The lamp was not intended to be some great "night light" so that the priests could find their way in the dark. It was far more important than that. It was to symbolize the presence of God and to remind them of God's constant watch care over them. Today, most churches are not concerned with keeping an oil lamp burning each night, although the image of God's continual presence and protection is still one we should hold dear. Instead of a lamp, the light of God is now to be carried forth in God's people. Christ said we are the light of the world. It is our job to keep the light of Christ burning before the nations. From our hearts, our words, our actions, and our attitudes, the presence of God should emanate. The truth of God's grace, love, and mercy should be so evident in the lives of each believer that when people look at us, the light still shines. In the darkest night of someone's life, the presence of a Christian friend should bring hope and peace. Are you keeping the light on? Does the very presence of Christ live in you so strongly that others are offered an assurance by your life?

Prayer

Father, use us this day to shine your light in the midst of our dark world. May our testimony of words and action give strength to someone who needs hope. Amen.

Day 78 — Exodus 28: Reminders of our Faith

> "You shall put the two stones on the shoulder pieces of the ephod, as stones of memorial for the sons of Israel, and Aaron shall bear their names before the LORD on his two shoulders for a memorial." Exodus 28:12 (NASB)

Observation
God gives Moses very specific instructions about the elaborate clothing that the priests are to wear when leading worship. These garments were to be made and worn for "glory and beauty" (Exodus 28:2b NASB). In other words, even the clothing articles of the priests were to glorify God. And so, God describes in great detail how the various pieces should look, the materials to be used, and the way the various pieces were to be worn together. The ephod was an apron-like garment that was worn over other clothing and that covered the breast and the back of the priest. In our focus verse, God instructs that two stones be woven into the fabric, one on each shoulder. On the stones the names of the 12 tribes of Israel would be engraved. When God looked down on Aaron, these two stones would serve as a memorial, reminding God of God's covenant people.

Application
First, does it make a difference to God what we wear in worship? This conversation comes up a lot these days as churches consider worship style, music, purpose, etc. Our clothing should always bring God honor. What we wear to worship should reflect our respect for God. The idea is that we should wear our best because we enter the presence of Almighty God. Does this mean that casual clothing is wrong in church? Not necessarily so. But I do think that what we wear on Sunday should be different from what we casually wear from day to day. Sunday is to be a distinctive day, and even our clothing should reflect an attitude that it is a special privilege to stand before God in worship. (There is a difference between casual and sloppy by the way.) Second, I like this idea of the "shoulder stones" that serve as a reminder each time the garment was worn. I think symbols and reminders of our faith are important for us to embrace. I hope that there are things you wear or items you place around your home that remind you of the importance of your faith. We need the visible and the tangible in our lives to remind us daily of God's presence in our lives. Maybe you carry a cross in your pocket or a gold cross around your neck. Maybe you even have a tattoo with religious significance. Let it mean something. Be reminded daily that you are loved by God and that God's deserves your remembrance.

Prayer
Father, as we travel to worship this Sunday, remind us that it is a privilege and an honor to stand in your presence. May our thoughts, our attitudes, and even our dress bring you glory. Amen.

Day 79 — Exodus 29: Doing the Wave

> "And you shall put all these in the hands of Aaron and in the hands of his sons, and shall wave them as a wave offering before the LORD."
> Exodus 29:24 (NASB)

Observation
In this chapter, God describes in great detail all that is to be done to consecrate Aaron and his sons for their role as priests in the tabernacle. Earlier in the chapter are instructions to dip the blood of a sacrificial ram and touch the blood to the right earlobe, the right thumb, and the right big toe of each priest. The symbolism was to show that the priests were to be consecrated from "head to toe" before the Lord. In our focus verse, Aaron and his sons were to present a "wave" offering before the Lord. The elements would be held high and then waved back and forth before the altar. The offering made clear that everything being offered was surrendered to God. (Unlike some sacrifices made, not all the parts of the animal were burned with fire. Some were held back to be consumed by the priests. Thus, the elements were "waved" before God and not all consumed.)

Application
I don't typically get up every morning and wave things before God. I don't hold up my wallet and wave it in God's presence. I don't grab my car keys and give them a shake. I don't wave a photograph of my family before the Lord. I don't wave my iPad in God's presence. I don't take my watch and lift it towards the heaven. I don't wave my reading glasses at the sky. I don't even take my smartphone and wave it toward heaven. But maybe I should... at least symbolically. Like the priests of old I need to make it very clear that I surrender all that I have, all that I possess before the Lord. I need to acknowledge that if God is Lord of all, then I should offer to God anything that would bring God glory. I wonder if "waving" things before the Lord would be a good discipline for us to undertake from time to time. I wonder if we don't need to take the things we hold most dear and wave them before God to acknowledge that we gladly surrender them for kingdom work. It might seem like a silly thing to do, but then again, it might remind us of how silly it is for us to claim anything as ours that in reality belongs to God. Our possessions, our time, our families, our vision, our conversations... it's all God's. Let's begin today by acknowledging God's lordship over all of life.

Prayer
Father, teach us today the meaning of lordship and surrender. May we offer our lives and our closely held things to you so that you will be glorified through our lives. Amen.

Day 80 — Exodus 30: Wash, Then Worship

> "Aaron and his sons shall wash their hands and their feet from it; when they enter the tent of meeting, they shall wash with water, so that they will not die; or when they approach the altar to minister, by offering up in smoke a fire sacrifice to the LORD." Exodus 30:19-20 (NASB)

Observation
Again in this chapter, God offers very specific and detailed instructions to Moses to share with the Israelites. Earlier in this chapter, God describes a large basin of water that was to be made and placed just outside the tabernacle. The priests were to use the water to wash both their hands and their feet before entering the tabernacle. God indicated that they were to wash, "so that they will not die." The idea was that these men were to be holy and clean before the Lord. The act of ceremonially washing prior to entering the tabernacle was a reminder of the importance of being pure as they stood in the presence of God.

Application
There is something to be said for being "pure and holy" as we stand in the presence of God. The ancient priests of Israel were to wash hands and feet or potentially die before the Lord because of the lack of their purity. Though God may no longer require a washing before we enter the sanctuary, God still requires the cleansing of our lives. How dare we stand in the presence of God when our hearts are not pure and our lives are not clean? My fear is that one of the prayers we most often neglect in our times of devotion before God, is the prayer of forgiveness. Because we have heard so early and often of the sacrifice of Christ for our sins, I am fearful that we may take such grace for granted. We assume God's forgiveness each day and rather than confess our sins and ask for grace, we just assume that God is always glad to give it and is even pleased by our blanket prayers in which we say, "and if you find any unclean thought or deed in my life, please remove it." Such a prayer puts the pressure on God to search our lives and not ourselves! We need to be careful to claim our sins. We need to name them with specificity. It is my belief that any unconfessed sin is unforgiven sin. That puts the burden on us to carefully delineate our transgressions before God. We need to name them and then ask for the cleansing of God to wash over us. It is no small thing to stand in the presence of Holy God. And though we are always welcomed in God's presence, we need to make sure that we wash ourselves thoroughly so that we are clean.

Prayer
Father, we ask this morning for your forgiveness... again. May we see our sins clearly and then faithfully pray for the grace needed to cover our iniquity. Amen.

Day 81 — Exodus 31: Sacred Sabbath

> "For six days work may be done, but on the seventh day there is a Sabbath of complete rest, holy to the LORD; whoever does any work on the Sabbath day shall surely be put to death." Exodus 31:15 (NASB)

Observation
At the end of the conversation on Sinai between God and Moses, God reiterates the importance of keeping the Sabbath. In fact, it is the only commandment that God repeats in the presence of Moses. And notice the severity of punishment to be offered to those who fail to observe the Sabbath... He "shall surely be put to death." God states that the Sabbath day is to be a day of "complete rest." It is obviously something we are to take very seriously.

Application
But do we? Do we take the concept of Sabbath rest seriously? Truthfully, most of us do not treat rest as an absolute commandment of God. For years, the discussion of observing the Sabbath meant the establishment of so called "Blue Laws" that kept businesses closed on Sunday. In my hometown, nothing was open on Sundays except a few restaurants. No department stores, gas stations, or offices opened their doors. It was just the culture in the Bible Belt to respect the day of worship. Of course, all that has changed through the years. For many retailers, Sunday is the busiest day of the week. Many argue that to close on Sunday would force a financial collapse.

But more than Sunday Blue Laws, I want to take a moment to consider the commandment to rest. Do we really value rest and do we make resting a priority? God knows that the human body needs time to rest, recover, and recuperate. And yet in defiance of God's design, we push ourselves and push ourselves and push ourselves to the point of absolute exhaustion. We "burn the candle at both ends" not taking the time to get the rest we need. By not resting, we sacrifice our health, we stress our relationships, and we strain our minds. More importantly, we violate a commandment of our Father. We justify our behavior with a sense of over-inflated ego... "I have to get this work done or surely the world will collapse!" God did not create your body just for you to abuse it with endless work. Learn the value of rest, not with a single week of vacation during the year, but with a day each week in which you rest and reflect and regain your very life. A friend once counseled me by saying, "If you don't plan your free time someone else will." He was right. Life and its demands will take control of our days and nights. We alone have the power to set the priorities. God commands us to choose rest with as much deliberate effort as we put forth in planning our work.

Prayer
Father, teach us this day the value of obedient, Sabbath rest. Amen.

Day 82 — Exodus 32: Our Golden Calves

> "They have quickly turned aside from the way which I commanded them. They have made for themselves a molten calf, and have worshiped it and have sacrificed to it and said, 'This is your god, O Israel, who brought you up from the land of Egypt!'" Exodus 32:8 (NASB)

Observation
This verse is taken, of course, from the story of the golden calf at the foot of Mount Sinai. While Moses was on the mountain with God, the people grew restless. Under the leadership of Aaron, the leaders collected all the golden earrings from the Israelites and Aaron fashioned the gold into a calf. The calf became the object of their worship. They made it into their god and danced around it with joy. When Moses returned and discovered their heinous sin, he smashed the two tablets on which the 10 Commandments were written and then destroyed the golden calf, grinding it to powder. Moses then cast the golden dust on the water and made the people drink it so that the bitter taste would remind them that what they had done was bitter before the Lord.

Application
Why would we think that God would react any differently towards the gods we create and worship today? Go back and read the story carefully and you will discover that God wanted to destroy the whole nation and start again by creating a new chosen people. Had it not been for the persuasive voice of Moses, God would have obliterated them all in the dessert. Even with Moses' plea before God, 3000 evildoers were slain because of their idol worship.

The story should say something to us about creating false gods. God has firmly declared that God alone is worthy of our worship and that we are not to create any gods. (See Commandment #1.) But we do… We tend to create those gods that quickly become the objects of our worship. Just look at the time we devote to certain hobbies, activities, and pursuits and you will discover a lot of false deities. Does it say something about our love of God when we can't find the time for daily devotion but can spend hours on social media each day? Does it say something about our love of God when we pour thousands into our vacations but only a few dollars flow to the church? Does it say something about our love for God when we read the paper religiously but seldom read scripture? Does it say something about our love for God when we worship our work, but play at our worship? They are out there, aren't they? The false gods. And we worship them all the time. May God forgive us for our worship of vain things, and may we find mercy from the wrath that should befall us.

Prayer
Father, remind us today, that you alone should be the object of our worship. Forgive our creation of false gods and rescue us from the punishment we deserve. Amen.

Day 83 — Exodus 33: A House of Worship

> "When all the people saw the pillar of cloud standing at the entrance of the tent, all the people would arise and worship, each at the entrance of his tent." Exodus 33:10 (NASB)

Observation
As the Israelites continued their journey away from Sinai and towards the promised land, Moses continued to meet God at the "Tent of Meeting" or tabernacle. Moses instructed the people to set up the tent, outside of the camp, and he would go and speak with God. When Moses entered the tent, the presence of God would descend on the tent in the form of a cloud that would remain at the entrance of the tent. When the people saw Moses worshiping at the tent of meeting, they would, in turn, each worship at the entrance of their own tent, where they were dwelling.

Application
Here's what I want you to see this morning... The people of God developed a routine of worship at the door of their own tent. They discovered ways to worship God at the very entrance of the place where they dwelled. Call it the first "house church" in history, but you get the point. They were to use their homes as a place of worship. Each dwelling was to be claimed in the name of the Lord.

Are we using our homes as a place of worship? Do we truly seek to acknowledge the Living God in the place where we dwell? Do we pray over our houses? Have we asked God to allow our home to be a place where God's presence can abide? There are things for which we must pray. Pray for peace within your home. Pray for grace to abound. Pray for the health of the people who live there. Pray for growing faith for those who live within its walls. Learn the importance of worshiping God in the place you live. You may not want to walk around your house each morning, singing hymns to the top of your lungs (neighbors might start to talk), but I would suggest that you offer your home to the glory of God. Let God's truth be spoken. Let God's name be mentioned. Let God's kindness abound.

Have you ever considered starting a small group Bible study in your home? Are there neighbors who might come to your home, who might not ever attend a local church? Could you use your "dwelling place" to start something special? There are certainly a number of trends that indicate many are disillusioned by the institutional trappings of the local church yet still long for a community of people with whom to share their faith experiences. Your home may provide a place for neighbors to experience a sense of church again. Think of your house as a tool that God could use if you are willing.

Prayer
Father, may you be glorified at the door of our homes. Amen.

Day 84 — Exodus 34: Changing Your Life a Day at a Time

> "It came about when Moses was coming down from Mount Sinai (and the two tablets of the testimony were in Moses' hand as he was coming down from the mountain), that Moses did not know that the skin of his face shone because of his speaking with Him." Exodus 34:29 (NASB)

Observation
In this chapter, God invites Moses back up on the mountain to replace the two stone tablets that Moses had shattered. God not only replaces that which was broken, but also reaffirms the covenant with Israel. God promises to do miraculous signs in their midst and promises to drive out the nations that possessed the promised land. When Moses comes down from the mountain, his face is glowing brightly because he had stood in the presence of God. In fact, the skin of his face was so bright that he had to cover his face with a veil when speaking to the people.

Application
Okay, let me get a little weird for a moment. Years ago, I was one of the adults leading our youth group from church on a summer camp experience. One night during the invitation, an older teenage boy for whom we had been praying responded to the love of Christ in a real way and committed his heart to the Lord. I will long remember the look on his face when he returned to our group after the service. His face was literally aglow with a special light of God's Spirit. There's just no other way to describe it. It was evident that God moved in his life.

Shouldn't there be evidence in our lives that we have spent time with God? Shouldn't something about our attitudes, our words, our actions, and even our very countenance change because we have spent time in the presence of the Almighty? Let's keep it real this morning... Most of us are not going to show up at work one morning with glowing face like Moses. People are not going to rush up to us with a veil to keep from squinting when they look at us. Our time with God seldom produces a celestial sunburn. But when we spend moments with God, things change. The anger leaves our lives. The resentment towards others melts away. The prejudice vanishes. The ugly words of gossip and backbiting are no longer used. Compassion returns. Grace abounds. Forgiveness is extended. People *will* notice the genuine change that only God can bring about. The key is to spend meaningful moments in God's presence. We will not be influenced by that with which we have no contact. But if we stand in God's presence each day, people will notice. I challenge you this morning to walk with God on the mountain each day and see how the conversations change your life.

Prayer
Father, thank you for your willingness to spend time with each of us. May we guard the time and discover how such moments can shape our lives. Amen.

Day 85 — Exodus 35: Your Skillset

> "Then Moses said to the sons of Israel, 'See, the LORD has called by name Bezalel the son of Uri, the son of Hur, of the tribe of Judah. And He has filled him with the Spirit of God, in wisdom, in understanding and in knowledge and in all craftsmanship.'" Exodus 35:30-31 (NASB)

Observation
God spent many days telling Moses about all the things that were to be made as a part of the tabernacle… the tent itself, the poles that supported the canvas, the Ark of the Covenant, the lampstand, the altar, etc. Not only did God indicate what was to be made, God also gifted individuals to do the detailed work. Bezalel, the son of Uri, was filled with the Spirit. God's Spirit working in him would give him the understanding and knowledge needed to do all that God asked.

Application
I'm not the greatest furniture maker on the planet. To be certain, I have crafted a few simple chairs, a bench, and a table or two… but nothing fancy. I always look at a finished creation and think, "If I just had the right tool, I could have made that better." By saying such a thing, I don't have to admit that I lack the proper skills… but I do. There are things that I do well and then there are things I can't do well. That's just the way I was made. I have some abilities, but not all abilities. None of us do. But we all have a few things we do well.

God always equips men and women to carry out God's work. God places skills, talents, and abilities in those lives in order to accomplish God's plan. The problem is that sometimes the God-given abilities are squandered. Sometimes, people see their gifts as simply a means of self-support. They take the talents of God and use them only to pad their wallets, establish their businesses, and create a reputation. To be sure, God intends for us to be good stewards of the things given to each of us. It would be foolish for us not to use our talents to prosper our lives and provide for our families. But… Let us never forget that making a living with our talents is only to be a by-product of our giftedness. Our priority is to honor God with our work and use our gifts to do what God has called us to do. So, my question this morning is this: Are you using what God has placed in your life as a way of accomplishing God's plan or as a way of accomplishing your plan? See the difference? Your life, with all its talents, has been created to serve a greater purpose. Before you spend your life's energy trying simply to make a buck or two, figure out why it is that God gave you such a gift. Invest in the kingdom. Pour out your life doing the things that God has created you to do.

Prayer
Father, thank you for investing in each of us. May we use our gifts and abilities for your glory and for your work. Amen.

Day 86 — Exodus 36: Giving Enough

> "So Moses issued a command, and a proclamation was circulated throughout the camp, saying, 'Let no man or woman any longer perform work for the contributions of the sanctuary.' Thus the people were restrained from bringing anymore." Exodus 36:6 (NASB)

Observation
Moses instructed the Israelites to collect an offering to provide for the materials used in the construction of the tabernacle. The people brought both gold and various fine linens and cloth to be used throughout the construction. The people became so excited in their giving and so enthusiastic about the work being done, that they gave more than was needed. Moses had to restrain them from bringing additional materials. Their gratitude to God was expressed through abundant giving.

Application
You don't see this kind of scenario played out very often, at least not in the life of the local church. How many times have you ever heard a preacher stand before his congregants and say, "You've given enough! Don't give any more!" And yet that is exactly what Moses did. Out of generous hearts, the people met and exceeded any vision Moses may have had for the offerings. My thought is that the people gave so abundantly for several reasons. First, they had stood in the very presence of God, and they realized that God was worthy of all praise and glory. Second, they had known first-hand God's blessings. They were liberated from oppression, led by God's Spirit in the wilderness, given food to eat, and provided with God's law. Third, they realized God's direct involvement each day in their lives. They could see the pillar of cloud and fire that led their journey. They could taste the manna that filled their stomachs each morning. So why would they not give both gladly and generously?

Why is it that we often give with reluctance and scarcity when we present our offerings to God? Do we not stand in God's presence each day? Have we not known God's blessings? Do we not feel God's direct involvement in our lives each day? When hearts are grateful, the giving is generous. I challenge you this morning, not simply to be a cheerful and generous giver financially to your church, but to be generous with the gift of your life as well. As an act of worship, volunteer some time. Mentor a child. Plug in to a local ministry. Find a way to serve others. Do you think that you are anywhere near hearing God say, "You've given enough! Don't give any more!"

Prayer
Father, thank you for the blessings we have. Give us generous and obedient hearts that honor you this day. Amen.

Day 87 — Exodus 37: Where Is the Ark?

> "Now Bezalel made the ark of acacia wood; its length was two and a half cubits, and its width one and a half cubits, and its height one and a half cubits" Exodus 37:1 (NASB)

Observation

Our focus verse describes the construction of the Ark of the Covenant. The Ark was the golden box that contained the 10 Commandments and upon which the "mercy seat" was located. The mercy seat was the spot just above the Ark where the presence of God hovered. What strikes me about the Ark itself is its size. A cubit is about 18 inches in length, the distance from the elbow to the end of your index finger. Do the conversion and you will discover that this box was relatively small... only about 4 feet long and 2 feet tall. In contrast, its significance was enormous. It represented the presence of God in the midst of the people. It became the most sacred object in all the world.

Application

What's interesting about the Ark of the Covenant is that no one today knows of its whereabouts. Somewhere around 587 B.C. when Jerusalem fell to the Babylonians and the Israelites were taken into captivity, it simply disappeared. It may have been destroyed by the Babylonians. It may have been hidden for protection by devout Jews. Some suggest that it was carried to Masada, which became the last Jewish stronghold against the Romans. Still some theorize that it was taken to Africa, for protection, to the modern-day region of Zimbabwe. It may have been transported into the exile and later lost or stolen. Who knows? The Ark may still be hidden deeply below the earth in some sacred and unknown spot.

Here's what has changed since those days of Moses. God's law is no longer written on stone tablets and placed in a gold box. Instead, God has placed the law in an even more sacred spot... the human heart. The living word of God is housed in the depths of the heart. We carry it with us each moment that we live. We protect it, we defend it, we share it... and some days we betray it. How is it that those of us who are charged with keeping the word of God, do such a horrible job of protecting it? Whenever we act with malice, or hatred, or prejudice, or envy, or jealously, or bitterness, do we not betray that sacred word that we claim to carry within us? You see, if we are going to carry the word, we must live the word. It must influence our actions, shape our thoughts, and govern our words. We are called to keep the word. May it dwell richly within us and let us pray that the day will never come when we betray that sacred trust and allow it to disappear from the planet once again.

Prayer

Father, entrust your word to each of us. May we be worthy vessels. Amen.

Day 88 — Exodus 38: There Are No Small Roles...

> "Moreover, he made the laver of bronze with its base of bronze, from the mirrors of the serving women who served at the doorway of the tent of meeting." Exodus 38:8 (NASB)

Observation

As Bezalel builds all the objects used for worship that are a part of the tabernacle, he constructs a large laver, or basin, of bronze that is to be placed just outside the "tent of meeting." The water contained in this large basin was to be used by Aaron and the priests to ceremonially wash themselves before going in to serve in the tabernacle. They were to wash both hands and feet before standing in the presence of God. Notice that the biblical record mentions women who served at the doorway to the tent of meeting. My thought is that these women were charged with keeping the water in the basin and with assisting the priests as they washed hands and feet.

Application

Why is such a detail important to mention? For me, it speaks of the value and importance of every person's role. To be sure, most of what took place in and around the tabernacle was done by the priests, those who had been set apart and consecrated for this specific work. But notice that for the work to be accomplished in the manner that God desired, that others were quietly doing their specific tasks so that the work of God could be accomplished. These women who served at the doorway of the tent of meeting obviously had a role to play and they served faithfully.

What is your role in God's kingdom? Are you playing that role well? God has ordained that each of us would have a variety of gifts, talents, and abilities to be used to accomplish God's purposes. Some of those gifts are displayed publicly, while other talents are used quietly, and often behind the scenes. The point is to take your sense of calling and contribution and use it to glorify God while helping the kingdom to grow. In other words, do your thing, no matter how seemingly great or small that it is, and do it faithfully as unto the Lord. Find your "service point" and work diligently to honor God through your effort.

And here's a word for those who long to do more or have a greater role in God's kingdom work. According to Luke 16:10, being faithful in the small things, will lead to faithfulness in the greater things. So today, prove yourself faithful, even in the smallest of kingdom contributions. God will notice and when the time is right, God will give even greater responsibility.

Prayer

Father, thank you for calling all of us into your work. May you be honored in both the small and great acts of service that we offer. Amen.

Day 89 — Exodus 39: Working Hard and Working Well

> "And Moses examined all the work and behold, they had done it; just as the LORD had commanded, this they had done. So Moses blessed them."
> Exodus 39:43 (NASB)

Observation
When all the construction and fabrication for the materials used in the tabernacle was completed, Moses inspected. We are not told the length of time needed to complete the work, only that the work had been done, "just as the Lord had commanded." The work obviously pleased Moses and honored the Lord and so Moses blessed those who had done all the work. What a joyful and proud moment it must have been for those workers to celebrate both the completion of the task and the blessings of the Lord.

Application
There is always great satisfaction in a job well done. It is exciting for a student to receive a good mark for a well-written paper. There's a sense of satisfaction or a salesman to receive a reward for a successful year. Parents are joyous when their child walks the stage at graduation. For a writer, signing off on the final version of a new novel brings both joy and relief. You get the picture... When a difficult task is completed and appropriate appreciation is shown, the worker finds a sense of joy, peace, and celebration.

What are you working on right now? A contract at work, the restoration of an old car, a hand-knitted garment, or a big sales presentation? I wish you well and hope you gain a sense of joy at the end of the process. Let me ask again, with a more existential twist... What are you working on right now? What are you longing and hoping to do with your life's energy? What is your greatest work? Your opus magnum? Is glorifying God in our calling a goal? What about raising our children well, loving our spouses devotedly, and building God's kingdom consistently? At the end of the day, we should seek God's favor. What a joy it will be for us to hear God say, "Well done, my good and faithful servant." There is an important mentality for every Christ-follower to adopt. It's this: All work is sacred work. In other words, to whatever work we put our hands we should do so with a sense of importance, excellence, and worth. Even the small tasks of each day should display the results of our best efforts as we do all things as unto the Lord. Don't settle for mediocrity. Don't be satisfied with a half-hearted effort. Always present your best. May God bless you this morning as you seek to live this day for God's glory. Work hard and find the success of a job well done.

Prayer
Father, may we strive to honor you today as we dedicate ourselves to the pursuit of your work for our lives. Amen.

Day 90 — Exodus 40: Serious Moments

> "Then the cloud covered the tent of meeting, and the glory of the LORD filled the tabernacle. Moses was not able to enter the tent of meeting because the cloud had settled on it, and the glory of the LORD filled the tabernacle." Exodus 40:34-35 (NASB)

Observation

God instructed Moses to erect the tabernacle on the first day of the first month. This initial set-up of the tabernacle must have been quite a display before the Israelites. To see all the parts fit together... to see all the poles and curtains and boards... to see the canvas material and its spectacular colors... to see the golden altar and lampstand... all must have been an exciting. And then suddenly, the glory of the Lord descended upon it and the people could see the visible cloud of God settle over it. Moses was prevented from even entering because the glory of the Lord filled the entire structure.

Application

Moses knew that the presence of God was not to be taken lightly. He knew better than to rush into God's presence at the moment God's glory filled the tabernacle. This amazing moment in time must have set the stage for the importance of worship in that place for generations to come. I wonder if at times we rush into the presence of God without forethought or preparation. Take worship for example. We are promised in God's word that whenever two or more gather in God's name, God will be uniquely present in that place. How should that inform the way we approach worship and the way we enter the space where worship happens? Do we give much thought to that moment? Do we purify our hearts and cleanse our minds before we step into worship? Most of us rush in with loud conversation and minds filled with the thoughts of a dozen different things. Some even come into worship with coffee in their hand. We should treat worship with great reverence and respect.

But what about when we enter God's presence for moments of private devotion? Those moments are also to be taken seriously. Often, we rush the process, reading and praying quickly because we have other "important" things to do. We abbreviate our time with God because we feel the rush of the on-coming day. Let me challenge you to value the time you spend in the presence of God. Prepare. Enter with a sense of awe. Enjoy the moments with your Father. Take the time to slow down your breathing, your heart rate, and your preoccupied mind. Commit yourself to a few moments of concentrated, fully-engaged moments with God, who has much to tell you. Take the time to listen.

Prayer

Father, teach us to value the moments we spend in your presence. Amen.

Day 91 — Leviticus 1: The Sweet Smell of Faith

> "Then the priest will burn the entire sacrifice on the altar as a burnt offering. It is a special gift, a pleasing aroma to the LORD."
> Leviticus 1:9 (NLT)

Observation
The book of Leviticus, named for the priestly tribe of Levi, details God's instructions through Moses for Gods' people. The purpose of the laws and regulations presented was to teach the Israelites how to maintain their purity before God so that God could live among them and so that they could worship God. This opening chapter describes the procedures needed to present a burnt offering before the Lord. The word "offering" is derived from the verb, "to bring near." Therefore, an offering was literally something that "brings one near to God."

Application
There is nothing better than walking through my neighborhood on a pleasant Saturday afternoon in the fall. About the time the sun begins to set, neighbors begin to fire up their grills. First, the scent of lighter fluid fills the air and then the hint of charcoal. A few minutes later the aroma of grilled meat begins to linger in the air, awakening the anticipation of a wonderful meal. Those with a discerning sense of smell can even distinguish the types of meat being prepared. One grill smells of burgers, another of barbeque ribs, still another gives off the aroma of grilled dogs… a personal favorite.

When the ancient Israelites gathered to worship, the air was surely filled with aroma of meat grilling on the altar. It was to be, as Moses describes, "a sweet aroma to the Lord." The scent surely found its way heavenward, but it also lingered among the community of Israel. It would not have taken long for the smell to become associated with worship. Each time the distinct smell found the noses of the Israelites, they were reminded that God was worthy of worship.

Paul writes in 2 Corinthians 2:15, "For we are to God the pleasing aroma of Christ…" (NIV). Just as the scent of sacrificed meat found its way through the community, shouldn't something of our influence find its way among the places where we live? Has not God called us to become the "salt and light" that affects the world around us? What about your aroma? Or better stated, "What about your influence?" Does your practice of faith reach the hearts of your community? Are people reminded through your attitudes, words, and actions, that there is a God who is to be worshipped?

Prayer
Father God, may we become good stewards of our influence, knowing that the authenticity of our faith, can draw others into your presence. Amen.

Day 92 — Leviticus 2: Remembering God

> "Season all your grain offerings with salt to remind you of God's eternal covenant. Never forget to add salt to your grain offerings."
> Leviticus 2:13 (NLT)

Observation

When presenting "grain" offerings on the altar before the Lord, the ancient Israelites used salt as a part of the preparation and presentation of the offering. Salt served two primary roles in ancient times. It offered purification and preservation. It was a symbol of longevity. The salt reminded the worshipper of his or her long-term commitment to serving God and God's long-term commitment toward God's children. (The use of the word "anyone" in verse 1 denotes that both men and women were invited to make offerings before the Lord.) Salt bore testimony to the purity of the relationship that God longed to established with God's people.

Application

If I bite into a French fry that seems a little bland, no one has to tell me to salt the rest. Put green beans on the plate without much salt and I will be reaching again for the shaker. I am accustomed to salt. It flavors. It enhances the taste. Talk to anyone battling blood pressure issues that has to cut back on sodium and they will tell you how difficult it is to give up salt.

Read the focus verse again. God doesn't require salt because of the flavor or because the priests will enjoy their portion of the grain offering a little better. No. God said to use the salt as a "reminder" of God's covenant. The introduction of the strong, savory flavor of salt was a teaching aid, reminding all of Israel of the permanence of God's covenant relationship. To be honest, I usually don't think of God's love each time I reach for the shaker. I don't dwell on God's lasting covenant with each sprinkle of the grains. It's not what reminds me of God's love each day. But the point is well taken. Each of us needs to consider faith reminders in the daily routine of our lives. We need small, tangible items that remind us of the love of God and of God's continual presence. Maybe God challenged the ancient Israelites to use salt because it was an item used each day.

What will remind you today of the presence and greatness of God? A song? A memory verse? A special photo? A moment in God's word? Like a sprinkle of salt, we need to flavor our lives with the reminders of God's love and grace. May God be found present in your life today.

Prayer

Father God, we thank you for the everlasting promises you offer to us… to love us, to save us, and to be present with us. May we be reminded of your connection to us even this day.

Day 93 — Leviticus 3: What We Give to God

> "You must never eat any fat or blood. This is a permanent law for you, and it must be observed from generation to generation, wherever you live."
> Leviticus 3:17 (NLT)

Observation
Moses offered words of instruction concerning "peace" offerings made to God. He told the Israelites never to eat the fat of the sacrificed animal. This detail may seem odd, but the fat was the most prized portion of the meat. It was never to be consumed by the one making the offering, it was to be given to God as a sign of "offering one's best." The blood of the animal was sprinkled on the altar. It represented the life of the animal and was the first step during the sacrificial process.

Application
Most of us don't have to be told not to eat the fat that surrounds a thick juicy steak. We know all about cholesterol and saturated fat intake and how unhealthy eating fat can be. But then again, we also know that a little "marbling" in the meat adds rich flavor. We want the lean stuff, to be sure… but a little fat to flavor our dinner never hurt anyone, right?

In this text, God didn't prohibit eating fat because it's unhealthy. Considered the prized portion, the fat was to be dedicated to God, because God deserves our best! Such dedication was to be taught from generation to generation. To honor God with the best of our lives is an instruction to be lived out before each new generation. Because we love God and long to follow with obedient hearts, we must continually offer God the best of our lives.

In Romans 12:1, Paul writes, "Present your bodies as a living and holy sacrifice, acceptable to God…" (NASB). The phrase "living sacrifice" intrigues me. A "living" sacrifice implies continual, intentional action. A living sacrifice is not a sacrifice made only once. It is a sacrifice that is offered continually, day after day. In other words, we are called to offer ourselves continually to God, submitting thought, action, will, and heart before God's authority. We offer God that which is best in us… this day, tomorrow, and the next.

If you want to provide a peace offering to God, then offer God all that you are. Give God the "good stuff." Be sure that God gets the best of your attention and gifts, and teach the next generation to do the same.

Prayer
Father God, I pray that this day, we will offer you the very best of who we are. Take our moments and our days… let them flow in ceaseless praise, let them flow in ceaseless praise. Amen.

Day 94 — Leviticus 4: Accidental Sin

> "If any of the common people sin by violating one of the LORD's commands, but they don't realize it, they are still guilty. When they become aware of their sin, they must bring as an offering for their sin a female goat with no defects." Leviticus 4:27-28 (NLT)

Observation

This entire chapter is devoted to the offerings needed to atone for sins committed "unintentionally." Moses speaks about people, priests, and rulers who have accidentally or unknowingly violated one of God's commands. As soon as guilt is recognized, there are steps to take to cleanse the heart and find right standing before God.

Application

There is an important truth in these verses. Moses affirms that those who sin accidentally are still guilty for their transgressions. There is an old expression that says, "ignorance is bliss." Not so in this case. Sin is a powerful divider. It will always separate us from God. Ignorance of the law is no excuse. Whether intentional or accidental, ours sins demand a response. In ancient Israel animals were slaughtered and the blood sprinkled on the altar to remove the transgression. In the language and theology of the New Testament, sins are removed, not by the blood of a lamb, but by the sacrifice and blood of THE Lamb. Christ himself becomes the atoning sacrifice for our sins. We confess our sins, and we find his grace.

As I age, I find myself reaching more and more for reading glasses. (Recently, while eating at a restaurant, I ordered by pointing at the menu because I had forgotten my glasses and was too proud to admit I was having trouble reading it!) Sometimes we need a glass lens to give us greater vision and sometimes we need a spiritual lens to give us greater insight. How many sins have we committed without realizing we have disappointed the Father? I believe that unconfessed sin is unforgiven sin. So, what happens when we sin in ignorance? First, I think we need to pray for the illumination of the Spirit. We need to ask the Spirit to give us a lens through which we might see our mistakes. We need to ask for help in seeing our sinfulness the way that God does. Second, we must confess discovered sin. I encourage you to ask for insight this morning in order that you might discover the hidden sins of your heart. When revealed, confess, pray, and find grace.

Prayer

Father God, we thank you for your provision for our sins. Give us insight this hour that we might see our "accidental" sins so that we might claim a very "deliberate" grace. Amen.

Day 95 — Leviticus 5: Testify!

> "If you are called to testify about something that you have seen or that you know about, it is sinful to refuse to testify, and you will be punished for your sin." Leviticus 5:1 (NLT)

Observation
In this chapter, Moses outlines several specific sins that require a special "sin" offering. He speaks of a failure to testify, touching something that is ceremonially unclean, making a foolish vow, or defiling the Lord's sacred property (like something used in tabernacle worship practices). He goes on to prescribe how to present the sin offering before the Lord. Remember that the word "offering" literally means "to bring near." The offering removes the sin and brings the worshipper into right standing with God.

Application
Sometimes parents require their children to "testify" about a recent breaking of the rules. It goes something like this, "Tell the truth, son, did you break momma's vase, or did you see who broke the vase?" The child is expected to describe what he has seen or done. Even if it means punishment, the child is expected to tell the truth. Moses went so far as to say to the ancient Israelites that to refuse to testify about something seen or known was in itself a sinful act. People were expected to testify.

Followers of Christ are to "testify" in a slightly different way. We have been called to proclaim the Good News of the kingdom each day, in as many ways as we can. We use our words, our actions, our thoughts, and our attitudes to demonstrate to others who Christ is. It is our Great Commission… our one command. "Therefore, go and make disciples of all the nations…" (Matthew 28:19 NLT). We make disciples as we proclaim God's truth. And here is the sticky part… it is a sin not to do so. Failure to go and do as commanded is rebellion. To quote Moses, "it is sinful to refuse to testify."

Most of us carry a little angst inside when it comes to faith-sharing. We always worry that our words will be inadequate, our Bible knowledge lacking, and our conversations too awkward. We tend to pull back and never fully demonstrate our Christianity. A failure to witness is surely a sin. So go forth this day with two thoughts in mind… first, God will present an opportunity for you to demonstrate your faith. Second, God will be with you as you do. Get it? You have not been thrust out into the world to change the world all by yourself. God's Spirit is already in you and already preparing the moment and conversation. Remember, it's a sin not to testify.

Prayer
Heavenly Father, may we have the vision today to see an opportunity to proclaim Christ and may we have the boldness to do it. Amen.

Day 96 — Leviticus 6: Keeper of the Flame

> "The fire must be kept burning on the altar at all times. It must never go out." Leviticus 6:13 (NLT)

Observation

Five times in the paragraph that contains our focus verse, the priests are instructed to keep the fire burning on the altar that was used for sacrifices. Some suggest as many as three reasons for this instruction. First, the original fire on the altar had come from God (9:24). Second, the perpetual fire symbolized the perpetual presence of God. Third, the presence of the fire reminded the people of their constant need for atonement and reconciliation. In other words, as they saw the fire they were reminded again and again to make needed sacrifices to be forgiven in the eyes of God.

Application

In episode 14 of season 2 from *The Andy Griffith Show*, Opie joins a secret club… the Wildcats. He is named the Keeper of the Flame. His job was to safely keep the candle and matches that were used as a part of the secret club meetings. When Jubal Foster's barn burns to the ground, Opie and the boys are accused of accidently setting it on fire when playing with the candle and matches. Barney Fife later discovers that Jubal has been brewing moonshine in the barn and the boys are exonerated.

Keeping the flame can be difficult. The priests in ancient Israel had to ensure that the fire never went out. Typically, a large sacrificial animal was placed on the altar at night to burn slowly until morning when more wood could be added to the fire.

Unless you are reading this while enjoying a weekend camping trip, odds are that you will not be charged with keeping a fire alive through the night. What you have been charged with is keeping the flame of faith continually burning in your life. Paul writes, "This is why I remind you to fan into flames the spiritual gift God gave you when I laid my hands on you" (2 Timothy 1:6 NLT). You and I have been chosen, as believers in Christ, to carry around in our lives the very presence, spirit, and love of Jesus. We are the keepers of the flame. In us, the Gospel must shine. In us, the love of Christ must be demonstrated. In us, the hope of salvation must dispel darkness. How carefully do we tend to the flame? Do we take our responsibility seriously? Do we take whatever measures are needed to ensure that the flame is fed, stoked, and protected? I encourage you to be a keeper of the flame. *"This little light of mine… I'm gonna let it shine…"*

Prayer

Heavenly Father, we thank you for the presence of Christ in our lives. May we guard it well and share it abundantly. Amen.

Day 97 — Leviticus 7: A Sacred Place

> "Any male from a priest's family may eat the meat. It must be eaten in a sacred place, for it is most holy." Leviticus 7:6 (NLT)

Observation
According to Mosaic law, when a guilt offering was presented before God, the fat and several vital organs were burned on the altar as a special gift to the Lord. The remaining meat could be consumed by the priest and his family. Because it was "holy" meat (distinct, different, set-apart), meaning that it had been used as a part of the atonement for one's sin, then care had to be taken for the way in which the food was eaten. Moses required that it be eaten in a "sacred place."

Application
Most of us don't consider the places we eat to be sacred in nature. We don't take off our shoes before we enter our favorite burger joint. We don't genuflect before we walk into the pizza place. We don't pause to take a reverent moment before we order our fried chicken. Though we might love those restaurants and patronize them often, they are not sacred places.

For me, one of the sacred places to enjoy a meal is the family dinner table. Remember when families spent time around the dinner table at the end of each day? There were no cell phones to interrupt the conversations. There were no televisions blaring in the background. There was just an honest sharing of life. Thoughts, opinions, and life-lessons were taught around the table.

It still happens at my house, just not as often. The kids are grown and married and have kids of their own. We don't get together as often as we did when they were young. It's safe to say that the meal takes a little more planning and coordination these days, but it's worth all the effort. The moments shared together around the table are vital times of communication, talking and listening, sharing the ups and downs, joys and struggles of everyday life. It is sacred space and should not be neglected nor undervalued.

Let me encourage you to carve out the time for your family to gather around the table. Make it a priority. Value the moments together. Listen more than you talk. Laugh more than you fuss. Invest in each other's lives. (The same lesson applies with your extended family of faith.) All that we have is a gift from God… even the food that we eat. Let's eat it in a sacred place.

Prayer
Heavenly Father, may we learn to value the moments we spend around the table with our families. May it be a sacred place. Amen.

Day 98 — Leviticus 8: A Sacred Life

> "Then Moses took some of its blood and applied it to the lobe of Aaron's right ear, the thumb of his right hand, and the big toe of his right foot."
> Leviticus 8:23 (NLT)

Observation
Chapter 8 opens with the ordination ceremony of Aaron and his sons as priests before Israel. The entire assembly of Israel is called together before the tabernacle. The priests are washed and adorned with special garments. They are also anointed with oil to set them apart for the task ahead of them. In our focus verse, Moses takes the blood of a slaughtered ram and he touches some of it to the ear, thumb, and toe of Aaron. By touching Aaron in these places, Moses was dedicating the "total" person to the Lord's work… literally head to toe.

Application
Recently, while walking my dog, I was caught in a summer downpour. Within seconds the rain was upon me and I had no option but to push ahead. By the time I got home I was drenched. My hair was wet. My clothes were soaked. My shoes squished. I left a puddle on the floor of my kitchen when I stepped into the house. Literally, I was wet… head to toe. There was not an inch of my body not dripping with water. Thoroughly, totally, completely wet.

Make the connection to the image of this ordination act described in scripture. Moses takes sacred blood and applies it to Aaron's ear lobe, his thumb, and then to his toe. It was a way of demonstrating that all of Aaron's life was to be committed to the work of the Lord.

When we commit ourselves to the lordship of Christ, we offer the totality of our lives before him. Though the preacher didn't sprinkle you with blood the day you first offered your life in faith, you have been called to give the totality of your being to the Lord. Head. Hand. Feet. First, you and I must offer the thought life before his throne. Every thought must be captive unto the word of God. We must ensure our thoughts are holy, our minds are clear, and our intellect is pure. In other words, we offer the very thoughts of our minds before the scrutiny of God. Second, our hands must also be dedicated to God's service. All of work should be viewed as sacred. Everything to which we apply our effort must in some way reflect his lordship. We must offer honest labor and ethical work. Third, wherever our feet take us must honor the God who longs to direct our steps. It matters how we spend our days. It matters where we go and how we influence others. We must be mindful of the steps. Let me encourage you to offer all that you all unto the Lord this day. Let your thoughts be pure, your work be ethical, and your journey pleasing in the sight of God.

Prayer
Heavenly Father, may we offer you the totality of our lives this day. Be glorified in what we think, how we act, and where we go. Amen.

Day 99 — Leviticus 9: Seeing God

> "Present all these offerings to the LORD because the LORD will appear to you today." Leviticus 9:4b (NLT)

Observation

This chapter of Leviticus records a very dramatic moment as the priests begin their time of service following their ordination week. According to the instruction of Moses, Aaron is to present several offerings before the Lord to consecrate both the priests and the people. He will offer sin offerings, burnt offerings, and peace offerings. The promise from Moses was that the Lord would appear to them on that very day. Read to the end of the chapter and you will discover that once the various offerings had been made, the glory of the Lord appeared in the form of a fire blazing forth from the Lord's presence in the tabernacle, consuming all the sacrificial offerings on the altar. The entire gathering of people saw the moment and bowed before the presence of the Lord.

Application

What an interesting promise... "The Lord will appear to you today." The Israelites certainly experienced such a moment on the day the priests began their work. What if you started this day with the same promise? "The Lord will appear to you today." Such a moment is more likely to happen than you might suspect. No... Don't look for God to appear as a flame shooting out of the front door of your church, but do look for God to appear. It is my belief that God appears to us in the small and even routine moments of our lives. Today God may appear to you in the beauty of the sunrise, or in the intricate blossoms of a flowering plant. God may appear in the answer to a long-recited prayer. Or God may also appear in the words of a friend who offers you counsel. God may even appear in tangible form.

Think about it... if human beings bear the image of God, then doesn't it make sense that God appears to us in the life of every person we encounter? Such a revelation gives such value and worth to every person who crosses our path today. God will appear to you today in the face of your child, the beauty of your spouse, and in the smile of your neighbor. God will also appear as a cashier at the store... a homeless man on the corner... a businessman in a clean, pressed suit... a nurse who listens to your aches and pains.

Moses was right. God WILL appear to you today. Look and listen for God's presence. See the worth of every person. Feel compassion for every need. Offer grace to those who are hurting. Understand who it is that stands before you.

Prayer

Father God, may we have vision this day to see your image reflected in the life of everyone we encounter. And as we do, may we in some way reflect your image before them as well. Amen.

Day 100 — Leviticus 10: Uh-oh...

> "Aaron's sons Nadab and Abihu put coals of fire in their incense burners and sprinkled incense over them. In this way, they disobeyed the LORD by burning before him the wrong kind of fire, different than he had commanded. So fire blazed forth from the LORDs presence and burned them up, and they died there before the LORD." Leviticus 10:1-2 (NLT)

Observation

Just after being told what to do and how to do it as priests, the sons of Aaron violated the procedures that Moses had outlined under God's instruction. Choosing a casual approach to worship, they caught the brunt of God's wrath. God demanded holiness and obedience. They flippantly ignored that command and suffered as a result. The fire of the Lord blazed forth from the tabernacle and both men were killed. When the news reached Aaron, the scriptures say that he "was silent." The point was surely made; God's commandments are to be taken seriously.

Application

Imagine that you have been given a task by God. The instructions are clear. The directions are easily understood. And then, rather than offer obedience, you offer ignorance. You ignore the instruction that God has provided. Are you foolish enough to think that God won't care?

Once, when Jesus was asked about the greatest of all commands, he immediately responded, "And you shall love the Lord your God with all your heart, and with all your soul, and with all your mind, and with all your strength. The second is this, 'You shall love your neighbor as yourself.' There is no other commandment greater than these" (Mark 12:30-31 NASB). This is no imaginary scenario. These instructions really are the God-given tasks to which we have been called. Have we taken them seriously? Consider the second commandment... that of loving your neighbor. How deliberate have you been about getting that done? Do you give yourself away unselfishly? Do you offer all that you have to meet their needs? Do you share without expectation of something in return? Do you love that person and provide for their needs with the same passion with which you love yourself? Nadab and Abihu were probably shocked that God's anger burned against them for their refusal to obey. Maybe they thought too casually about Almighty God and God's instructions. Maybe we do as well. Think about loving your neighbor today. Pour out your life. Give your heart. Offer your service. You just may provide yourself with a little fire insurance.

Prayer

Father God, teach us today to take all your commandments as seriously as you do. Amen.

Day 101 — Leviticus 11: Avoiding Contact

> "If such an animal falls into a clay pot, everything in the pot will be defiled, and the pot must be smashed." Leviticus 11:33 (NLT)

Observation
Chapter 11 of Leviticus is filled with instructions about which animals, which birds, and which fish are considered "clean," and which are considered "unclean." Clean animals could be eaten and used in the various offerings. Unclean, of course, could not. These regulations all pertained to purity. The idea was twofold. First, because God is pure, God's people must live lives of purity, which certainly includes the type of food they consume. Second, these dietary laws were part of the way in which the Israelites distinguished themselves from surrounding nations. Their fidelity to God, demonstrated even in the food consumed, bore testimony to the importance of God in their lives.

Application
In our focus verse, Moses and Aaron are giving specific instructions about animals that scurry along the ground; specifically, rats and lizards. Not only were the people not to eat or touch the dead body of such a creature, but if one fell into a clay pot, the pot would have to be destroyed. Just the contact with such a creature would ruin the pot and render it no longer useful.

Most likely, the biggest problem you face today will not be eating food prepared in a pot that a lizard once inhabited. (At least I hope not!) But the problem of "contact" may be a real issue for most of us. Because God is holy, God's continual desire is for us to be holy. We are to be distinct, different, and set apart. We are to honor God with every word and deed. Sometimes, however, it is our contact with the darkness around us that renders us a little "unclean." These ancient rules were a summons to purity… a call to live a life that honored God. It is not food that renders us impure, but rather the other vices we contact each day that erode our purity. Sometimes we let the search engine of our browser go a few pages too deep. Sometimes, we let the movies we watch take us down a dark road. Sometimes we allow negativity, anger, and bigotry to steer our thoughts. Sometimes we go to the wrong place and make poor decisions. It's the contact with such things that slowly destroys the purity that God longs to find in our hearts. In verse 45 of this chapter, God declares, "You must be holy, for I am holy" (NASB). I challenge you to be careful of that which contacts your life, your heart, and your very spirit. You are to bear the image of God and not the darkness of human depravity.

Prayer
Father God, give us a desire to live lives of purity. May we guard our hearts knowing that your Spirit longs to dwell within us. Amen.

Day 102 — Leviticus 12: A Delicate Matter...

> "On the eighth day the flesh of his foreskin shall be circumcised."
> Leviticus 12:3 (NASB)

Observation

Chapter 12 of Leviticus deals with laws regarding motherhood. In the birth process, a mother was rendered ceremonially unclean because of the flow of her blood. In the case of a male child, the mother had to wait 33 days before she could go through the rites of purification. For a female child, the time was doubled to 66 days. Though no explanation is given for the difference between the sexes, it is thought by some commentators that additional time was set aside when a daughter was born because the daughter one day would experience a similar flow of blood. There was nothing sinful about childbirth... God had instructed mankind to be fruitful and multiply. Mosaic law did however make a distinction between sacrificial blood (blood used for worship practices), and all other occasions when blood was present. Thus, the need for a special purification when a child was born.

Application

The focus verse dictates that on the eighth day of life, male children were to be circumcised. Circumcision was a sign of God's covenant with Israel. The cutting of the foreskin would be a distinctive act not practiced by the surrounding pagan nations. Thus, even with one's anatomy, God's people would be different from the world around them. One could make the point that even the most personal, intimate part of a man's body was to be controlled in such a way that God would be honored. In other words, how a man controls his sexual urges should display a fidelity to God's vision for proper human relationships.

Mosaic law indicated that circumcision would be practiced on the eighth day of life. There is a very important and practical reason for this guideline: by that time an infant's blood had developed clotting factors sufficient to make the procedure safe. Think of it... long before the days of modern medicine, long before sterile surgical procedures and vital medicines, our creator God commanded an eight-day waiting period, knowing precisely what would ensure a safe observance of the instruction. It's another affirmation that we are fearfully and wonderfully made and that every detail of human life is known and ordained by a deliberate creator God.

God understands the importance of details. Nothing in our lives escapes God's notice. I hope that this day, you will enjoy the assurance that in all the moments of your life, both great and small, God is watching over you.

Prayer

Father God, we acknowledge that we are indeed fearfully and wonderfully made. Thank you for your amazing creativity and scrutiny. Amen.

Day 103 — Leviticus 13: Unclean People or Unclean Thought?

> "He shall remain unclean all the days during which he has the infection; he is unclean. He shall live alone; his dwelling shall be outside the camp."
> Leviticus 13:46 (NASB)

Observation
According to the Law of Moses, the role of the priest in ancient Israel extended beyond the duties of scripture reading and worship leadership. Priests were also vested with the responsibility of diagnosing certain diseases and infections. Those suffering from various infections or diseases, like leprosy, would present themselves to the priests. The priests would examine the patchy skin or infected area. If there was a question of wellness, the person would be isolated for a period of time. This was not punitive but diagnostic. Within a week or so, the priest could determine whether or not a condition was improving or becoming chronic. Those who were thought to be contagious were forced to live outside the Israelite encampment for two reasons: first, to avoid any further contamination of the infection, and second to ensure that nothing "unclean" would inhabit the camp. Remember that the tabernacle was considered the dwelling place of God. To keep the encampment ceremonially clean, anything considered unclean had to be removed.

Application
It may seem to us, in our modern-day context, a bit cruel to isolate sick members of the community away from everyone else. When we think of compassionate care, we think of the ways in which human touch and contact can certainly heal a wound and give great comfort. Before we become too judgmental of the ancient Israelites, let's remember that their exclusionary tactics were not judgmental, but a way of safeguarding the community from the spread of further disease.

We too tend to isolate various people within our communities. The problem for us however has nothing to do with health concerns or the threat of disease. We tend to isolate and segregate out of fear, out of ignorance, and out of prejudice. We tend to reject anyone who doesn't look like us, speak our language, practice our religion, or share our ideologies. We may not go so far as to drop such folks off at the city limits, but we do find ways to exclude them from conversation, from community, and from contact. We have been slow to understand that when called by Christ to love our neighbor, he was demanding of us an ethic and attitude that welcomes the stranger, that engages diverse thought, and that loves in spite of the differences. Let me encourage you to become intentional about inclusion. Until you are willing to reach beyond your comfort zone, you will close off relationships that could enrich your life, heal your community, and broaden your perspective.

Prayer
Heavenly Father, may we display the welcoming embrace of your kingdom. Amen.

Day 104   Leviticus 14: Restoration

> "Thus the priest shall look, and if the infection of leprosy has been healed in the leper, then the priest shall give orders to take two live clean birds and cedar wood and a scarlet string and hyssop for the one who is to be cleansed." Leviticus 14:3-4 (NASB)

Observation
This chapter of Leviticus describes in great detail the process needed to provide cleansing and restoration to someone healed of leprosy. When the priest determined that the infection was no longer present, a very elaborate process was put into place to atone for sin and bring the recently-healed-person back into the encampment. For 20 verses, the narrative describes a very long and detailed process of restoration. In the later verses of the chapter instructions are also provided detailing the steps necessary to rid one's home of leprosy. (This may be a reference to a dangerous mold.) The cleansing of the house could be as extreme as tearing it down and rebuilding the entire dwelling. It is clear that restoration is not an easy process.

Application
Sometimes I get caught up in watching those television car shows in which an old, rusted-out car is brought back to life through a very meticulous restoration. A junkyard wreck becomes a showroom masterpiece. The rust is sanded away. The dents are straightened. The leather is replaced. To do it well takes a lot of time and a lot of money, but the end result is stunning.

Though most of us will never have to deal with a case of leprosy, we will have to deal with the problem of sin. Because of poor choices and regrettable decisions, our lives become marred, broken, and damaged. We lose our hope and often decide that we are destined to live a life of remorse and shame. We wish things were different… that we could begin again.

The good news is that we can. Through his infinite grace, Christ offers us new life. Through his atoning sacrifice for our sins, he offers us forgiveness. A junkyard wreck can become a showroom masterpiece again. But remember… restoration is not an easy process. Christ offered his life to make the process plausible. And from us, restoration also makes its demand. We have to take deliberate steps to tear down and rebuild. We can no longer continue down a destructive road of disobedience and poor choice. We have to be willing to let the transformative Spirit of God begin to reclaim and remake our lives. We must abandon the strongholds of our selfishness, our pettiness, and our remorsefulness so that we can be made new through the power of God at work in our lives. God has been healing lives for thousands of years. Why not let God start to work on yours?

Prayer
Father God, through the blood of Jesus Christ, make us new again. Amen.

Day 105 — Leviticus 15: Wash Up!

> "Thus you shall keep the sons of Israel separated from their uncleanness, so that they will not die in their uncleanness by their defiling My tabernacle that is among them." Leviticus 15:31 (NASB)

Observation

This chapter of Leviticus seems to deal more precisely with practical matters of health and hygiene. The verses describe any number of bodily discharges that could occur both from men and women. These discharges could include pus from an infection, semen, diarrhea, menstrual fluid, or blood. The concern seems to focus on the prevention of spreading germs or diseases that could be present in those discharges. The law indicated procedures to be followed so that household items like chairs, beds, and even saddles for horses could be cleaned and maintained properly. The emphasis in this chapter does not seem to focus on how to atone for transgressions of God's will and way, but rather, it focuses on more practical issues related to hygiene. The focus verse seems to indicate that God demanded a certain level of cleanliness from those who were involved in tabernacle worship.

Application

There's an old expression here in the South when it comes to ridding your hands of the day's dirt: "I need to wash up." That means a person needs to go wash his hands before he sits down to eat. All of us have been there. Before we sit down to enjoy a nice meal, we want to ensure that we wash off all the dirt, grime, and germs that we might bring to the table. Certain surfaces are just covered with germs and we feel the need for a good cleansing to wash them all away. In my office, I keep a bottle of hand sanitizer close by. Several times a day, I will make sure that I am "germ free." More than just a matter of hygiene, we also feel better psychologically when we are clean.

I grew up singing one of the great hymns of faith that carried this line, "What can wash away my sins? Nothing but the blood of Jesus. What can make me whole again? Nothing but the blood of Jesus." As important as it is to be physically clean… hands and body washed well, it is more important to be spiritually clean. Our walk through life soils our very souls. Sin collects on our hearts. Disobedience stains our psyche. Mistakes cloud our self-perception. We need to be washed. First John 1:9 affirms, "If we confess our sins, He is faithful and righteous, so that He will forgive us our sins and cleanse us from all unrighteousness" (NASB). We have the ability to stand faultless before the Throne of God… not because we deserve to be there… not because we are without sin… not because we haven't made mistakes. We are able to stand before God because we are clean. Our lives have been washed by the atoning sacrifice and abundant grace of Jesus Christ. What wonderful grace. Maybe it's time for you to get washed up.

Prayer

Father God, thank you for the cleansing grace of Jesus Christ. Amen.

Day 106 — Leviticus 16: Our Scapegoat

> "Then Aaron shall lay both of his hands on the head of the live goat, and confess over it all the iniquities of the sons of Israel and all their transgressions in regard to all their sins; and he shall lay them on the head of the goat and send it away into the wilderness by the hand of a man who stands in readiness." Leviticus 16:21 (NASB)

Observation
This chapter outlines a unique and important observance, the "Day of Atonement," or in Hebrew, "Yom Kippur." As you may recall, the tabernacle, which was the precursor of the Temple, contained two rooms, separated by a huge veil. The outer room, where the priests carried out daily duties, had three main features... a golden lampstand, 12 loaves of bread on a table, and an altar on which incense was burned. The inner room, known as the Holy of Holies, housed the Ark of the Covenant which contained the 10 Commandment stones. And as described in verse 2, God appeared in that place in the form of a cloud. It was in that inner room, where the High Priest (Aaron) could go once a year to make atonement from himself and the sins of the people. In addition to the sacrifice of ceremonial animals, a scapegoat was used to transport the sins of the nation away from the presence of God and into the wilderness.

Application
According to our focus verse, a goat was used to symbolically remove the sins of Israel from the presence of God. The sins were transferred to the animal and the animal led away to the wilderness. The image of a scapegoat vividly displays the work of Christ. Recall for a moment the prophetic words of Isaiah 53:6, "We all, like sheep, have gone astray, each of us has turned to our own way; and the LORD has laid on him the iniquity of us all" (NIV). Or bring to mind the words of 2 Corinthians 5:21, "God made him who had no sin to be sin for us, so that in him we might become the righteousness of God" (NIV). Because of God's desire to remove the barrier to humanity that sin creates, God made a way for our sins to be removed. By placing our sins on the head of Jesus, those sins are transferred away from our lives and completely forgiven. Jesus becomes the scapegoat who bears the penalty for our sins.

Imagine that you take the time to record on index cards all the sins of your life... each mistake, each impure thought, every moment of disobedience. The cards are boxed up, sealed with tape, and dropped off at the local post office and sent to a destination where they will never be remembered by God again. How freeing would that be? What joy in having the burden lifted? It happens every day... not through a parcel sent in the mail, nor a goat sent out into the wilderness, but through the atoning blood of Jesus Christ.

Prayer
Father God, thank you for taking away our sins through Jesus. Amen.

Day 107 — Leviticus 17: Throw Out Your Goats

> "They shall no longer sacrifice their sacrifices to the goat demons with which they play the harlot. This shall be a permanent statute to them throughout their generations." Leviticus 17:7 (NASB)

Observation

This chapter of Leviticus has much to say about the importance of blood, especially the way in which it was used to make atonement for the sins of individuals. The chapter affirms that there is life in blood. We need blood to live. Because it is a life-giving substance, God considers it sacred. This chapter speaks of the proper ways that blood is to be treated. It was not to be consumed at any time. In fact, any blood not used as a part of the atonement process was to be poured out onto the ground and covered with dirt if not offered at the door of the tabernacle.

Application

It's hard to read a chapter like this one and not have your eyes drawn to the words, "goat demons," right? In the ancient cultural context in which Israel was placed, the Canaanites especially were known for pagan worship practices that often involved goats. Goats were a symbol of fertility. The warning of our focus verse is that of guarding one's faith and worship practice. There was to be no association with false gods. To worship any god other than Yahweh, was to commit "spiritual adultery." No other deity was worthy of worship, praise, or sacrificial offering.

Let's be honest, none of us will struggle with worshipping a goat demon today. It's just not on our agenda. But what we will struggle with is our tendency to create other gods to worship and pay our allegiance. Though we might never admit to the creation of a false deity, surely we have raised up a few of our own. We bow to the gods of social media. We genuflect before the god of television. We worship our work. We even worship our leisure activities. If you doubt me, keep a log for a week and chart out the way you spend your time. How many hours are spent on your smartphone? How many minutes on social media? How much time and money are invested in your favorite hobby? The things we treasure become the objects of our worship. And the more we devote our lives to the unimportant, the more we eliminate God from our schedule. Be mindful of the ways in which you invest your life. You may just be offering a sacrifice to latest goat demon that has walked into your world.

Prayer

Father God, may we never, ever substitute a false god as the object of our worship. Amen.

Day 108 — Leviticus 18: The Rub of Culture

> "You shall not do what is done in the land of Egypt where you lived, nor are you to do what is done in the land of Canaan where I am bringing you; you shall not walk in their statutes. You are to perform My judgments and keep My statutes, to live in accord with them; I am the LORD your God."
> Leviticus 18:3-4 (NASB)

Observation

Chapter 18 is a call for Israel to live by a different ethic and morality than the nations surrounding them. Specifically, Moses speaks about laws that condemn certain relationships which were accepted and practiced in the land of Egypt and Canaan. Both cultures observed all kinds of pagan worship practices, some of which even included various forms of prostitution and human sacrifice. These nations had defiled themselves with their practices (verse 24). God's people were to live differently. Specific to this passage, God's people were not to practice immoral sexual relationships. The chapter outlines several perversions, practiced by the surrounding cultures, that were not to be mentioned among the Israelites.

Application

I heard a rather unusual report recently on NPR about the decline of "cargo pants" as a staple in men's fashion. (Quite honestly, I didn't realize that it was such a big deal!) Apparently, starting about the mid 1990s, cargo pants became the "go to" fashion for shorts-wearing men here in America. Once the fashion caught on, millions of men bought into the idea that cargo pants were the way to go. The trend has lasted for almost a quarter century. But, according to the report, fashion trends are moving toward a different look and cargo pants are going the way of mullet haircuts, bell-bottom jeans, and wide neckties. Here's the point, using fashion trends as an illustration. We are impacted by the culture in which we live. We are easily influenced and affected by the world that swirls around us.

For the ancient Israelites to maintain a holy posture before God and a distinctiveness before other nations, they could not allow the cultures of the pagan nations to seep into their hearts, minds, and even daily life. Unfortunately, the problem of damaging cultural influence has not gone away. Voices outside the sphere of Spirit and scripture continue to call us to compromise, asking us to adopt a different set of values. We feel the pressure to lean into compromise, mediocrity, and a "everything goes" mentality. God demands more of us. The flow of influence should move from us to the world around us. We are called to change the world, not be changed by it. So be mindful today of the influence of the world around you. Be as salt and light and work to transform your corner of it in a way that honors God.

Prayer

Father God, teach us how to offer our world a better way of thinking, living, and acting. Amen.

Day 109 — Leviticus 19: The Hard Work of Inclusion

> "The stranger who resides with you shall be to you as the native among you, and you shall love him as yourself, for you were aliens in the land of Egypt; I am the LORD your God" Leviticus 19:34 (NASB)

Observation
Chapter 19 of Leviticus offers a wide variety of teaching. The opening verses speak specifically about idolatry and the ways in which no other gods are to be made or created. The remainder of the chapter deals with various topics such as, the right way to harvest crops, when to eat the produce of newly-planted fruit trees, a prohibition of tattoos, how to groom a beard, and the importance of using accurate weights and measurements for trade purposes. It's a lot to take in. All of it points to the distinctive character that the children of God are to embrace. Our focus verse for the day speaks of the way immigrants are to be treated.

Application
A lot is being said these days in various political circles about immigration. Opinions vary greatly in terms of treatment, acceptance, and incorporation into American life. In his day, Moses argued for a rule of hospitality that welcomed the stranger, pointing to the earlier days when every Israelite was a foreigner living in the land of Egypt. Because they knew what it was like to live a marginalized life, they were to offer a greater acceptance and welcome as the redeemed people of God. Notice the "love your neighbor as yourself" ethic written into this verse.

Interesting, is it not, the way that the truth of scripture speaks in timeless fashion to the people of every generation. Certainly these words should somehow enter the hearts of God's people as we debate the merits of welcoming the foreigner into our land. There is a rule of hospitality that we cannot ignore. There is a golden-rule mentality that we must adopt. There is a civility and respect that must be a part of the conversation. As people of faith in a loving God, we must move beyond the prejudices and fear of human nature and adopt a Godly obedience that welcomes the outsider. We must choose to live a better ethic and provide a more welcoming community. In the face of fear based in ignorance and hatred based in selfishness, we must love those who are struggling to find their way in a strange land. It's as simple as a word a welcome, a shared meal, or the offer of friendship. I heard recently about a small group at a local church, whose single-minded purpose is to adopt, befriend, and incorporate a refugee family into their midst each year. They are changing the conversation about immigration one family at a time. It's a good approach. Considering the problems connected to refugees and immigrants, what do you need to be doing?

Prayer
Father God, teach us to welcome the stranger in our midst. Amen.

Day 110 — Leviticus 20: One Red Car

> "You must be holy because I, the LORD, am holy. I have set you apart from all other people to be my very own." Leviticus 20:26 (NLT)

Observation

This chapter outlines several sins so heinous in the mind of God, and so destructive to the reputation of Israel as a light to the surrounding nations, that they were capital offenses. For example, specific instruction is given to the nation about offering child sacrifices to a pagan god named Molech. Anyone who did such a thing was to be put to death. God, through Moses, went on to say that if the community of Israel was unwilling to carry out the sentence, that God would destroy that person. (vs. 4-5) The entire chapter points to a greater truth. God demands holiness from God's people. We are made in God's image, and if we are God's image-bearers before the nations, then something of our lives should reflect God's holiness. We are to be distinct in order to celebrate our God who is unlike any other god.

Application

Years ago, while vacationing at the Georgia coastal island of St. Simons, I rented a plane and flew around the area, including the Port of Brunswick. (Yes, I have a pilot's license.) There is a special dock where huge freighters off-load thousands of cars, primarily from Asia and Germany. They park the cars in massive lots until they can be loaded onto trucks and railcars to be distributed across the nation. These lots contain thousands of cars. I flew over one section that must have held 5000 cars... all of them the very same make and model and even color. Envision 5000 white Hyundai Elantras. But for whatever reason, in middle of the lot someone had parked one red car. It stood out. It was distinct. In a sea of white, it was the single, red, car that drew my focus. Being different can make a real impression.

That was God's point to the nation of Israel. Until they stood out from the various cultures and nations around them, the story of the Almighty God would not be told. God called them to a "radical difference." We continue to share that same calling. We are to be radically different from the world around us. We are to love where there is hate. We are to unite where there is divide. We are to forgive when others clamor for revenge. We are to heal where there is strife. We are to lift oppression while others demand it. We are to give light where there is darkness. If we fail to represent the God with whom we are in a dynamic, loving, and destiny-altering relationship, how will others ever know of that love?

Prayer

Father God, may we be radically different... not to look at others with condescension, but to offer others a glimpse of who you are and how you love. Amen.

Day 111 — Leviticus 21: A High Calling

> "They must be set apart as holy to their God and must never bring shame on the name of God. They must be holy, for they are the ones who present the special gifts to the LORD, gifts of food for their God."
> Leviticus 21:6 (NLT)

Observation
Our focus verse explains all the rules and regulations outlined in chapter 21 related to the life and work of the priests. Throughout the chapter, there are several parameters established for the descendants of Aaron as they carry out their important work. The rules outline a diversity of regulations including a prohibition on touching dead bodies, cutting one's hair, and shaving one's beard. There are also rules about whom a priest could marry and what to be done to a wayward daughter to atone for her sins. The point of all the rules was to ensure that the priesthood maintained a very high standard of conduct because of the sacred work placed upon them as they mediated the relationship between the holy God and sinful men.

Application
It is easy to remove ourselves from the instructions provided, reasoning that these rules only applied to the "professional clergy" of the day and not to the common Jewish citizen of Israel. We tend to hold minsters and pastors to a very high ethical standard, and so we should. Those who lead the people of God are admonished "to live beyond reproach." However, the call to responsible, moral, and ethical living does not apply simply to the paid professionals of religion. It applies to all of us. Notice the resounding call in our focus verse to be set apart as holy, not bringing shame upon the name of the Lord our God.

We must constantly guard our integrity, our actions, and our motivations, knowing that all of us bear testimony to Christ. He is either honored or dishonored by the way in which we conduct our lives. People are always watching. The scrutiny is constant. We cannot afford to let down our guard and allow any compromise. Let's be clear, no one is perfect. "For all have sinned and fall short of the glory of God" (Romans 3:23 NASB). We will not live a sinless life. There will be times when we stumble. But holy living is the goal towards which we should strive. It should be our daily resolve and fervent prayer to honor Christ in all that we do.

Sometimes, when we fail to meet the expectations and fall way short of the glory of God, we develop a defeatist mentality. We reason, "I've messed up my life and have lost the ability to serve as anyone's role model or guiding influence." Have we forgotten the God of the second chance? Let me encourage you this day, not to look back with regret, but to look forward with the resolve to honor Christ to the best of your ability this day.

Prayer
Dear Heavenly Father, forgive us when we fail, strengthen us for better living. Amen.

Day 112 — Leviticus 22: Help with the Big Decisions

> "If a priest's daughter marries someone outside the priestly family, she may no longer eat the sacred offerings." Leviticus 22:12 (NLT)

Observation

This chapter contains laws that pertain to the role of the priesthood. These rules and regulations cover a wide variety of topics, from the type of animals to be used in sacrifices to the types of activities that would render a priest temporarily unclean and thus unable to fulfill his duties. Some of the rules are interesting, like those outlined in verses 29 and 30 that require the priests to consume all the meat offered in a thanksgiving sacrificial ceremony before the next morning. (Party on!) Our focus verse deals with food offerings that were presented before the Lord. The priests were allowed to eat this food along with the members of their household. It was considered part of the payment for their work. Notice however, that if a daughter married someone outside of the priestly family, she was no longer able to benefit from the food offerings.

Application

As the father of two married daughters, I have to chuckle a little bit when I read this verse. Both of my girls have married great young men and we (my wife and I) are very proud of them. And no… we haven't cut them off because they no longer live with us. In fact, it's been a joy for us to watch them become more independent and build families of their own. Like all of you who are parents, we will continue to support and nurture our children for as long as we live.

Some decisions we make carry a price. In the ancient world of the Israelite priesthood, to marry out of the family business meant being cut off from the food chain. It was a choice that I'm sure was carefully considered and thought out. The decision to marry carried a price. The decisions you will make today probably won't affect your food supply, but they probably do carry a price. Decisions lead to our well-being or our demise. They lead to wealth and prosperity or to ruin. They lead to healthy relationships or to brokenness. They lead to better opportunity or to the squandering of a moment. Decisions really are important. The problem is we lack the wisdom to always choose well. James offers this suggestion… "If you need wisdom, ask our generous God, and He will give it to you" (James 1:5 NLT). In light of our inability to choose well, and knowing that even today there will be many choices to make, doesn't it make sense to seek the wisdom of God in all that we do. Both in the large and small matters, let's be careful to seek the wisdom of our Father who has promised to give us wise counsel.

Prayer

Dear Heavenly Father, thank you for your willingness to give us clarity in the choices we will make today. Amen.

Day 113 — Leviticus 23: A Call to Remembrance

> "You shall live in booths for seven days; all the native-born in Israel shall live in booths, so that your generations may know that I had the sons of Israel live in booths when I brought them out from the land of Egypt. I am the LORD your God." Leviticus 23:42-43 (NASB)

Observation

Chapter 23 contains a very detailed and complete list of the religious festivals to be observed by the Jewish people. These events are considered "holy convocations" in which the entire nation interrupts the usual routine of life in order remember the deeds of God and to honor God's name. This chapter outlines Sabbath law, the observance of the Feast of Unleavened Bread and Passover, the Feast of Weeks or Pentecost, Rosh Hashana (Head of the Year), the Day of Atonement (Yom Kippur), and the Feast of Booths. Throughout the entire year, the Israelites were challenged to remember and celebrate the various acts of God in their midst.

Application

You've heard the saying, "Those who cannot remember the past are condemned to repeat it." This saying comes from the writings of George Santayana, a Spanish-born American author of the late nineteenth and early twentieth centuries. We read that phrase and are reminded that we will continue to repeat former mistakes if we do not learn from them. In fact, I have often counseled people who have come to me confessing some transgression with these words, "The tragedy is not in making mistakes, for we all do. The tragedy is not learning from those mistakes." History needs to be our teacher. We would do well not to repeat past mistakes. However, in our focus passage, God is reminding the people of the importance of remembering, not for the sake of avoiding mistakes, but for the sake of honoring and remembering God's miraculous deeds. Specific to our focus verse is the commandment to build and live in a tent for week, to be reminded of the way in which the Israelites lived in tents during their journey to the promised land. God called the nation into remembrance and celebration.

I wonder how well we have done at remembering and honoring the key moments in our lives when God has acted on our behalf. Do we dedicate moments to glorify what God has done? Do we set aside a holiday just to recall God's blessings? Do we even set aside a day each week to rest and reflect on God's providential care in our lives each day? Here is my fear... if we are not intentional about remembering God's movement among us, we may soon forget how intertwined God's presence is with our lives. I'm not suggesting that you go live in a tent today, but I am suggesting the creation of your own celebrations to honor what God has done in your life.

Prayer

Father, help us to remember and honor the moments you have been at work in our lives.

Day 114 — Leviticus 24: Continual Light

> "Then the Lord spoke to Moses, saying, 'Command the sons of Israel that they bring to you clear oil from beaten olives for the light, to make a lamp burn continually. Outside the veil of testimony in the tent of meeting, Aaron shall keep it in order from evening to morning before the LORD continually." Leviticus 24:1-3a (NASB)

Observation

In the tabernacle, just in front of the veil that separated the Holy of Holies from the rest of the space, a golden lampstand was placed. In addition to the lampstand, a golden table stood with 12 loaves of bread placed on the top. (The bread was replaced each Sabbath as an offering before the Lord. The priests alone were allowed to eat it at the end of each week.) Our focus verse outlines the instructions for the lamp. Filled with clear and clean olive oil, it was the duty of the priests to keep the lamp burning continually. This eternal flame was symbolic of the presence of God among the people, and the lamp was to burn continually from generation to generation throughout every night.

Application

Sometimes what we can't see in the dark frightens us a little. We hear a strange noise—the house creaks, a dog barks, a baby cries—and we stare into the darkness and allow our minds to race in a thousand different directions. Then we turn on the light and the fear is dispelled in a moment. The dark shadows contain no monsters, the dog is at rest again, and the baby settles in. It's the presence of light that makes the difference. It doesn't matter if we are 7 years old or 70 years old, having a little light during the dark hours of the night helps us to rest a little more securely.

God understands human nature. The light that symbolized God's presence during the night surely gave comfort when the Israelites trembled in the darkness. We are no different. We too find assurance in the presence of light. Let's be honest, there are a lot of dark moments that fill our lives. Maybe you are walking in some deep darkness of fear even this morning. We feel the darkness when relationships are broken, when finances are tight, when health concerns are raised, or when the news of the world seems so heavy upon our hearts. As we grope in the darkness, we would do well to remember the presence of God. Though we don't keep a candle burning at night, we do keep a relationship growing strong. It's the relationship with Christ who proclaimed, "I am the light of the world" (John 8:12 NLT). So if your world seems a little dark and scary today, turn on the light by recalling the promise of Jesus' continual presence. The darkness will be dispelled by the power of his light.

Prayer

Father, may we be reminded today of your continual presence. Amen.

Day 115 — Leviticus 25: Ready. Set. Celebrate!

> "You shall then sound a ram's horn abroad on the tenth day of the seventh month; on the day of atonement you shall sound a horn all through your land." Leviticus 25:9 (NASB)

Observation
This speaks to both Sabbath rest and the year of Jubilee. God commands a year of rest for the land the Israelites farm. The land is to remain fallow with no crops sown or harvested. This would ensure that the land would remain fertile. God promised that the harvest from the sixth year would more than sustain the nation during the year of rest. The narrative then shifts to the idea of the Year of Jubilee. After seven cycles of seven years, the 50th year was to be a special year unlike any other. During the Year of Jubilee, all debts were wiped away, slaves were set free, property reverted to the original owner, and homes that had been sold could be bought back if desired. The Year of Jubilee was a momentous year when things were set right again and people were able to unshackle themselves from their past.

Application
The Year of Jubilee started on the Day of Atonement, which always fell on the seventh month of the year. It began with a trumpet blast. The priests blew a ram's horn to mark the beginning of the celebration. The word "jubilee" actually means "ram's horn" and refers to this single moment every 50 years when the celebration began. It's hard to even compare that moment to anything in our context. It was bigger than the fireworks on the fourth of July. Bigger than the ball drop on New Year's Eve. Bigger than the celebration Memorial Day, Labor Day, and President's Day all rolled into one. It was a huge celebration that reunited families, cancelled oppressive debt, and returned land to the original owner. Surely the people counted down the days and hours… waiting to hear the trumpet blast, knowing that it meant freedom and salvation and hope.

The scriptures speak of another blast of trumpet sound. The Book of Revelation speaks of seven trumpets that will sound announcing the Day of Judgment and the second coming of Christ. The scene becomes more intense with each trumpet sound. The seventh trumpet is described this way: "Then the seventh angel sounded; and there were loud voices in heaven, saying, 'The kingdom of the world has become the kingdom of our Lord and of His Christ; and He will reign forever and ever'" (Revelation 11:15 NASB). Talk about a moment in time… What a day of rejoicing will come at that moment for those who are in Christ Jesus. Broken relationships will be mended. The oppressive debt of sin will be cancelled. The kingdom of Heaven will be claimed by the faithful. It's not here yet… but it's coming. Get ready to celebrate.

Prayer
Father, we thank you today for the bright hope of that great day of celebration. Amen.

Day 116 — Leviticus 26: Cause & Effect

> "I will set My face against you so that you will be struck down before your enemies; and those who hate you will rule over you, and you will flee when no one is pursuing you." Leviticus 26:17 (NASB)

Observation
Chapter 26 is a very sobering chapter to consider. It is all about the result of obedience versus the disaster of rebellion. Simply stated, the theme is, "Obedience brings blessing, rebellion brings curses." In the initial verses of the chapter, God reveals to Moses all the ways blessings will pour out on those who practice fidelity to the ways and will of God. There is strength, prosperity, abundance, and blessing. Just the opposite is outlined in the latter part of the chapter. Rebellion brings terror, illness, and defeat. Eyes will dim and the soul will diminish. Enemies will eat the harvest. There will be fear, anxiety, and restlessness. Notice the language of the focus verse, "you will flee when no one is pursuing you." It's the image of a paranoid sense of panic. The contrast is made very clear... those who pursue the righteousness of God will know a peace, a joy, and a quality of life that the disobedient can't even image.

Application
All of us are familiar with the principle of cause and effect. Certain actions bring certain results. For example, consider your eating habits. If you eat nothing but junk food, consume too many sugary drinks, and avoid all things green, your body will respond in negative ways. The unhealthy habits will result in everything from obesity, to high blood pressure, to even a shorter life expectancy. It's the cause and effect of what you place into your body. Here's another example. Let's pretend that you neglect your car's maintenance. You never change the oil. You never inflate the tires properly. You never maintain the coolant. Sooner or later bad things are going to happen. The breakdown will be the result of poor choices.

All of us have choices to make in terms of our faith and how passionate we are about pursuing an obedient relationship with God. Obedience will have its result. When we invest in the word, spend time in daily prayer, worship with fellow believers, and serve those with need, the result will be a faith that works... a faith that strengthens and fortifies us... a faith that will provide answers to the challenges we face. But if we choose to neglect our faith, or even worse, willfully choose disobedience, the results can be tragic. We will find no peace. We will hold no assurances. We will discover every facet of our lives is headed into ruin. So choices have to be made... willful, deliberate, daily choices. It's as simple and timeless as the words of Leviticus. Obedience brings blessing, rebellion brings curses.

Prayer
Father, teach us today the joy and reward of obedience. Amen.

Day 117 — Leviticus 27: Ground Rules

> "These are the commandments which the LORD commanded Moses for the sons of Israel at Mount Sinai." Leviticus 27:34 (NASB)

Observation
This is the final chapter of Leviticus ends. Throughout this book, God, through Moses, has been setting forth the ground rules for the nation of Israel. God's intent has not been to draw restrictive guidelines that hold the nation in bondage. Why would God free them just to enslaved them again? The intent is for God's children to have the best life possible. The laws provided defined a framework for living that offered the best life imaginable. When followed with sincerity, both earthly and heavenly relationships would find success. In this final chapter, Moses outlines regulations for Offerings of Dedication. At times, the Israelites offered a vow or made a promise to God, hoping for God's blessing or answer. If the vow was a foolish one, or if the person who made the vow could not keep the promise, the vow could be retracted or bought back, with a penalty imposed. The person who made the vow paid the price set by the priest. The price varied according to the object of the original vow. For example, if the vow involved a person, the amount would vary according to the age and sex of the person involved. The intent was to keep at a minimum the making of foolish vows.

Application
Ground rules are important. Knowing the boundaries and expectations of any job, relationship, or activity provides for success. For example, in my role at work, there are certain guidelines in place. There is a start time and an ending time. There is a place to park. There is a policy for monetary expenses. There are expectations of dress and decorum. Knowing the ground rules makes it easy to assess my compliance. A good employee plays by the rules. Every sport has a set of rules that governs play. There are boundaries, time limits, and guidelines to follow. Can you image a game of baseball without any rules? Would base runners follow the base paths? Would pitchers refrain from throwing at players? You get the point. Ground rules define the way a game is played.

Ground rules are especially important for human conduct and Godly living. There are expectations. There are rules. There are boundaries. God has set forth expectations to offer us the best life possible. God's guidelines are not punitive, but prescriptive. When followed closely, relationships flourish, worship increases, compassion rises, and our desire to love our neighbors becomes paramount. We become better people... not because God forces us into a relationship of coercion and fear, but because God provides us with a way of living that provides success.

Prayer
Heavenly Father, today may we know the joy of living within your design. Amen.

Day 118 — Numbers 1: Where Are You Standing?

> "So when the tabernacle is to set out, the Levites shall take it down; and when the tabernacle encamps, the Levites shall set it up. But the layman who comes near shall be put to death." Numbers 1:51 (NASB)

Observation
Numbers marks the beginning of the journey from Sinai to the promised land. It is the journey from slavery to nationhood. The book opens with a census of the people. Particularly in this opening chapter, the fighting men are all numbered according to their clans. Those 20 years of age and older were deemed eligible to participate in the conquest and were thus counted in the census. The total number of fighting men was 603,550.

The latter part of the chapter gives specific instructions to the tribe of Levi. Set apart as the priestly tribe, they were not counted among the fighting men. Their chief duty was to care for the tabernacle and support its functions. Remember that the tabernacle was a large tent-like structure that was the focal point of the Israelite encampment. It was the place of worship and, as our focus verse indicates, it was so holy that those unauthorized to approach it were to be put to death if they did.

Application
I grew up in the grand age of southern hospitality and my mother was a rock-star. She was always well dressed, gracious, and knew how to do things according to the rules of etiquette. Our living room was a testimony to her sense of decorum. It was beautifully decorated and pristinely kept. It was not a place for us boys to play. In fact, it was set aside for company and rarely did we dare step foot inside. It's not that we were forbidden to do so, it was just that we knew it was important to mom to keep it ready for guests.

Ever step into a place where you felt as if you didn't belong? Ever been somewhere that seemed so holy, so dignified, and so important that you felt unworthy to be standing in that place... maybe a sanctuary, or a cemetery, or even in the office of some great leader? Most of us have had that feeling of being unauthorized, or ineligible, to stand in such a place. Consider the kingdom of heaven for a moment. Who among us has the right to stand in the presence of God? None of us. But who among us can have the joy of being there? All of us. We are not worthy. We have not earned a place. We come into that holy place with our feet tracking in the mud of our very imperfect walk through life. And yet, because of the grace shown to us through Jesus Christ, we stand in God's presence, forgiven, invited, and welcomed. This morning as you start your day, take a moment to thank God for the privilege of standing in God's holy presence.

Prayer
Father God, thank you for counting us worthy to be welcomed into your Glory. Amen.

Day 119 — Numbers 2: Marching Orders

> "Thus the sons of Israel did; according to all that the LORD commanded Moses, so they camped by their standards, and so they set out, everyone by his family according to his father's household." Numbers 2:34 (NASB)

Observation
This chapter outlines the instructions for the arrangement of the Israelite encampment at each stop along the wilderness pilgrimage. The tabernacle was always placed in the middle of the camp. Closely surrounding it, were the tents of the Levites, who served the tabernacle activities. According to the word of the Lord given to Moses, the remaining 11 tribes were given specific places to camp according to their clans. Some were to camp to the North, others to the East, others to the South, and the others to the West. The chapter also gives the marching order whenever God directed the nation forward in their journey. Those in the East would lead the way, followed by those in the South. The Levites, who carried the tabernacle, would find their place next, right in the middle of the procession. The tribes from the West from then join the line-up, followed at last by those tribes encamped in the North.

Application
You are no doubt familiar with the phrase, "marching orders." Although no one seems to know the original etymology of the phrase, perhaps its roots could trace all the way back to this word of instruction from Numbers 2. God certainly gave the nation the order that they were to march as they journeyed to the promised land. In normal use, the phrase "marching orders" has a relatively negative context. It is usually connected to someone's job loss. When fired from his/her position, they are given their "marching orders."

But let's use the phrase in a different way. Let's think of marching orders as the assignment of a task or duty. We have been given a task to complete and now we are sent out to do the work. Is not the Great Commission a set of marching orders? "Therefore, go and make disciples of all nations, baptizing them in the name of the Father and of the Son and of the Holy Spirit" (Matthew 28:19 NLT). Is not the Great Commandment also a set of marching orders? "Jesus replied: 'Love the Lord your God with all your heart and with all your soul and with all your mind.' This is the first and greatest commandment. And the second is like it: 'Love your neighbor as yourself'" (Matthew 22:37-38 NIV). So, how should you arrange your day in light of your marching orders? Maybe it's not about your pursuit of wealth, health, or enjoyment. Maybe it's more about a pursuit of Almighty God who calls you to bear God's image before the world this day.

Prayer
Father God, may we be obedient to the tasks to which we are called this day. Amen.

Day 120　　　　　　　　　　　　　　　Numbers 3: A Part to Play

> "Now the duties of the sons of Gershon in the tent of meeting involved the tabernacle and the tent, its covering, and the screen for the doorway of the tent of meeting, and the hangings of the court, and the screen for the doorway of the court which is around the tabernacle and the altar, and its cords, according to all the service concerning them."
> Numbers 3:25-26 (NASB)

Observation

According to the instruction of God, Moses dedicates the tribe of Levi as the priests over Israel. Not only were they to administer the various offerings and sacrifices, but they were also responsible for the care, up-keep, and transportation of the tabernacle. Within the tribe of Levi, there were a number of family groups. In Numbers 3, Moses charges each group with their specific responsibility. Our focus verse describes the duties assigned to the sons of Gershon who were essentially charged with the fabrics that covered the tabernacle and the courts. A careful reading of the entire chapter will offer a glimpse at what the other descendants of Levi were charged with doing.

Application

I grew up within a "family on wheels." Everything from wagons, to cars, to motorcycles filled our garage. It all started with trikes and bikes and eventually moved into motorized vehicles like mini-bikes and go-carts. I had a bike without fenders and with little paint that became my "jump" bike. I would build ramps in the backyard, race down the driveway, and see how far I could fly through the air, ala Evil Knievel. Sometimes my brother would lay down at the end of the ramp and let me jump over him. (He never was too bright.) There were times when the chain on my bike would break. One of the links would fail and a quick repair job was needed to get things back in working order.

Sometimes kingdom work involves a lot of small parts joined together to do a great thing. God takes our individual gifts, talents, and abilities and arranges them in a way to accomplish things about which we can only dream. But here's a critical point... it takes all of us making the "willing investment" of our lives to move the kingdom forward. Even though our contribution may seem small and insignificant, the truth is, it's vital. Just as one missing link can stop a bike from rolling, one person's lack of obedience can thwart the way God longs to work in a situation. So, what is it that you are called to do? What is your contribution, and have you offered it to God's glory? You have a part to play. Life is just not the same without you.

Prayer

Father God, thank you for giving each of us a role to play in your grand design. May we be faithful with your gift. Amen.

Day 121 — Numbers 4: Holding the Most Holy Things

> "When Aaron and his sons have finished covering the holy objects and all the furnishings of the sanctuary, when the camp is to set out, after that the sons of Kohath shall come to carry them, so that they will not touch the holy objects and die. These are the things in the tent of meeting which the sons of Kohath are to carry." Numbers 4:15 (NASB)

Observation
The Kohathites were direct descendants of the tribe of Levi. Aaron and his sons were members of this group. This clan of individuals was given a very specific task related to the moving of the tabernacle when it was transported from one spot to the next. They were entrusted to carry the "most holy things." These objects included the Ark of the Covenant, the table of the bread, the golden lampstand, the golden incense altar, and the altar used for sacrifice. Before these objects could be carried, Aaron and his sons carefully covered each object in blue cloth, then wrap them in leather. The sons of Kohath were not to see the objects nor touch them directly. To touch the objects would bring death. Because these items were sacred and reserved for worship, they required special attention.

Application
I have a friend who used to fly corporate jets for the Humana Health group. Occasionally, his passenger list included more than just some guys in business suits. Sometimes he was called upon to transport organs from one site to another for delicate transplant procedures. Most often it was a donor-heart that needed to be rushed from one city to another. He was always fascinated by the process. These human hearts were placed on ice and carried around in a cooler, just like the coolers you use to carry your drinks to the lake. Can you imagine? Something so precious carried around in something so common...

I find it interesting that God takes the most precious and vitally important message ever conveyed and places it for safe keeping in the hearts of fragile and flawed human beings. As Paul writes, "But we have this treasure in earthen vessels..." (2 Corinthians 4:7 NASB). The greatest story, the greatest message, the greatest hope is carried around in each of us. It is not wrapped in blue cloth or fine leather... just in frail human flesh. How well do we safeguard the story? It is fascinating to me that we safeguard the message, not by selfishly holding it in secret, but by lavishly and intentionally giving it away. The more we share Christ in both word and deed, the more we protect the message. You carry something of great worth in your life this day. Guard it by giving it away.

Prayer
Father God, we praise you for including us in your kingdom work by asking us to both hold and share the story of Jesus. Amen.

Day 122 — Numbers 5: When Confession Isn't Enough

> "When a man or woman commits any of the sins of mankind, acting unfaithfully against the LORD, and that person is guilty, then he shall confess his sins which he has committed, and he shall make restitution in full for his wrong and add to it one-fifth of it, and give it to him whom he has wronged." Numbers 5:6-7 (NASB)

Observation
There are several words of instruction offered in this chapter. The chapter opens with a decree that those who are defiled by leprosy, discharge, or contact with dead bodies are to be placed outside the camp. The reasons for doing so are to create ceremonial purity and to safeguard the camp from possible spread of infection or disease. Further in the chapter, a test is prescribed for a woman believed to have been unfaithful to her husband. She is to drink a mixture of water and dust from the floor of the tabernacle. If guilty, she would become barren and her abdomen would swell! Our focus verse centers around the topic of restitution for a transgression committed against someone. The guilty party was to confess the sin and then "make things right" with the offended person by offering an additional 20% restitution.

Application
Let's be honest… we all make mistakes, all the time. We miss the mark. We sin against others and in so doing we sin against God. And we certainly try to practice the old adage "confession is good for the soul." In fact, we cling to the promise of 1 John 1:9 that reminds us "If we confess our sins, He is faithful and righteous to forgive us of our sins…" (NASB). Those who have found a maturity of faith can certainly testify to the freedom and cleansing that comes when we practice confession as a discipline of our faith. But here's where it gets a little sticky… we can easily offer our confession to God. We know that God loves us and will grant us the cleansing of grace. It's the confession to those we have wronged that makes us a little more uncomfortable.

It's hard to tell someone that we have sinned against them. It's hard to admit to our spouse that we were wrong, or to our child that we messed up, or to a friend indicating that we were not the kind of friend we should have been. Confession clears the air. But sometimes it isn't enough. Sometimes we have to make restitution. Sometimes we have to verify our claims of confession through demonstration. I'm not suggesting that you give flowers, or buy a lunch, or promise your child ice-cream. I'm suggesting that you earn the trust again with intentional acts of repentance. Change your behavior. Honor your word. Channel your emotions in a healthier way. Sometimes it's not enough to confess poor behavior, it takes restitution.

Prayer
Father God, make us intentional about our confessions. Make us better. Amen.

Day 123 — Numbers 6: Be Different

> "Speak to the sons of Israel and say to them, 'When a man or woman makes a special vow, the vow of a Nazirite, to dedicate himself to the LORD...'" Numbers 6:2 (NASB)

Observation
Chapter 6 describes in detail the provisions of a Nazarite vow. The word Nazirite means, "to separate." This voluntary vow allowed men or women to set themselves apart for the Lord. Vows were taken very seriously in ancient times as a well-established means of expressing devotion or gratitude to God. This vow could be temporary or permanent. It had three provisions. It involved refraining from alcoholic drinks, hair cutting, and contact with dead bodies. Nazirite restrictions gave members of non-Levitical tribes a way to enter a more demanding and highly respected relationship with God. The Nazirite vow is probably best known because of Samson (Judges 13–16). If a vow had been taken for a specific amount of time and the person swearing out the vow broke the vow, he would have to make sin and guilt offerings, and then start the process all over again.

Application
The point of making a Nazarite vow was for a person to show extreme dedication to God. The vow was a very public demonstration of someone's faith commitment. The refusal to drink wine in a culture where wine was the prevalent drink, would distinguish a person. To grow one's hair to extreme length would also be quite visible. The refusal to touch a dead body, even that of a loved one, would also signify a person's vow. The three aspects of the vow were intended to make a person distinct, different, and set-apart so that others would know of their devotion before God.

There are things that distinguish us from the people around us. We are known by our looks, our hair, our gait, our voice, maybe even our clothing. I work on a hall with a dozen other people. No one gets confused over identity. We are distinctively different. That's how we are made. But in terms of our faith commitment, are there distinctive qualities that set us apart? I think there should be. Those who belong to Christ should be different from those who don't. The distinctive characteristics should be in place, not to develop a moral superiority, but to point to the Christ who is our Savior and Lord.

I'm not asking you to swear out a weird vow this morning. I not suggesting that you refuse to cut your hair or change your drink selection. But I am asking you to consider what it is about your life that will make you distinctively Christian today. Your Christian character will be demonstrated by the words you use, the attitudes you express, and the acts of generosity you display. So, go and be different. The world should know to whom you belong.

Prayer
God, allow our difference to show today so that you will be glorified. Amen.

Day 124 — Numbers 7: Where to Hear from God

> "Now when Moses went into the tent of meeting to speak with Him, he heard the voice speaking to him from above the mercy seat that was on the ark of the testimony, from between the two cherubim, so He spoke to him."
> Numbers 7:89 (NASB)

Observation

This chapter records the day when the construction of the tabernacle was completed. Moses anointed it and the people dedicated it. Every tribal leader brought an offering to the Lord and placed it before the altar. The extravagant offerings gave testimony to the greatness of God and to the importance of the tabernacle as the dwelling place of God's presence. Each tribe brought silver dishes, bowls, and golden incense containers. Additionally, they brought bulls, rams, lambs, and goats to offer as sin offerings and peace offerings. The description of the dedication is recorded 88 verses. Obviously, it was a huge deal. After wading through much of those details, a blessing for the reader is found in the final verse. Moses goes into the tent of meeting (tabernacle) and there he heard the voice of God speaking to him.

(The Ark of the Covenant was a golden box that contained the 10 Commandments. It was positioned in the inner room of the tabernacle known as the Holy of Holies. The top cover of the Ark had two golden angel figurines whose wings pointed towards each other. The space created between the outstretched wings was said to be the Mercy Seat... the very place where the presence of God hovered above the Ark.)

Application

Where do you go to hear from God? For Moses it was in the inner sanctum of the tabernacle. If you continue to read the Biblical narrative, you will discover that on many occasions Moses encountered the presence of God in that place and God spoke to him. It was a spot where Moses consistently heard from God. We should long for such a place. Yes, God is omnipotent. God is all around us and the Holy Spirit is in us. We can certainly hear from God in a thousand different places in a thousand different ways. But is there a place where you can consistently go to pour out your heart in God's presence and let the Spirit whisper into your heart? I want to encourage you to seek out such a place. Find that quiet place of respite, that inner room, that private closet where all the distractions are closed off and the unimportant thoughts dissipate. We need to be alone with God. We need moments to sit in God's presence. We need an inner sanctum where the Spirit of God can find our longing hearts. Be intentional about finding a place and go there often. God is always waiting to chat.

Prayer

God, may we allow the creation of time spent with you to become a priority in our lives. Amen.

Day 125 — Numbers 8: Directing the Light

> "The Lord said to Moses, 'Give Aaron the following instructions: When you set up the seven lamps in the lampstand, place them so their light shines forward in front of the lampstand.'" Numbers 8:1-2 (NLT)

Observation

God gives specific instructions to Moses to be forwarded on to Aaron concerning the golden lampstand that was to be placed inside the tabernacle. Because it contained no windows, the interior of the tabernacle was shrouded in darkness. This large lampstand (menorah) would cast much needed light into the interior space. According to the instructions in Exodus 25:31-40, the lampstand was to be made from seven pounds of pure gold. It would contain seven individual lamps, fashioned in the shape of almond blossoms. The shape was a possible reflection back on the Garden of Eden. Notice that the light of the lamp was to be focused in a specific direction. It was to be directed out into the room to provide maximum illumination.

Application

My dorm room at Samford University was plain and simple. All the fixtures were built into the walls. There was a bed, a closet, three drawers for clothes, and a desk with several shelves above it. Above the desk a lamp was affixed to the wall. It was one of those flexible, metallic, goose-neck kinds of lamp with a metal cone on the end. For those moments when I actually did want to study, the lamp could be positioned to shed light directly on the desk. At other moments, when the room required greater light, the lamp could be directed to shine upward towards the ceiling. You get the point. The light could be directed where it was needed.

When Jesus offered his instruction to those gathered on the mountainside, among the first words he spoke were: "You are the light of the world" (Matthew 5:14 NASB). Can you imagine the impact those words would have had on those listening in that moment? Just think of Jesus looking into your eyes and into the depths of your heart and saying, "You, yes you... You are the light of the world." Surely it shook his audience down to their foundations. And surely it must do the same to all of us who claim him in this generation. We are the light of the world. If the world's darkness is going to be dispelled, it must happen through us. We must direct the light where it is needed. Into the crevices of brokenness, prejudice, injustice, slavery, intolerance, anger, and hatred, the light of Christ must shine. The light offers hope, grace, and redemption. Are we willing to be directed so that we might provide maximum illumination? This day, when you can and where you are, be the light.

Prayer

Father God may the grace of Jesus Christ shine through us today. Amen.

Day 126 — Numbers 9: Waiting on Wisdom

> "Moses answered, 'Wait here until I have received instructions for you from the LORD.'" Numbers 9:8 (NLT)

Observation

The first half of this chapter is a response to a very practical question about the observance of Passover. When the time came to celebrate, some of the men who had come into contact with a dead body, thus rendering them unclean, were unable to join the Passover celebration. These men approached Moses and Aaron to ask them what could be done in their situation and if they could somehow participate in the celebration. Moses petitioned the Lord on their behalf. The answer was to delay their personal Passover observance for a month. When the time came, they were to celebrate and observe the rituals as the rest of the nation had done the previous month.

Application

There is a good model to observe in the way Moses handled this situation. Not knowing nor presuming to give Godly advice or counsel, he took the matter before the Lord. He sought wisdom from God before responding to the question concerning Passover. Those who were seeking an answer were told to wait until the Lord had spoken. Bound up in this process is both seeking and waiting.

About the time I first obtained my driver's license, "prestige tags" started being offered in the state of Georgia. Now referred to as "personalized license plates," these tags could have your name, your initials, or some other word as long as it was seven letters or fewer in length. Long before the days of computerized automation, a paper form had to be completed by hand indicating a first, second, and third choice and then submitted by mail. Then, patience was required when waiting for a response to come in the mail from the state. There was seeking and waiting involved.

The book of James clearly tells us that if we lack wisdom, we can ask God, who will gladly pour wisdom into our lives (James 1:5). The problem is that we are not good at asking, nor waiting. Most of us struggle each day with tough choices and big decisions. Often, our "go to" methodology is to rely on our own intuition, experience, or wisdom. Knowing that God is interested in every facet of our lives, doesn't it make sense for us to seek God's input into both the great and small decisions we face? I feel like we could avoid the clean-up from a lot of poorly made choices if we just sought the counsel of God before we acted. And to be honest, for many of us the problem is not in waiting to hear from God, it's slowing down long enough to ask for God's wisdom before we ever make our choices.

Prayer

Father, forgive our foolish ways and grant us greater wisdom that we might honor you.

Day 127 — Numbers 10: Listen for the Alarm

> "Now the LORD said to Moses, 'Make two trumpets of hammered silver for calling the community to assemble and for signaling the breaking of camp.'" Numbers 10:1-2 (NLT)

Observation
In the final words of instruction just before the Israelites are to set out from Sinai and begin their journey to the promised land, Moses is told to make two silver trumpets. These trumpets would serve as the mass media of the day. Heard from a great distance, these trumpets would be used to alert the camp. Depending on the number of trumpet blasts given, the nation would know to either assemble at the tabernacle for a special word of instruction or to begin the process of breaking camp to move forward. The trumpets were also used at other times… to sound the alarm when going into war, to mark the beginning of annual festivals and offerings, to celebrate special moments in the life of the Israelites. The sound of the trumpets was always significant and when heard, the people needed to respond.

Application
All of us have smoke detectors in our homes. We rarely pay attention to them until the battery grows weak. They begin that shrill, quick, chirp, signaling that some attention is needed. I have learned over the years to keep a supply of 9-volt batteries on hand to reset the smoke alarms when they start to make noise. But more than responding to the chirp, we know to respond to the full alarm when it sounds. Hopefully, the only time yours will ever sound is when something in the oven gets a little too done. But in the event a fire ever does occur, it's nice to have the assurance that the alarm will sound and your family will be safe.

Though we may not hear trumpet blasts from Moses, I wonder if we pay attention to the alarms that go off around us? In our culture we should pay attention to key signals that alert us to dangerous trends. For example, when we hear the alarms of violence and anger that arises out of racism, are we careful to respond with words of reconciliation, involvement, and healing? When we hear the alarms and stories of human trafficking, do we invest our energies into a greater awareness of the problem and work toward solutions? When we hear the alarms of discrimination and hatred towards those whose gender identities mark them for abuse, do we respond with civility and respect? When we hear the alarms from the voices of immigrants who are met with derision rather than welcome, do we respond with open arms? When we hear the alarms of melting icecaps and shrinking forests, do we engage the conversation or write it all off as a political hot potato? There are many other alarms sounding all around us. Do they call us to action or are we content to ignore their sound and pretend the dangers don't exist?

Prayer
Father, give us hears to hear the alarms and the courage to face the foes. Amen.

Day 128 — Numbers 11: Help with the Burdens

> "I will come down and talk to you there. I will take some of the Spirit that is upon you, and I will put the Spirit upon them also. They will bear the burden of the people along with you, so you will not have to carry it alone."
> Numbers 11:17 (NLT)

Observation
In this very interesting chapter, the anger of the Lord is provoked and demonstrated among the people. The chapter opens with the nation complaining about the lack of meat in their steady diet of manna. God's anger sends forth a fire into the camp and some of those who complained are consumed. Later in the chapter, once God has responded to their desire for meat by sending quail, several Israelites are struck with a plague as they gorge themselves by eating too many of the birds. Those who had complained about the lack of meat died because of complaining against God. But sandwiched in the middle of the narrative is a brief story of relief for Moses. He feels the enormous weight of leading the Israelites. In our focus verse, God instructs Moses to set aside leaders from every tribe. God places the Spirit upon these leaders so that their leadership will lessen the burden on the shoulders of Moses.

Application
A number of years ago I first heard the following story from a friend who participated in the event. It seems that a family, living just on the outskirts of Mars Hill, North Carolina, needed a little assistance when moving their home. The house was to be loaded onto a large trailer and moved to a different, nearby location. There was a problem with the former site. Because of its position on the lot, a truck and trailer could not gain access. So, what to do? The local college football team was called in to help. The strong young men surrounded the small house, lifted it, and carried it a few steps to load it onto the awaiting trailer. Teamwork accomplished something that no single individual could do.

It's that way with life as well. None of us have shoulders broad enough nor backs strong enough to carry the intense weight of life. Burdens are heavy. Responsibilities weigh a lot. Concerns and problems can bring enormous pressure in our lives. Foolishly, we often attempt to carry all the weight on our own. We want to be self-reliant and not bother those around us. How foolish. The truth is that we were created for community. God has placed us in a world filled with family, neighbors, and friends who are equipped to help us shoulder the load of life. We need their help at times even though we are reluctant to ask. And sometimes, we are the ones whom God will use to give support in the life of another. It's a give-and-take kind of proposition. Learn the lesson. You do not have to carry all the oppressive weight of life by yourself. Others have been sent to help. And when the time comes, offer the same support.

Prayer
Father, thank you for the supporting cast in our lives. Amen.

Day 129 — Numbers 12: Poking the Bear

> "Then Miriam and Aaron spoke against Moses because of the Cushite woman whom he had married (for he had married a Cushite woman); and they said, 'Has the LORD indeed spoken only through Moses? Has He not spoken through us as well?' And the LORD heard it."
> Numbers 12:1-2 (NASB)

Observation
This chapter opens with a declared opposition to the actions of Moses. Miriam and Aaron, Moses' siblings, speak out against Moses and, in so doing, speak out against his authority. Their complaint is that Moses has married a non-Jewish wife, probably a reference to Zipporah who was of Midianite descent. The opposition is a result of either disappointment in Moses, or a result of jealousy. Arguably, Miriam is the most powerful woman in Israel. Perhaps she is jealous of the influence that Zipporah has on Moses. The problem with her outspoken complaint is that "The Lord heard it." God's anger burns against her insolence, and she is struck with leprosy and placed outside the camp for seven days. God has chosen Moses as leader. To speak ill of Moses was to reject the purpose of God.

Application
Those of you who are old enough to remember the 1970s might remember the Chiffon Margarine commercial in which an actress, portraying Mother Nature, dips her finger into the margarine and says, "Ah, my sweet, creamy butter." When the off-camera voice reveals that it's not butter, but Chiffon margarine, the actress declares, "It's not nice to fool mother nature!" And with a wave of her hand, the sky darkens, lightning flashes, and animals start to stampede. Mother nature has been riled-up.

In this scene, it's the anger of God that gets poked. Verse 3 describes Moses this way… "Now the man Moses was very humble, more than any person who was on the face of the earth" (NASB). God had obviously found a righteousness and obedience in the heart of Moses. God entrusted him with the leadership of the Israelites. To question Moses's ability to lead was to question God. And so, Miriam is taught a very poignant lesson about questioning God's purpose.

To be honest, most of us are not going to have our limbs diseased by leprosy today, but most of us will question God's leadership. We will wonder about God's timing. We will dismiss the Holy Spirit's prodding to action. We will try to insert our plans in opposition. We will yield to human nature over Godly counsel. In other words, we will find ways to question God's leadership. That's never a good idea. God's purpose and plan are designed for our well-being. God desires what is best for each of us. When we turn a deaf ear to God's voice or ignore God's gentle prodding in our lives, we must be willing to accept the consequences of our foolishness.

Prayer
Father, may you find both righteousness and obedience in us today. Amen.

Day 130 — Numbers 13: Good News, Bad News

> "Then they came to the valley of Eshcol and from there cut down a branch with a single cluster of grapes; and they carried it on a pole between two men, with some of the pomegranates and the figs." Numbers 13:23 (NASB)

Observation

This chapter is well known to those who study the history of the Israelites. As the scene opens, Moses sends 12 leaders into the land of Canaan to spy out the territory. He wants their assessment concerning the productivity of the land, the strength of the people, the fortification of the cities, and the harvest of the trees. They discover that the land is fruitful and productive. In fact, according to our focus verse, the grape clusters are so large that a single cluster can only be carried by two men who suspend it from a pole. They also discover that the people are physically large and strong. When asked about the potential of an invasion, all the spies except Caleb tremble at even the thought. Caleb alone indicates that the time has come for them to begin the conquest.

Application

We, after having read the rest of the story, often applaud Caleb for the courage he displayed in the face of opposition. We scorn those who rejected the idea that with God's power the army of Israel could not have moved forward. We know that as a punishment for their lack of faith, their generation would wander in the wilderness for 40 years. As much as we like to criticize their actions, I wonder if we would have come to the same conclusion. "The enemy is too great. The walls are too strong. Our resources are too scarce." Sound familiar? It should. It's the same language we use in the face of our day-to-day struggles with the strongholds of culture. We see the strong force of peer pressure and we turn and run. We see how the majority lines up against us and we tremble. We see all the barriers and declare them to be insurmountable. Even knowing that the presence of Almighty God indwells our lives, we still struggle with the courage to move forward in our pursuit of God's purpose.

Consider the heart of Caleb for a moment. He alone attempts to stem the tide. He alone calls the nation to move forward. And it will be Caleb 40 years later who stands beside Joshua to lead the nation in conquest. God rewarded him with long life and strength because of his faithfulness. Sometimes a single voice can make a difference. Sometimes the power of one can defeat the power of many. Sometimes all God needs is a single voice that will proclaim God's power when all others shout defeat. Think about those looking to your example. Do they see evidence of a strong faith? Do they hear words of Godly courage? Do they see the heart of a leader? What is your assessment of evil's strength? Can we defeat the foe?

Prayer

Holy Father, may I have the courage today to be bold in my actions. Amen.

Day 131 — Numbers 14: Living in the Meantime

> "So they said to one another, 'Let us appoint a leader and return to Egypt.'"
> Numbers 14:4 (NASB)

Observation
This chapter explains the reason for the 40 years of wilderness wandering on the part of the Israelites. In essence, the long journey is a death sentence for the current generation. Once the people heard of the strength of the awaiting enemy in the land of Canaan, they began to grumble against Moses and Aaron suggesting that it was a mistake to ever leave Egypt. In fact, they want to appoint a new leader in the place of Moses and head back to the land of Pharaoh. Meanwhile, Caleb and Joshua continue to insist that God will go before them in the conquest and that the nation should immediately rise up and attack. The people rebel and suggest that their children would "be as plunder," believing that the army of Israel would surely fail. In response their lack of faith, God declares that all those above the age of 20 will eventually die in the wilderness. An entire generation will pass away before the land of promise is claimed.

Application
It is often hard to live in the meantime. We sometimes find our lives stuck between the euphoria of the good old days when times were seemingly better, and the hope of the future when things will be better again. Living in the present moment brings the stress, fear, and anxiety to the forefront of our minds. We awaken in the night with anxious worry over finances, relationships, and problems at work. We stress over unresolved tensions. We fret and strain under the weight of a difficult chapter in our lives. We wring our hands and let all hope and joy slowly drain from our lives. Look at how the ancient Israelites responded. They were so distraught about living in the meantime that they wanted to overthrow Moses as their leader and head back to Egypt. They forgot for a moment that the God Who had led them out of bondage would be the same God Who would lead them in triumph. As soon as their resolve was tested, they abandoned their belief in the provision of God.

Maybe we do the same. Whenever we are caught living in the meantime, which can really be *mean*, we let our hearts grow faint and our faith become dim. We forget that the God who has always been with us, is with us still, and will continue to lead our lives. We lose our perspective and thus we lose our hope. As you read this devotion thought, you may be living in the midst of a very difficult chapter in your life. Things are hard. Answers are illusive. Pain is real. I get that. But the storms of life are not the time to abandon your faith, but rather they signal the moment to grip your faith even tighter. God has not forgotten you, nor has God abandoned you. Stay strong.

Prayer
Father God, may we have the assurance of your watch care over us today. Amen.

Day 132 — Numbers 15: Willful Disobedience

> "But the person who does anything defiantly, whether he is native or an alien, that one is blaspheming the LORD; and that person shall be cut off from among his people." Numbers 15:30 (NASB)

Observation

This chapter is a very forward-looking chapter for the nation of Israel. God is setting forth instruction for the various offerings that will be a part of worship when the Israelites enter the promised land. There is a code of conduct... expectations of proper behavior set forth in these verses. In this passage, God makes a distinction between sins committed unintentionally and those committed defiantly. For sins committed unintentionally, provision is made for atonement and reconciliation. The guilty party may confess his/her sin, make appropriate sacrifices, and find reincorporation into the life of the community. But for those who willfully and defiantly commit sin, there is no such provision. They are to be "cut off" from the rest of the people. Verses 32-36 tell a brief account of a man found gathering sticks on the Sabbath. His sin is not committed in ignorance but in defiance of God's commandment. God decrees that he is to be stoned to death! The message is clear... God demands obedience and any willing departure from such action will result in punishment.

Application

As good parents, we demand obedience from our children. Every household sets a standard of behavior and expectation. For example, you may teach your children to say, "yes ma'am," and "no ma'am." You may forbid them to run in the house. You may require them to make up their beds or clean their rooms. You may demand that they respect their elders. The intention of the rules is important. The boundaries and expectations are not punitive in nature but designed to help them grow-up in a respectful and mature way. The guidelines lead to a better life.

It's the same in terms of our relationship with God. God's ways, God's rules, God's expectations are not meant to lessen our lives or burden us with over-bearing pressure. The goal is to lead us into making good choices and conducting ourselves with responsible action. Thus, obedience becomes the path to a better life. Obedience leads us to enjoy the fullness of life that God wills for us to have. We are commanded not to covet so that we will not spend our days chasing after things we think will offer us pleasure and joy but come up empty. We are commanded not to commit adultery so that we can focus on loving our spouses. We are commanded not to steal so that we can avoid a life of crime and punishment. Obedience leads to the best life possible, not a life of oppression and limitation. As you begin this day, let me challenge you to live obediently before God. Obey God's word. Obey God's prompting.

Prayer

Father God, give us a heart of obedience this day. Amen.

Day 133 — Numbers 16: The Cost of Rebellion

> "They assembled together against Moses and Aaron, and said to them, 'You have gone far enough, for all the congregation are holy, every one of them, and the LORD is in their midst; so why do you exalt yourselves above the assembly of the LORD?'" Numbers 16:3 (NASB)

Observation
This chapter tells the story of what is often referred to as "Korah's rebellion." A man named Korah, along with several others, rebelled against the leadership of Moses and Aaron. They convinced 250 other key leaders to join them. They questioned Moses' authority and right to lead. As a member of the tribe of Levi, Korah and his followers already had a special calling from God to assist in the work of the tabernacle and yet they grumbled against the position that Moses held among the people. God was angered by their rebellion and, as a result, the earth suddenly split open and the families, tents, and possessions of the three key instigators were swallowed up. Additionally, fire went forth from the tabernacle and the 250 other rebels were consumed. The next day, the people murmured against Moses insisting that he had caused the death of their fellow Israelites. God's anger was again stirred and a plague went through the camp, killing 14,700. The real sin of the people was not in their rejection of Moses' authority, but in their rejection of God's leadership.

Application
When I was in middle school, I attended Darlington, a private, and at that time, all-male school. It was a great school with a lot of emphasis on honor and good behavior. My social studies class was taught by one of the high school football coaches named Mr. Booker. Mr. Booker had played college football and was a large and imposing individual, but he possessed a gentle nature and was well-liked. One morning during class, he was summoned to the office to take a phone call. He left with the instructions for us to stay in our seats and quietly work. Yeah, right… I thought it would be funny to encourage the class to hide from Mr. Booker, to exit the rear door of the classroom and hide along the hillside behind the school. So, I led the rebellion and everyone followed. Let's just say it was the best of times and then suddenly it became the worst of times. Ever been paddled by college linebacker?

Rebellion is never a good idea, especially when we choose to rebel against God. Our rebellion can be a rather subtle thing. It is usually not our habit to boldly stand and reject the leadership of God in the big moments of our lives. It happens in the small things. It happens with our thoughts, our attitudes, and our words. We make choices that don't honor God. We reject God's counsel. You get it. Whenever we refuse God's lordship, we commit our acts of rebellion. And it never goes well…

Prayer
Father God, forgive us of our rebellion this day. Join our hearts to yours. Amen.

Day 134 — Numbers 17: Looking for God

> "It will come about that the rod of the man whom I choose will sprout. Thus I will lessen from upon Myself the grumblings of the sons of Israel, who are grumbling against you." Numbers 17:5 (NASB)

Observation
The event recorded in Chapter 17 had its genesis in the narrative recorded from the previous chapter. The Israelites had grumbled against the leadership and authority of Moses. God has grown weary with the bickering about who should lead the nation in various leadership positions. All the leaders from the 12 tribes are told to bring a rod to the tabernacle, with their names inscribed. All 12 are placed before the presence of God. The next morning the rod of Aaron, who is the leader of the tribe of Levi, had sprouted with buds, blossoms appeared, and ripe almonds were visible... all in one night! It was a powerful demonstration that God had chosen the tribe of Levi to serve as priests before the people. The goal was to lessen the grumbling of the nation.

Application
Sometimes, we just need proof. Sometimes we just need a sign from God about the direction of our lives, or a decision with which we are struggling. Sometimes we just need God to show up in an undeniable way so that our minds will find clarity and our hearts will know peace. I suspect that the problem does not lie with God's ability to move among us, but in our ability to discern God's movement among us. Sometimes we miss the message because we have not turned our attention in God's direction.

Let's be careful this morning. Though we might always desire to see a "visible" sign from God, that may or may not be the way God communicates with us. Sometimes God speaks in a whisper to our inner heart. I have often had the experience of having an undeniable prompting of the Spirit directing the course of my day. Sometimes God speaks through God's word. Again, I have often had the words of scripture all but leap off the page at me during some trial or difficult decision. Sometimes God speaks through the words of a friend who has been carefully placed in our path. And yes, sometimes, God does choose to be revealed in a miraculous way that cannot be explained with any other language.

The point is to look and listen for God. It is not that we should test God or become angry when we can't see God's way. It is that we should live each day with the assurance that God is moving in our lives and that God may be revealed in a special way. So keep your eyes open today... you might see God at work.

Prayer
Father thank you for being active in our lives. Amen.

Day 135 — Numbers 18: Shared Responsibility

> "But as the Levites go about all their assigned duties at the Tabernacle, they must be careful not to go near any of the sacred objects or the altar. If they do, both you and they will die." Numbers 18:3 (NLT)

Observation

In giving further instructions about the ministry of the tabernacle and those who served there, God speaks directly to Aaron about the role of the priests and the Levites. I find it interesting that twice in this chapter the narrative indicates that God speaks directly to Aaron about his duties. Moses is not the only one who receives a direct word from God. In this chapter, there are instructions about the duties of both the Levites and the Priests. All the priests came from the tribe of Levi. But a special responsibility and honor was given to the direct descendants of Aaron. The descendants of Aaron would serve as priests, mediating the conversation between God and men, offering the prayers and sacrifices of the people. The Levites, (tribe of Levi but not direct descendants of Aaron), served the priests as they performed their duties. The Levites maintained the various equipment used, the tabernacle tent, and other items required by the priests.

Application

Notice the very strict rule outlined in our focus verse. The Levites were forbidden to go near the sacred objects or the altar. If the priests allowed that to happen, both the priest and the offending Levite would die! In terms of the tabernacle, God demanded strict boundaries to maintain the holiness of worship. God's rules were not to be taken lightly. What I want for us to notice in this passage is the shared sense of responsibility. Priests and Levites were inextricably connected. What each did affected the other. Disobedience of one, would result in punishment for both.

Sometimes we fail to see how interwoven our lives are with fellow believers. Whether we like it or not, the reputation of the Church and even the reputation of the Lord depend on how well we live out our lives and maintain our Christian character. When one of us stumbles, all of us share in the rippling effect. When one of us betrays his/her Christian witness, the kingdom is wounded. Knowing that others are depending on the reputation and witness we offer before the world, shouldn't it challenge each of us to live our best selves? Is it not important for all of us to deny the selfish behavior of human nature and embrace the demands of the Gospel so that the Church moves forward? My goal this morning is not to burden you with guilt or shame, but to call you to an intentional living out of your faith. Your witness matters to me and to all the people of God.

Prayer

Father God, may we bear carefully the responsibility of authentic Godly living. Amen.

Day 136 — Numbers 19: Tag. You're It!

> "Furthermore, anything that the unclean person touches shall be unclean; and the person who touches it shall be unclean until evening."
> Numbers 19:22 (NASB)

Observation

This chapter of Numbers describes a purification ritual involving the ashes of a red heifer. According to the word of God received by Moses and Aaron, Eleazar, who is serving as the high priest, is to take a red heifer and slaughter it outside of the camp. It was then to be burned along with cedar wood, hyssop, and scarlet material. The ashes were to be collected and kept. These ashes were to be used to ceremonially remove impurity, especially impurity related to the touching of dead bodies. For example, if someone died inside of a tent, the ashes were to be mixed with water and sprinkled over the tent to remove the impurity. Those removing the body would also undergo a cleansing process involving the use of the sacrificial ashes.

Application

I'm a little intrigued by our focus verse, which happens to the be the final verse in the chapter. According to Mosaic law, anyone touching a dead body was considered unclean until a purification ceremony could be conducted. But notice what this verse states: Anyone who touches an item touched by the unclean person would also be considered unclean until evening. It's sort of like the spread of "cooties" when I was a kid. If someone who had these imaginary germ-like "cooties" touched you, you had them and then you could pass them along to someone else. In ancient Israel the practice of ridding items that were considered "unclean" was more practical than just imaginative. Obviously, germs and disease could be spread by contact with a dead body. The process of cleansing made both ceremonial and practical sense.

This story speaks of influence. We are influenced by those with whom we have contact. Their stories, words, and attitudes intersect with our own. Whenever we encounter a person with negativity, anger, or pettiness, the same attributes tend to rub off on us. If we are not careful, we can pick up the poor aspects of someone's personality. The key is to guard our hearts carefully. We need to be aware that people around us can make us "unclean" if we are not careful. I'm not suggesting that we avoid everyone that is having a bad day, but I am suggesting that we continually monitor the influences that can potentially "rub-off" on us. When we encounter a negative attitude or an angry countenance, we need to be careful to deflect such emotion from overtaking our lives. Rather than receive it, we need to look ways to offer such a person a better perspective or a more hopeful word. Even a momentary prayer for that individual is a much better response than letting the "cooties" get on us.

Prayer

Father God, make us aware of the influences around us. May we guard our hearts well.

Day 137 — Numbers 20: The Cost of Disobedience

> "But the LORD said to Moses and Aaron, 'Because you have not believed Me, to treat Me as holy in the sight of the sons of Israel, therefore you shall not bring this assembly into the land which I have given them.'"
> Numbers 20:12 (NASB)

Observation
This chapter records one of the key moments in the life and leadership of Moses. The narrative begins with the nation stopping in the wilderness of Kadesh. Moses' beloved sister, Miriam, dies and is buried. Typical to form, the people begin complaining again about the harshness of their journey and the lack of water. Moses and Aaron pray before the presence of the Lord and God tells them to stand before the rock and speak to the rock. By God's power water will begin to flow from the rock. Yet when the moment comes, Moses strikes the rock with the rod in his hand rather than speaking to the rock as God had commanded. What may seem like a small infraction is a huge mistake for Moses. His actions seemed to glorify his own strength and initiative rather than displaying the power of God. He displayed disregard for the holiness of God. As a result of his disobedience God declares that neither Moses nor Aaron will lead the people into the promised land. In fact, the chapter ends with the story of Aaron's death on Mount Hor, just after his priestly garments have been placed on the shoulders of his son, Eleazar.

Application
It is no small thing to disobey God's instructions. Written consistently throughout the pages of scripture is the call to listen and respond to the leadership of God. Also recorded are the negative consequences for not doing so. For most of us the problem of obedient living never surfaces in the huge moments of our lives. Most of us are not called to lead a nation out of bondage, part the sea, or provide water from a rock. Our problem tends to surface in the small, day-to-day choices that we make. We are called to obedience to God in our relationships, our business ethics, and our interactions with people. If we dare to look and listen, God will prompt us into action. God will reveal the steps we are to take, the conversations we are to hold, and the compassion we are to express. The problem is not our ability to discern the will of God in each moment... the problem is in our willingness to obey the Spirit's prompting. Let's be careful as we interpret this passage. I don't want us to live in fear each day, thinking that every misstep will bring the wrath of God crashing down on our shoulders. What we miss out on when we fail to live obediently are the blessings that God longs to give to each of us. Moses missed out on the promised land because of his lack of judgment. What joys might we miss as we choose a lack of obedience this day?

Prayer
Father, may I spend this day aligning my life with your will. Amen.

Day 138 — Numbers 21: Snakes on a Plain

> "The LORD sent fiery serpents among the people and they bit the people, so that many people of Israel died." Numbers 21:6 (NASB)

Observation
This chapter depicts the Israelites as they begin to make their way ever closer to the promised land. It tells of victorious battles against the Canaanites, the people of Sihon, and the people of Og. In each case, God gives them victory over their enemies. But woven into the narrative is yet another instance where the Israelites grumble and complain about their adversity. They complain about the food and water situation once again. The Lord's anger is kindled and the resulting punishment "fiery snakes" that invade the camp. Many people are bitten and die, and the people quickly repent. To end the plague, God instructs Moses to make a bronze snake and place it on a pole in the middle of the camp. All who are bitten and then gaze upon the bronze snake are healed of their bites.

Application
Sometimes our memories tend to be a little short-term. Scientists say that there is a reason for such phenomena. Because our brains tend to multitask as they process any number thoughts at once, whenever a task is completed, our minds tend to dismiss the time and energy devoted to that task in order to devote more energy to the next area that needs attention. In other words, as soon our minds sense a completed task, they switch to the other items needing attention. It's like having a long "to-do list" on your desk. As soon as a task is complete, you mark it off and move on to the next thing. And so, our memories of completed tasks really do tend to be short-lived.

It is interesting to me that as a part of the healing process, God instructed the Israelites to look upon the bronze serpent on the pole. Maybe the people needed a continual reminder. They needed to see how the wrath of God came to the camp because of their sinfulness. The bronze snake kept the memory alive so that they would not forget how they had sinned and would strive to live more faithfully.

The most prominent symbol of the Christian faith is the cross. We place one around our necks, or hang one on the walls of our homes, or suspend one from the ceiling of our churches. We display the symbol prominently. Why? Because we need to remember. We need to remember both our sin and the method of our salvation. We simply cannot allow ourselves to forget, even for a moment, how desperately we need the grace of God. So, gaze upon the cross of Christ, and as you do, find the healing of your brokenness.

Prayer
Father God, thank you for the cross… the visible reminder of your grace. Amen.

Day 139 — Numbers 22: The Strange Voice of God

> "When the donkey saw the angel of the LORD, she lay down under Balaam; so Balaam was angry and struck the donkey with his stick. And the LORD opened the mouth of the donkey, and she said to Balaam, 'What have I done to you, that you have struck me these three times?'"
> Numbers 22:27-28 (NASB)

Observation
Whenever I have the opportunity to teach "Intro to the Old Testament" to students here at Belmont University, this passage is one of my favorites to share. Let me set the scene… The Israelites have made their way into the land of Moab, camping near the Jordan River, just opposite the city of Jericho. Balak, who is the king of Moab, is fearful of this large migration of people and so he sends for a man named Balaam to come and pronounce a curse on the Israelites. Balaam is believed to be a prophet and so those whom he blesses, are blessed. Those whom he curses, are cursed. But as the story goes along, an interesting event occurs. While on the way to curse the Israelites, Balaam's journey is interrupted by the appearance of an angel of the Lord. The donkey on which Balaam is traveling is able to see what the prophet cannot. Three times the donkey stops in her tracks because of the presence of the angel. Then things get really interesting. The Lord opens the mouth of the donkey and she is able to speak! She tells the prophet about all what she has seen. Finally, the eyes of the prophet are opened and he understands more clearly what his role is to be.

Application
Sometimes God speaks in the most unusual and unexpected ways. Take this story for example. God speaks through a donkey! God's voice comes from the mouth of a common beast of burden, offering instruction to Balaam. How will God's voice reach your ears today? It may not be in the way you think. Most often God speaks to us through scripture, or through the proclamation of some inspired preacher or writer. At times, it is even through the words of a friend that we hear God's voice. But let us not forget that a sovereign God can use anything to convey God's message.

Let's be honest… I really don't expect God to speak to me today through the barking of my dog, or the chirping of a bird, or the mooing of a cow. That's crazy talk, right? But then again maybe God will use something or someone that I am not expecting. Maybe God will be revealed in my thoughts today, or through things that come into my view. God may speak through some observation I make or through a conversation I overhear. Who knows? God speaks in a lot of ways. I just pray I have the wisdom to hear God's voice whenever and however it comes.

Prayer
Father God, speak to us today through the mysterious workings of your kingdom. Amen.

Day 140 — Numbers 23: Not Taking No for an Answer

> "But Balaam replied to Balak, 'Did I not tell you, "Whatever the LORD speaks, that I must do"?'" Numbers 23:26 (NASB)

Observation
This chapter continues the story of King Balak and the prophet Balaam. Remember that Balak had summoned Balaam to come and pronounce a curse upon the nation of Israel. Balaam tells the King that he will seek the will of God in the matter and the King is instructed to set up seven altars on a hillside and appropriate sacrifices are made. The Lord speaks to Balaam and in response, Balaam blesses Israel. The king is angered and takes Balaam to another hill, builds another set of altars and, again, instructs him to speak to God. The result is the same. Rather than curse Israel, Balaam pronounces a blessing. Still not satisfied, the chapter ends with the King taking Balaam to yet another spot where he will build more altars to seek the will of God in the matter. The focus verse reveals Balaam's response to the King, that he can only do what the Lord says to do, not what the King wants.

Application
You can see where this is going, right? The King does not like the response that God has provided through Balaam and so he asks a second time. And when that answer doesn't suit him, he asks a third time. Like most of us, the King is a little stubborn. When he doesn't get the answer that he wants, he just keeps asking for a different answer. This story reminds me of the game children like to play when one parents says "no" to a request. The child then goes to the other parent hoping for a different answer. Like a petulant child wanting a different answer, the truth is that sometimes we are not going to receive the answer we want to receive from God. We pray our prayers and make our requests based on the ways we think God should respond, or at least the way we want God to respond. We make our requests based on human intellect. God, who is all-wise and all-knowing, sometimes answers our prayers in a different way. When we don't get the response we want, we begin to question God. We momentarily forget that God's knowledge is vastly, infinitely superior to our own. Isaiah writes, "'For My thoughts are not your thoughts, nor are your ways My ways,' declares the LORD" (Isaiah 55:8 NASB).

What we may perceive as being a non-responsive and non-caring word from God turns out to be a better response than we could even imagine. It is not that God refuses to answer our prayers, it is that God hears our prayers and then responds in the ways that are best for us even when we cannot fully understand God's ways. Let us not become angry with God over prayer responses we don't like. Let us instead pray faithfully, listen carefully, and respond obediently knowing that God's answers are always right.

Prayer
Father God, teach us to patiently embrace your response to our prayers. Amen.

Day 141 — Numbers 24: One Little Spot...

> "Balaam said to Balak, 'Did I not tell your messengers whom you had sent to me, saying, "Though Balak were to give me his house full of silver and gold, I could not do anything contrary to the command of the LORD, either good or bad, of my own accord. What the LORD speaks, that I will speak'?'" Numbers 24:12-13 (NASB)

Observation
As the narrative of Balaam and Balak continues, Balaam continually seeks a word from the Lord. It becomes very clear to Balaam that he is to bless the Israelites, which he will do three times. King Balak is angered. It is the last thing that he wanted to have happen. In these two focus verses, Balaam reminds the King of what he has previously said to the servants who had been sent to bring him before the King. The message was clear, "What the Lord speaks, that I will speak." There was nothing vague about it. Give credit where it is due. Even though obedience might cause the prophet financial loss, he stubbornly speaks the Lord's will and way.

Application
Integrity. We demand it of pastors, political leaders, teachers, and business managers. In fact, a lack of it can be a deal breaker for us. If we can't trust someone, we will refuse to patronize their business, attend their church, or vote for their candidacy. Even in our marriages, when trust is broken between spouses, marriages can quickly dissipate. The question for us to wrestle with this morning is this: "Am I trustworthy? Can people believe my word? Will they accept my testimony? Will they listen when I speak or turn a deaf ear to my words because of the inconsistencies in my life?"

We prove our integrity in the great and small moments of our lives. If we are willing to compromise on a little issue, what keeps us from compromising on the greater things? We have to say and do the right thing, no matter the cost and no matter the situation. Every decision, every action, and every word reflects on our character. Let me illustrate it this way... As most of you know, I am a car nut, especially when it comes to keeping my car clean. I hate trash on the inside and dirt on the outside. When my car is all clean and shiny, I find myself in my happy place. Sometimes when I wash my car, I think I have done a fine job only to discover later that I missed a spot. It could be a really small section, low on a door... but once my attention is drawn to that spot, it changes my whole image of the car until I can get to a towel and wipe it clean.

You get the point... It only takes one small stain to ruin our reputation and betray our Christian character. So, strive for integrity. Be a person of honesty. And when you falter... and you will... ask for grace and work towards restoration.

Prayer
Father God, help us to learn the value to consistent character. Amen.

Day 142 — Numbers 25: The Slippery Slope

> "These women invited them to attend sacrifices to their gods, so the Israelites feasted with them and worshiped the gods of Moab."
> Numbers 25:2 (NLT)

Observation
While encamped at Acacia Grove, some of the men of Israel began to notice the women of Moab. Many of the men began to have sexual relations with these women. The relationships formed then led the men to join in Moabite pagan worship practices, and they bowed down to the god named Baal of Peor. God's anger was kindled against these men and Moses was ordered to slay all the evil doers. As the story continues, another Israelite man draws a Midianite woman into his tent to sleep with her. Phinehas, the grandson of Aaron the High Priest, witnesses this, and he runs a spear through both the man and the woman as they lie together. Phinehas' actions are rewarded by God and a plague, apparently the result of Israel's sinfulness, is halted.

Application
This story illustrates the pattern of poor choices that sometimes govern our actions. Notice the slippery slope. It all began as these Israelite men began to notice, speak with, and eventually befriend these foreign women. They allowed themselves to begin a relationship with women who were strictly off-limits according to God's instruction. One bad decision quickly led to other bad choices. Not only did they sleep with these women, but also they chose to worship foreign deities. One bad choice led to another and then to another. Because these men allowed themselves to explore the possibilities of sinful behavior, soon their actions were out of control.

When Christ was instructing his disciples about prayer, one of the most important words of admonition he offered was to pray, "And do not lead us into temptation, but deliver us from evil" (Matthew 6:13 NASB). Christ reminded his disciples of the continual, relentless onslaught of temptation. His words are meant for us as well. Daily we should pray that we will not be drawn in, victimized, or enticed by temptation's allure. It is an ever-present danger in our lives. Our prayer should be for strength to stand firm so that we will be delivered from evil and the result of temptation in our lives. So, learn the lesson. The time to stand up to temptation is when the battle first begins, before too many choices are made and too many decisions lead to poor action, guard your heart and your mind. Pray for strength to redirect your thoughts, for courage to redirect your path, for wisdom to rethink your priorities. Temptation does not have to win. Stand strong. Be brave. Pray for strength.

Prayer
Heavenly Father, don't allow us to be led into temptation. Deliver us from evil. Amen.

Day 143 — Numbers 26: The Hope of a New Generation

> "Not one person on this list had been among those listed in the previous registration taken by Moses and Aaron in the wilderness of Sinai. For the LORD had said of them, 'They will all die in the wilderness.' Not one of them survived except Caleb son of Jephunneh and Joshua son of Nun."
> Numbers 26:64-65 (NLT)

Observation
After a recent plague, which is described in the previous chapter, the nation of Israel is camped on the plains of Moab, just across the Jordan from the city of Jericho. The time of the conquest is about to begin. The Lord instructs Moses and Eleazar, son of Aaron, to count all the men of Israel who are 20 years of age or older. This is the second census taken of the nation. The first was taken years earlier while at Sinai. The chapter lists every tribe and the number of men who are of warrior age from each tribe. The total is 601,730. Now reread the focus verses. In the span of 40 years, an entire generation has died. Along with Moses, only the two men who had once counseled the nation to seize the "land flowing with milk and honey" are left (Numbers 13-14). God raised up a new generation with the desire to be faithful, courageous, and loyal.

Application
Every once in a while, I get in the mood to build something. Maybe it's a guy thing. Maybe it's just the joy of getting to use power tools. But not too long ago I decided to build wooden Adirondack chairs. I didn't consult any do-it-yourself book or look up plans on the internet. I just starting thinking, scheming, and cutting. With a little trial and error the first chair was finished. It had a few flaws. There were some aspects that needed a little rethinking. I built a second chair and it was better. Then I built a third. It, too, was much improved. I learned a few things along the way and now I can build a pretty nice chair, if I do say so myself.

When I look at this history of the Israelites, I think that maybe the new generation had learned a few things along the way. I think that the lessons of obedience and God-dependency were carefully woven into the fabric of their psyche. Although they still had to learn a few lessons during the conquest, some of the ways of God started to sink in.

So what about us? How are we at learning to obey? It's a little trial and error for most of us… mostly error. But here's the good news. God has not abandoned us, nor our generation. In Christ, God offers forgiveness, redemption, and the second chance. We are God's new generation, the one into which God has placed hope. Let's learn. Let's grow. Let's obey.

Prayer
Father God, may we have the good sense to follow your ways this day. Amen.

Day 144

Numbers 27: Succession

> "Moses laid his hands on him and commissioned him to lead the people, just as the LORD had commanded through Moses."
> Numbers 27:23 (NLT)

Observation
This chapter opens with the daughters of Zelophehad petitioning Moses for an allotment of land when the promised land is claimed. The daughters are direct descendants of Manasseh, who died without any sons, and they were concerned that Manasseh's name and his clan would die off without any provision. Moses appealed to God and God heard their petition and instructed Moses to grant the land that they deserved. In the second part of the chapter, God instructs Moses to climb the hills east of the Jordan. God will allow Moses to see the land of promise, but tells him that he will die on the mountain. Moses pleads for God to appoint a new leader to guide the people. Joshua is chosen and Moses commissions him to lead the people.

Application
Succession is always an important conversation in the life of any successful institution, business, university, or similar organization. As an entity gains momentum and strength under its current leadership, the question always hangs around somewhere in the minds of the stake holders, "Who will lead once our current leader steps down or retires?" It's an important question to ask. Some organizations put a succession plan in place years before the current leader retires.

Moses obviously had a lot "skin in the game." He had led the nation for 40 years. He had orchestrated the liberation, chartered the desert path, and instilled the laws of God. What a proud moment it must have been for him to stand above the plains of Jericho and see the destination for his people. When God told him that his days were numbered, his concern was not about his own destiny, but for the continued success of his people. He cried out to God for a leader to take his place that would continue to lead the people effectively.

I want us to consider this question of succession in terms of where the Christian faith is headed. I am a believer in Christ because of the faith commitment of the generation before me. Dedicated individuals loved me enough to tell me the story of Jesus and demonstrate his compassion by their attitudes and actions. They made sure that the faith would be carried forward. I hope I am doing the same. I hope that I have consistently taught and modeled the faith so that it continues ever onward. This succession of faith is not automatic. The Christian faith moves from one generation to the next only with great intentionality. Let us commit our lives to the future leaders of the faith, ensuring that we have done our task well.

Prayer
Father God, my we instill in generations to come, the glorious news of the Gospel. Amen.

Day 145 — Numbers 28: God's Daily Bread

> "Give these instructions to the people of Israel: The offerings you present as special gifts are a pleasing aroma to me; they are my food. See to it that they are brought at the appointed times and offered according to my instructions." Numbers 28:2 (NLT)

Observation
Chapter 28 provides a list of various offerings that are to be made to God by the people of Israel: daily offerings, Sabbath offerings, monthly offerings, Passover offerings, and Festival of Harvest offerings. The daily offerings consisted of two lambs, a grain offering, and a liquid offering, made once in the morning and once in the evening. They were to be offered as a "sweat aroma" unto God, but surely the aroma penetrated the entire camp as well. As the people smelled the delicious fragrance of the cooking meat and baking bread, they would be reminded of the continual blessings and presence of God. Each time the scent hit their nostrils, their thoughts should have reflected for a moment on the provision of God.

Application
As I read this focus verse, the one phrase that leapt off the page at me came at the end of the first sentence… "they are My food." The word translated "food," is the Hebrew word, "lechem." It literally means "bread," as in daily bread. God was saying that the offerings of God's people were God's daily bread. I don't think that God experiences physical hunger in the way that we do. I don't think God craves caloric intake. But what God does long for is interaction with creation. God longs to enjoy a relationship with each of us. We feed God when we remember God and as we obediently follow God's commandments. For the Israelites to provide daily offerings meant that each day they would remember God. Each day they would be obedient before God. Each day they would continually feed their relationship with God. In many ways, God was sustained, nurtured, and satisfied by the daily interaction.

Think about this… you and I have the opportunity today to "feed" the Father. God no longer requires burnt sacrifices on the altar. God doesn't need a plate at the dinner table, or a packed lunch. But what will bring God great satisfaction is the dedication of our lives, the pure motivations of our hearts, and the giving away of ourselves to the needs of others. So, remember God today. Obey God today. Continually feed the relationship today. It's the kind of food God enjoys.

Prayer
Heavenly Father, today may the gift of our lives be the offering that blesses you. Amen.

Day 146 Numbers 29: Holiday or Holy Day?

> "You must present these offerings to the LORD at your annual festivals. These are in addition to the sacrifices and offerings you present in connection with vows, or as voluntary offerings, burnt offerings, grain offerings, liquid offerings, or peace offerings." Numbers 29:39 (NLT)

Observation
Chapter 29 details a number of Holy Days to be celebrated by the Nation of Israel. Beginning on the seventh month, a Jewish New Year was to be celebrated with the Festival of Trumpets. This New Year's Day is referred to as Rosh Hashanah. Also, included in this seventh month was the Day of Atonement and the seven-day Festival of Shelters. Specific instructions are given throughout this chapter describing the various ways each of these holy days are to be observed. The Israelites were to do "no ordinary work" on these days. They were to sacrifice bulls, rams, and lambs along with giving grain and liquid offerings. These days were set apart as special days of worship and celebration.

Application
Let's talk about the difference between a Holy Day and a holiday, at least in the eyes of the American public. We get the concept of holidays. We look forward to those days on the calendar when we do not have to work. We enjoy the time off from our labor. Here at Belmont University, like most other businesses and institutions, we are given several paid holidays throughout the year... New Year's Day, MLK, Labor Day, etc. Most of us spend those special days trying to squeeze a little enjoyment into the normal routine of our usual work lives. We cook out. We travel. We gather with family and friends. We try to take full advantage of the time away from work. But if we are honest, rarely are the holidays what we would describe as being holy days.

Holy days are those special moments when we give careful reflection to our faith. Easter and Christmas are examples of days set aside for reflection on faith. I wonder, however, if we should recapture some of the thought behind the holy days described in Numbers 29. I am not suggesting that we suddenly embrace the Jewish calendar and celebrate days like Yom Kippur or Rosh Hashanah. But I am suggesting that even on the holidays when we kick back to relax, that we should honor God in things that we do. We should be thankful to God for the chance to be with family. We should be grateful for the good food we eat. We should celebrate that we have work that provides for the needs of our family. You see, even the holiday should always be as a holy day. So, the next time you have a day off, why not take a moment to reflect on the God who has blessed you with family, work, provision, and a home. We are truly blessed and highly favored.

Prayer
Father, teach us to be grateful for days of work and days of rest. Amen.

Day 147 — Numbers 30: Keeping Your Word

> "A man who makes a vow to the LORD or makes a pledge under oath must never break it. He must do exactly what he said he would do."
> Numbers 30:2 (NLT)

Observation

This chapter outlines laws that pertain to the making and keeping of vows or promises. There are stipulations given for men, women, and daughters. The overarching principle is clear: Vows made by the people of God, especially those vows in which the name of the Lord is invoked, must be kept. The people of God are to be trustworthy in the promises that they make. This passage obviously speaks to the gravity of the promises made. Integrity must remain a distinguishing characteristic for the people of God.

Application

Read that focus verse again... "A man who makes a vow to the Lord or makes a pledge under oath must never break it. He must do exactly what he said he would do." Our Christian character is on trial with every promise we make, both large and small. How well we live out our commitments speaks volumes about our integrity.

One of the great stories of a promise kept is about the bones of Joseph. (You remember Joseph. He was the boy with the coat of many colors, sold into slavery in Egypt, and later saved his family and the land of Egypt from famine.) According to Exodus 13:19, Moses took the bones of Joseph with him on the way out of Egypt because of an oath the Israelites had once made, promising to return his bones to the land of Israel. Most likely, Joseph had been dead for nearly 400 years when the Exodus occurred. His bones had been kept all that time. And then, through the 40 years of wilderness wanderings, Moses lugged them through the desert. Finally, at the end of the period of conquest, according to Joshua 24:32, the bones were finally laid to rest in Shechem. Though it took the better part of 500 years to do so, the promise had been kept.

Most of the promises we make will not require 500 years to complete, but they will require effort and energy from us, including the prioritization of our agendas. Some promises are easily kept... "I promise to be home in time for dinner." "I promise to take you on a bike ride this Saturday." "I promise to write the thank-you note." Others take the greater commitment of our lives and energies... promises like the ones we make to our spouses and children, "I promise to love and cherish you." "I promise to always take care of you." And then there is the huge promise of discipleship, "Lord Jesus, I promise to follow you always." The demands are great. Are you keeping your promises? Are you a person of integrity?

Prayer

Father, teach us to honor every vow we make both great and small. Amen.

Day 148 — Numbers 31: Protection

> "We, your servants, have accounted for all the men who went out to battle under our command; not one of us is missing!" Numbers 31:49 (NLT)

Observation
This chapter outlines the destruction of the Midianites. Previous chapters told the story of how a number of the Israelite men had been lured into relationships with some of the Midianite women, which in turn caused these men to slip into the practice of idolatry, worshipping pagan deities. It is important to understand the moment in time created by this event. God was preparing the nation for the conquest of the promised land. He longed for a nation of people who would be obedient, faithful, and true. Just as the nation was in the final stages of preparation, along came this Midianite distraction. To demonstrate God's unwavering desire to create a holy people, God orders the destruction of the Midianites. Twelve-thousand soldiers are sent forth led by Eleazar, the High Priest. All five kings of Midian are killed in battle. All the towns and villages are burned. Only the younger women are spared and brought back to Israel to become servants. To demonstrate God's power, not a single Israelite soldier is lost in battle.

Application
For me, the take-away from this narrative is the protection of God over those who were following God's plan. Because the army went forth at God's command, obeying every facet of God's instruction, the soldiers found success. Not a single man was lost. Twelve thousand went out and twelve thousand returned.

It's a pretty sure bet that you will not be called by God today to engage the Midianites in battle. They've been gone for a long time. But you may well be called of God today to go forth in God's name to fight some other cause in which God needs your involvement. Maybe the battle is against the ills of our culture and time. Maybe God needs your strength to take on homelessness or hunger, abuse or racism, addiction or discrimination. There are many evil forces that try to dehumanize and devalue human life. There are systems that allow for abuse. There are policies that marginalize people created in the image of God. Maybe it's time for you to engage the enemy and join the battle. And notice from our focus verse that whenever you take on the causes of God, that God's presence and protection go with you. You are never alone, nor do you act in your own strength or wisdom. That does not mean that you are to live without prudence or act without wisdom. But it does mean that God pays attention to those who act in God's name. God gives power, protection, and plans. So, go forth and face the challenges. Declare victory in God's name.

Prayer
Father, remind us that there is indeed, strength in the name of the Lord. Amen.

Day 149 — Numbers 32: The Lost City of Nobah

> "Meanwhile, a man named Nobah captured the town of Kenath and its surrounding villages, and he renamed that area Nobah after himself."
> Numbers 32:42 (NLT)

Observation

As the nation of Israel prepared for the time of conquest, representatives from the tribes of Rueben, Gad, and Manasseh approached Moses and asked if they could settle in the land east of the Jordan in the territories already conquered by the Israelites. Apparently, the tribes of Rueben and Gad had large numbers of flocks and herds and the typography of the land was well suited for grazing. At first, Moses is angered by their request. He sees the request as a break in the unified front needed when the Israelites invade the promised land. The dilemma is solved as the representatives of these tribes pledge to join the fighting forces in the conquest, committing to return to their flocks only after the days of conquest are complete.

Our focus verse points attention to a man named Nobah, who is part of the half-tribe of Manasseh. He has taken territory in the region of Gilead, capturing the town of Kenath, renaming it after himself.

Application

Ever been to Nobah? I haven't either. Apparently, no one has in a very long time because it ceased to exist many centuries ago. Most internet searches will tell you that the location of the city is probably near the modern-day city of Kunawat. The point I want to make is that this town, named after the man who conquered it, is no longer around. Perhaps it's a lesson in folly and frustration when we try to take ourselves a little too seriously.

Can you imagine taking over a town and then naming it after yourself? How self-absorbed could you be? But before we judge Nobah too harshly, maybe we should consider that way that we attempt to take credit for things that are blessings from God and not the product of our own hands. I talk all the time about "my" car. I live in "my" house. I love "my" family. I live on "my" street. I keep "my" money in the bank. You see where this is going, right? We claim the blessings of God as though they are ours to own. We arrogantly act as though all we have is the result of our hard work, our intellect, or our initiatives. This is not "our" world and we do not have the arrogant right to act as though it is. If all that we have is a result of God's blessing, then it is only right to use those blessings as God directs. We are called to look beyond self, to live beyond greed, to love beyond expectation of return. So, the next time you are tempted to claim something as being "yours," maybe you should stop and consider for a moment how God wants to use the things God's has placed in your hands to briefly hold as a way of helping others.

Prayer

Father, thank you for your blessings and our opportunities to share. Amen.

Day 150 — Numbers 33: Preventing the Irritant

> "But if you fail to drive out the people who live in the land, those who remain will be like splinters in your eyes and thorns in your sides. They will harass you in the land where you live." Numbers 33:55 (NLT)

Observation
Chapter 33 recounts the various places where the Israelites had camped during their 40-year trek across the wilderness. God had told Moses to carefully record the names of all the places they stopped along the way. Moses' journal begins the morning they left Egypt after the Passover event. He lists every small town, village, region, or oasis where the people stopped along the way. There are more than 40 places listed in Moses' writings. Just imagine… more than 40 times they pulled up stakes, packed up the tabernacle, and moved the nation. As they camp at their final staging area on the plains of Moab, God gives specific instructions about the conquest. God tells the people to drive out all the people and destroy the carved and molten images of their worship, along with the pagan places of worship. A failure to do so, according to our focus verse, will result in continual harassment and irritation for the people of Israel.

Application
A few weeks ago, I was cutting my grass when a small piece of debris flew up from the mower and struck my eye. It was quite painful. My eye watered for over an hour and stayed red for about two days. Finally, things returned to normal. My wife, who had to put up with my complaints about my eye, suggested that I think about wearing safety goggles when I cut the grass. I even had a pair hanging above my tool bench. So, I took her advice and ever since, I have been protected from any further eye-gouging debris.

Notice God's warning to the Israelites… "If you fail to drive out the people who live in the land, those who remain will be like splinters in your eyes…." The instruction was clear and simple: If you fail to protect your heart and community from the influence of pagan deities, they will continue to cause problems. We need to hear that message. As long as we are willing to live with, allow, and flirt with dangerous temptations and distractions, we will suffer as a result. When we fail to distance ourselves from potential danger, we will have to deal with the consequences produced by its presence. So, ask yourself this question, "What are the distractions to my spiritual life that keep me from walking faithfully and obediently after God?" Is it a lack of schedule prioritization? Is it a lack of internet discipline? Is it a poor attitude caused by social media overload? Is it a lack of attention to matters of faith? Until you begin to address the things that disrupt your walk of faith, you will continue to be irritated by the problems those things drop along your path. It's time to protect your heart.

Prayer
Father, help us to see the distractions in our spiritual lives and eliminate them. Amen.

Day 151 — Numbers 34: Boundaries

> "Then the LORD said to Moses, 'Give these instructions to the Israelites: When you come into the land of Canaan, which I am giving you as your special possession, these will be the boundaries.'" Numbers 34:1-2 (NLT)

Observation
In a very interesting chapter, God reveals to Moses the boundaries of the promised land. God clearly defines the southern, eastern, northern, and western limits of the land the Israelites will possess. God declares that the 9½ tribes will live in this portion of land while the tribes of Rueben, Gad, and the half tribe of Manasseh will live on the east side of the Jordan River, as prescribed in earlier chapters. With the help of a chosen leader from each tribe, the land will be granted to the tribes according to the size of each tribe.

Application
Let's talk about boundaries. Boundaries define the limits, the borders, even the rules that govern our lives and our behavior. The plot of ground on which my home is placed is defined by property lines or boundaries. When I drive to work, the lane I drive in is defined by white lines. My office at work has walls and a door that define my workspace. The city of Nashville has city limits that define the metro area. Go to any sporting event and notice how carefully the boundaries are marked. There are sidelines and end lines and goal lines. The game is played within those boundaries. Even the airspace overhead is defined by certain limits.

It's a simple concept. But rather than think in terms of geographic boundaries, let's think for a moment on relationship boundaries. There are limits that should govern both our thoughts and our behavior. Let's begin with God. That boundary is that relationship is exclusive. We are not to have any other gods. We are not to serve any other created deities. Our focus is to be solely upon God. Let's talk about human relationships. Marriage defines the boundaries of behavior between spouses. For those of us who are married, we live our lives defined by the exclusive relationship we have with one other. We pledge a fidelity to the total investment of our lives only to each other. There are also boundaries in friendships. We are governed by honesty and compassion in those relationships. We hold confidences and work for what is best for one other. There are certainly boundaries with our children, whom we nurture and support, and for whom we pray. In return, they respect, honor, and obey us.

The list of boundaries goes on and on. It is important to understand why they exist. It is not to limit our lives, but to set the parameters that will offer us the best life possible. So, pay attention to all the boundaries. They will define your best life.

Prayer
Father, help us to see and live within the important boundaries of our lives. Amen.

Day 152 — Numbers 35: Holy Ground

> "You must not defile the land where you live, for I live there myself. I am the LORD, who lives among the people of Israel" Numbers 35:34 (NLT)

Observation

This chapter outlines the provision to be made for the Levites who were not entitled to a land grant. The other tribes were to give them cities in which to live, along with plenty of room for their livestock, flocks, and cattle. There were 48 towns designated for the Levites, six of which were set aside as "cities of refuge." These cities of refuge were to provide protection for anyone who accidentally killed another individual. They could flee to one of these cities and find protection until a proper law proceeding could take place. The avenger, who was the closest relative of the slain person, could seek revenge unless the offender found his way to one of these cities. The guilty person could live in the city indefinitely and at the death of the High Priest, they could leave the city because no further threat of revenge could be enacted.

Application

At the end of all the instruction about the cities of refuge and who could enact revenge, the final verse of the chapter is rather interesting. God demanded that things be done properly so that the land would not be defiled by sinful action. It was important to keep the land holy and pure because, "I live there myself." I like the image of Holy God living among God's people. That image teaches me that God is with us, living among us, desiring fellowship with us.

I have the joy and privilege of having really good neighbors. Some have lived on the cul-de-sac as long as our family has lived there… more than 20 years. My neighbors are solid people. They care for one other. They look out for other's children, property, etc. When there is a need in the group, all the others respond. It's good to know that there are people living close by that will help when called upon, that will give strength and support in times of need. Though it may be a bit absurd to think of God in anthropomorphic ways, I like the image of our focus verse that tells me God lives among us. No, God doesn't have a house on my street and no, God doesn't own property in our neighborhood. But God is very much with us in this journey of life. God's presence gives comfort. God's Spirit gives direction. God's grace offers mercy. God's love brings us joy. Because God lives among us, there is nothing that we will face today that will come as a surprise to God. It might surprise us… but not God. And God is certainly walking beside us through any experience we face. It's good to know that not only are there good people living close by today, but to know that our Heavenly Father lives in this place as well.

Prayer

Father, thank you for your continual presence in our lives. Amen.

Day 153 — Numbers 36: It's All About the Details

> "None of the territorial land may pass from tribe to tribe, for all the land given to each tribe must remain within the tribe to which it was first allotted." Numbers 36:7 (NLT)

Observation
In this final chapter from the book of Numbers, the descendants of Manesseh approach Moses with an important question. Although provision had been made earlier in the narrative decreeing that the daughters of Zelophehad would receive a land grant in the distribution of land, there was a question about what would occur if the daughters married outside of their ancestral tribe. Would the land then be transferred to the tribe of their husbands? If so, would the land grant in effect be diminished? Moses instructed the daughters to marry within their own tribe to ensure the ancestral land would always remain in the hands of the descendants of Manesseh.

Application
You are probably asking, "What possible difference does it make to me that the daughters of Zelophehad were able to hang on to their clan's land grant?" I mean, it's not like such an action is going to reduce the cost of your lunch today, or put more gas in your tank, or help you to resolve an issue at work. It's just a rather insignificant detail buried in the pages of an ancient text. No big deal, right? Maybe there is more to the story than we first imagine. It is important to note that Moses insisted on the property rights of these women because the distribution of the land mattered to God. Moses was taking precautions to make sure that God's will and purpose for the Israelites was carried forward.

It has been my experience during my working career that some people tend to be the "dreamers" in an organization, while others are the "detail-oriented" ones. Both are certainly needed to ensure the success of the business or organization. To be honest, I'm more of the big-picture, dreamer type. I need people around me who think on the detail level. Dreamers alone can't accomplish much. Detail people, on the other hand, can get lost in the minutia of a project and never see the bigger goal. In this story, Moses paid attention to the details because to do so was to pursue God's plan for Israel. So, take a moment to examine your life. Ask yourself what role you are currently playing in God's kingdom work. Are you dreaming dreams or are you the detail person? Both are vitally important. So, if you are feeling a little stuck in the finessing of the details, take heart, God needs your tedious work. If you have lots of good kingdom dreams but can't seem to get going, don't despair. If God has given you a plan, God will lead you to a detail person to get it moving.

Prayer
Father, encourage all of us today with the knowledge that dreamers and detailers are both a part of your work. Amen.

Day 154 — Deuteronomy 1: Missing the Moment

> "But you were unwilling to go up; you rebelled against the command of the LORD your God." Deuteronomy 1:26 (NIV)

Observation
Written by Moses, the book of Deuteronomy records Moses' final words as he reminds the Israelites both of their history and of the law of God. These words were recorded 40 years after God gave the laws on Sinai. An entire generation has passed away and Moses is reminding the new generation of God's commands as they prepare to enter the promised land. As the book begins, the nation of Israel is encamped in the plains of Moab, just east of the Jordan River, preparing for the conquest of the land.

Our focus verse is a part of the history lesson that Moses offers. Early in the wilderness experience, God had commanded the Israelites to go into the land of promise and take it. God had promised to lead them in victorious battle. Twelve spies were sent to evaluate the land and its people. Upon hearing their report of strong cities and mighty warriors, the nation cowered in fear and refused to begin the conquest. Because of their stubbornness, God decreed that none from that generation would see the promised land. And so, for the next 40 years, the people wandered in the desert until that generation died out.

Application
The story is a lesson in obedience. When God directs our thoughts, outlines our path, and points us in a direction, our response should not be that of questioning the call of God or even offering excuses for our delay. We are to go. Whenever God reveals God's plan, obedience should be our response. The ancient Israelites found themselves at a pivotal moment. God had led them to the promised land. God had arranged the journey, provided for their needs, and promised protection and strength. By refusing to move when called upon to do so, they lost the opportunity for success and missed the moment of God's intervention. They spent the next 40 years regretting their disobedience.

What about your life? What is God calling you to do? How is God directing your path? What are the opportunities that are placed before you by God's providential leadership? Maybe your land of promise is just beyond the horizon. If God has called, you need to go. If God is leading, you need to obey. Why live with the regret of having missed the moments that God has ordained? It's a bold and brave adventure, this life to which we are called. Are you listening? Are you going? It is better to step out in faith, courageously walking into the uncertainty of where you are going with God at your side, than to look back years from now with regret having missed the moment for which you were chosen.

Prayer
Father, as you choose to reveal yourself to us and show us the next step of our life journey, may we be courageous enough to respond now, not later. Amen.

Day 155 — Deuteronomy 2: Created to Matter

> "You have made your way around this hill country long enough; now turn north." Deuteronomy 2:3 (NIV)

Observation
The words recorded in our focus verse are drawn from a very pivotal time in the wilderness experience of the Israelites. For almost 40 years, the nation had wandered and meandered her way across the desert. The moment came when God called the nation to begin a definitive march toward the land of promise. The Israelites had mired in the sand long enough. God was now calling them to action by providing direction and purpose. The disobedient generation had died off and so the march of the promised land was underway.

Application
Sometimes we need to take deliberate, purposeful steps. If we are not careful, it is very easy for any of us to become bogged down in a spiritual quicksand that slows our pace and obscures our vision. We get trapped in the mire of complacency, apathy, and indifference. We get tired of the pursuit of the Christian life. We grow dull to the idea of boldly living the faith. We lose our vision, our motivation, and our zeal. We wander aimlessly through the desert, resigned to the fact that our faith has become lackluster and our passions have grown cold. It's easy to do. Well-meant routines have a way of evolving into ruts if we are not careful about keeping them fresh and exciting. Sometimes we just need to change it up a little.

Faith doesn't have to be boring nor stale. God has not called us to merely survive, but to thrive. So how do we reclaim direction and bolster our faith-passions? Look at the focus verse again... "Now turn North." It's a call to claim a new direction. It's a call to begin a new journey. It's a call to live boldly enough to set a new course, dream a new dream, and start a new life. Think carefully and thoroughly about claiming a Spiritual goal. Maybe consistent church attendance is where you need to start. Maybe actually joining a church and learning to serve is where you need to land. Maybe you need to start a home Bible study. Maybe you need to volunteer at an organization that strives to build the kingdom by meeting human need. Maybe you need to start a consistent plan for the reading the Bible. Maybe you need to start journaling your thoughts or praying daily for a very specific thing. Let's admit it... We all get trapped in spiritual ruts from time to time. We keep circling the same of mountains over and over again. It's time to head north. It's time to pray for a vision to start something new. Risk. Volunteer. Write. Pray. Start a class. Invest. Claim a passion and pursue it until it blesses you. You were not created for mediocrity. You were created to matter. Set a new course and climb out of the rut.

Prayer
Father, give each of us a vision, a purpose, and a pursuit. Amen.

Day 156 — Deuteronomy 3: When to Stop Praying...

> "But because of you the LORD was angry with me and would not listen to me. 'That is enough,' the LORD said. 'Do not speak to me anymore about this matter.'" Deuteronomy 3:26 (NIV)

Observation

In our focus verse, Moses is reminding the Israelites about a conversation that he had with God just before the beginning of the conquest. Joshua will soon be commissioned to the lead the nation into battle as they cross over the Jordan River. Moses had been told by God that he is to climb mount Pisgah and look over into the land, but that he himself will not be allowed to cross over the Jordan. Moses tells the Israelites that because of them, the Lord was angry with him. In fact, Moses receives a rebuke from God saying not to speak about this matter any longer.

Application

This verse is a little different, isn't it? Read it carefully and you will discover that God's patience with Moses is exhausted, at least regarding conversations about entering the promised land. God had already revealed to Moses that he would not lead the nation into the time of conquest. Moses had served his role and his life was about to end. Apparently, Moses had continued to plead with God, hoping to change God's mind and Moses be allowed to enter the land. But the response is firm and clear... "Do not speak to me anymore about this matter." Yikes. I am forced to wonder if we, at times, exhaust God's patience. There are moments when God clearly and undeniably answers our prayers in ways we don't like, and because we don't get OUR way, we continue to pester God. Such a strategy never gets us very far. Who are we to dare argue with God? Let's be clear... God always longs to hear from us. God enjoys the moments that we share. What God does not enjoy is our impudence. When God answers, matters are settled. Not only because of who God is, but because God's wisdom is always superior to ours. God's answers are always right, even if we would prefer a different response. Take a moment to consider whether you are continuing to pray about something that God has already answered. Maybe your prayer should change from one of petition, to one of obedience in which you ask God to give you the grace to accept God's plan. Please don't misunderstand... I am not advising you to ever end the discipline of prayer. We should pray consistently, daily, confessionally, and specifically. What should end is our desire to usurp the plans of God in exchange for our own agendas.

Prayer

Father, forgive us when we overstep our place. Teach us boldness in our prayers along with the humility to accept your answers. Amen.

Day 157   Deuteronomy 4: A Cry from the Far Country

> "But if from there you seek the LORD your God, you will find him if you seek him with all your heart and with all your soul."
> Deuteronomy 4:29 (NIV)

Observation
As Moses offers one of several farewell speeches in the book of Deuteronomy, he gives an important word of both warning and promise. He warns the Hebrews not to drift away from God and fall into the trap of worshipping false idols. For if they do, they will surely be scattered from the promised land. Then comes the promise. If they have indeed forsaken God and have found themselves in a distant land, even there, God will be present. They will find God if they seek with both heart and soul. It is a promise of God's presence even in the foreign land.

Application
Our God is always discoverable. The promise of scripture reminds us that we can never flee from God's presence. We can never find ourselves in a place where God is not present. Therefore, the promise of Moses holds true. If we seek the Lord with sincerity of heart and with the passion of our souls, we *will* find God. The God who longs to be revealed *will* be. First, a word about what the distant land might resemble. We really could be physically at some point in our lives in a place where Christianity is unknown and where God is not mentioned. With the ease of world travel and with the globalization of many businesses, your journeys could take you to a non-Christian nation. Most likely, however, the distant land is one that we create in our hearts and minds each time we deny the lordship of Christ. When we flee from his presence, disobey his words, and fail to pattern our lives after his heart and Spirit, we will find ourselves vulnerable to the worship of false idols and perverse doctrine. We will awaken one day to discover that we have traveled to the distant land within ourselves where God is not honored.

But now a word about seeking God's presence... The promise is that even in such a place of rebellion or state of mind, that God can be found. Remember the story of Jonah? Even from the belly of a whale in the depths of the sea, while fleeing the presence of God, God heard Jonah's prayer. Learn the lesson. Whenever and wherever we turn our hearts to God, seeking to know God with intentionally and purpose, we will discover God's quick response. God does not desire for us to languish in darkness. God is with us. Seek God and you will discover God's presence. That's not just a hope... *it's a promise from God*. If you have found yourself adrift, struggling a little to connect with God, do not worry. God will hear your heart's cry.

Prayer
Father, forgive us when we willfully or subconsciously turn our hearts away from yours. Thank you for your willingness to run to us whenever we seek your presence. Amen.

Day 158 — Deuteronomy 5: Responsible Living

> "You shall not bow down to them or worship them; for I, the LORD your God, am a jealous God, punishing the children for the sin of the parents to the third and fourth generation of those who hate me, but showing love to a thousand generations of those who love me and keep my commandments." Deuteronomy 5:9-10 (NIV)

Observation

In this chapter, Moses reminds the Israelites of the 10 Commandments that he received from God on Mount Sinai. He encourages them to follow them to exacting standards so that they will please the Lord God. Our focus passage is a portion of the 2nd Commandment, that of not making any false idols to worship. God is to be worshipped exclusively. We are not to create any gods or idols that would draw our focus away from God.

Application

We should be careful to observe in these instructions the "rippling effect" of our actions. Notice that God declares that children will be punished for the sin of the parents to the third and fourth generation of those who hate God. We need to understand that our bad habits, our vices, our attitudes, our prejudices, and our sins have a way of reaching down to the next generation and the generation beyond that. Children and grandchildren have a way of adopting the habits of their fathers and mothers, grandfathers and grandmothers. Whatever we value and whatever ill we harbor often finds its way into the psyche of future generations. If we have placed other things above our love for and our allegiance to God, why should we expect our children to act differently? If we have sinned by worshipping the false of gods of our culture, more than likely our children will do the same, sometimes for many generations to come. The influence of our bad actions can linger many years.

But notice the flip side of this coin. Those who love the Lord and who keep the commandments can affect the lives of a "thousand generations." Our passion for God and for the kingdom will long be remembered. Our legacy of faith will be passed on to our children and our grandchildren. Each of us has the potential to make a huge difference in the lives of future generations by living faithfully and authentically. You will make your mark "then," by how you choose to live "now." Want to bless your family for a thousand generations? Want to leave a legacy of faith? Love the Lord your God with all your heart, soul, mind, and strength. When you walk faithfully, your children will walk in your footsteps. When you model grace, the message is clearly conveyed.

Prayer

Father, may each of us assume the responsibility for the future generations of our families. Teach us that to love you now, will bless them for generations. Amen.

Day 159 — Deuteronomy 6: A Few Reminders...

> "Hear, O Israel: The LORD our God, the LORD is one. Love the LORD your God with all your heart and with all your soul and with all your strength. These commandments that I give you today are to be on your hearts. Impress them on your children. Talk about them when you sit at home and when you walk along the road, when you lie down and when you get up. Tie them as symbols on your hands and bind them on your foreheads. Write them on the door frames of your houses and on your gates." Deuteronomy 6:4-9 (NIV)

Observation
This passage from Deuteronomy 6 is vitally important to the message given by Moses to the Israelites. It is referred to by many as the "shema," which is drawn from the Hebrew verb, "to hear." Faithful Jews continue to repeat this phrase at least three times each day. To acknowledge that God is one and that God is to be loved with heart, soul, and strength, is the greatest of all commandments. God demands that these words should "be on our hearts." They must be inextricably linked to every moment, every thought, and every action.

Application
Our love for God is to find expression throughout each day that we live. Notice the emphasis on what we are to do with God's commandments. We are to teach them to our children. We are to keep the words on our lips when we sit at home and when we travel about. They are to be the last words we remember when we retire at night and the first words we recite when we awaken. They are even to be written on the door frames of our homes so that they are constantly before us. I find written between the lines of this passage two simple messages. First, the word of God is vitally important to each of our lives. It is our guide, our path, our instruction, our teacher, our hope, and our salvation. Our fidelity to God's word will force us into faithful discipleship. Second, the word of God should be visibly present in our lives, reminding us constantly of the God who offered it and of the Spirit that empowers us to live it. What daily reminders are present in your life to keep the word before you? Is it written on the doorpost of your home? Is a verse taped to your mirror, or stuck to your refrigerator? Does a verse sit on your desk? Is there a screen saver with a Bible text? There really should be constant, visible, consistent reminders placed strategically throughout our day, lest we forget for a moment by whom we are claimed and under whose authority we live. Let me challenge you today to discover places in the routine of your life where you need to place the words of God, lest you forget.

Prayer
Father, may we value your word so strongly, that it is never absent from our sight for very long. Amen.

Day 160 — Deuteronomy 7: Take No Prisoners

> "When the LORD your God brings you into the land you are entering to possess and drives out before you many nations—the Hittites, Girgashites, Amorites, Canaanites, Perizzites, Hivites and Jebusites, seven nations larger and stronger than you—and when the LORD your God has delivered them over to you and you have defeated them, then you must destroy them totally. Make no treaty with them, and show them no mercy."
> Deuteronomy 7:1-2 (NIV)

Observation

There is both warning and hope in Moses' words about the conquest of the promised land. The hope is the promise that God will give their enemies into their hand. Keep reading the rest of the chapter and you will notice that God even describes how this will slowly and steadily come to pass. The warning is wrapped around how they are to defeat their enemies. The enemies are not to be taken lightly. They are to be utterly and completely destroyed. Such a decree seems harsh at times. We often ask, "How can a God of love demand destruction?" Remember that God was in the process of creating a holy and chosen nation. Without complete obliteration, the temptation to adopt some of their culture, ways, and worship would be too great. And so, the marching orders are to show no mercy.

Application

"Make no treaty with them, and show them no mercy." Obviously, we are not in a life and death struggle with the former nations of the Land of Canaan. Seldom do we encounter any Girgashites or Jebusites! But make no mistake, we are in a life and death struggle. The struggle is one of good and evil… The ways of God and the ways of culture. The dangers to us are just as caustic as the dangers to the ancient Israelites on the brink of conquest. If we dare to treat our enemies lightly, or ignore their potential influence in our lives, we will surely be overcome. There is an ever-present danger, and we need to treat it seriously. We must keep a constant vigil over our hearts to ensure that they will not become tainted with compromise or mediocrity. God longs for a people who are devoted to God's kingdom. Compromise is always a slow fade. First, we become a little relaxed in one area of our lives, and then another. We slowly but surely drift away from our convictions and commitments. The warning is to defeat the enemy completely. Allow no room for infiltration or defeat. Don't let the voices of compromise even find a place of rest within your mind for a moment. Remember you don't fight the battle alone. The same God who allowed the Israelites to march boldly into the promised land will help you to defeat your foes. Go boldly. Go in the strength of the Lord.

Prayer

Father, teach us the value of total commitment to your word and your ways. May we refuse to give in to the tempting voices of our culture. Amen.

Day 161 — Deuteronomy 8: Credit, Where Credit Is Due

> "But remember the LORD your God, for it is he who gives you the ability to produce wealth, and so confirms his covenant, which he swore to your ancestors, as it is today." Deuteronomy 8:18 (NIV)

Observation
Moses offered the people a little advice in terms of self-sufficiency and how that relates to God-dependency. His fear was that the prosperity of the people would cause them to forget the Lord's blessings. He wanted them to remember that any success they gained or any wealth they accumulated, would not be the result of their own doing, but simply the outpouring of God's grace. His hope was that they would never think more highly of themselves than they should. All that they had or ever hoped to attain would be bound up in God's provision.

Application
Let me offer a quick word about who deserves credit for the successes we attain. Guess what… it's not us. To be sure, there are many of us who would like to think that we are "self-made," that we have gained our success by our work ethic, intellect, or business savvy. The truth is that we are who we are because of God's blessings. It is God who has given us the ability to reason, to think, to understand, to plan, to live. As Moses writes, God has given us the ability to produce wealth. So, if the blessings come from God, wouldn't we do well to praise God daily for all that we have? It is simply inappropriate for us to take credit for the things that we haven't done. We are simply the caretakers of what God has placed in our hands for a while. We get to "hold the gold" for a few moments in time. The point is not to forget that God alone has given us the ability to work and earn a living. Whenever we forget that simple truth, we abuse God's gifts in our lives.

And, if all that we have is a result of God's grace, then shouldn't we truly be "cheerful givers?" Is it not an abuse of God's grace in our lives to be the recipients of God's blessings and then fail to bless those around us? We have not been blessed by God to simply fill our purses and spend with needless extravagance. We are blessed in order to bless the lives of others. How can we see needs around us while holding the means with which to make situations better and be unmoved? The most joyful people I know are not those who have saved a lot of money, but rather those who have learned to give much of it away. Let's live this day, conscious of our blessings as we acknowledge the one from whom they come. And out of a spirit of gratitude, let's seek ways in which we can bless the lives of others through our wealth.

Prayer
Praise God from whom all blessings flow. Praise him all creatures here below. Praise him above ye heavenly hosts. Praise Father, Son, and Holy Ghost. Amen.

Day 162 — Deuteronomy 9: Facing the Giants

> "Hear, Israel: You are now about to cross the Jordan to go in and dispossess nations greater and stronger than you, with large cities that have walls up to the sky. The people are strong and tall—Anakites! You know about them and have heard it said: 'Who can stand up against the Anakites?' But be assured today that the LORD your God is the one who goes across ahead of you like a devouring fire. He will destroy them; he will subdue them before you. And you will drive them out and annihilate them quickly, as the LORD has promised you." Deuteronomy 9:1-3 (NIV)

Observation

Moses offered words of encouragement to the Israelites regarding the foes they were about to face. When they crossed the Jordan, they would encounter great and strong nations, mightier than they. The enemies seemed too great, too strong, too formidable. But the promise of Moses was clear: God would go before them and would bring victory.

Application

When I was playing high school football, I faced a few giants. My senior year I weighed in around 127 pounds. The problem was I had to block opposing players who were much bigger. One, in fact, weighed 255 pounds and we played his team twice my senior year! My only plan was to aim for his knees and hope for the best. I was overmatched, to say the least.

God calls us to face some pretty strong enemies. The foes we face each day in trying to live Godly lives, role-model our faith, and defend the word of God are great and strong and mighty. But don't forget the promise. We never fight alone, nor in our own strength. We go with the power of God undergirding our lives. The victory will come. Our problem may not be in our belief concerning the power of God, but in our unwillingness to engage the battle. Sometimes we trudge along in the desert sand for years when just over the next horizon is a land flowing with milk and honey. Do you get it? We can't claim victory until we are willing to fight the war. There are plenty of "side-liners" out there... Those people who curse the darkness and wish things were different. They can articulate what is wrong... They just are unwilling to help make things right. There are, however, the courageous among us who are willing to wage the war by proclaiming truth, refusing to compromise, and rejecting mediocrity. Where do you see yourself? Are you living a life of courage or a life of compromise? One life changes the world. The other is changed by the world. There are big battles to face. Be strong in the Lord and be of good courage.

Prayer

Father, in the face of those enemies that threaten the ways of Christ and assail the Church, may we find the courage afforded us by your Spirit to march boldly, courageously, and carefully. Give us the victory of faith. Amen.

Day 163 — Deuteronomy 10: Guarding the Treasure

> "Then I came back down the mountain and put the tablets in the ark I had made, as the LORD commanded me, and they are there now."
> Deuteronomy 10:5 (NIV)

Observation
In this chapter, Moses continues to offer both important reminders of God's provision and teachings about God's purposes. Read the chapter carefully and you will discover some important words about defending the fatherless and the widows and extending hospitality to the foreigners in the land. Our focus verse this morning deals with the second set of stone tablets on which the 10 Commandments were written. Remember that the first set was destroyed when Moses threw them to the ground in anger over the rebellion of the Hebrews concerning the golden calf. This replacement set was placed in the Ark of the Covenant (golden box kept in the tabernacle) where they remained secure at least until the time Moses writes these words.

Application
What a powerful symbol those tablets must have been to the ancient Israelites! Imagine knowing that in the encampment, the stone tablets, engraved by the very hand of God, were always just a few feet away. Each time that the priests carried the Ark from one spot to another, the people must have found great comfort and strength by looking at the golden box. They knew that God's commandments had been carefully written on the tablets that were contained in the Ark and that they were always present in their midst.

Somewhere in the history of Israel, those stone tablets disappeared. Were they destroyed when Jerusalem fell and the Temple destroyed in 587 B.C.? Were they hidden to protect them during some battle? Are they still buried somewhere in the earth waiting for an archeologist's trowel to uncover them? Does it matter? The better question this morning is to ask, "Where is God's word now written and where can it be found in the midst of our communities?" No longer written on stone but on human hearts, the word of God surrounds us, carefully engraved in the heart of every believer. The word is enshrined in each of us. We are called to carefully preserve its message and defend its truth. Somehow the message written on the inside of each of us must find expression on the outside. We best guard the treasure as we live out its demands each day sharing the love and joy of the Savior in authentic and practical ways. We protect the treasure each time that we teach it to others. We protect the treasure when we pass it along to our children. It is to be safeguarded in the human heart and proclaimed by human voices and lived out by human action. So be careful to guard your heart this day. It safeguards a mighty treasure.

Prayer
Father, may we be careful guardians of the treasure placed in our hearts for safe keeping.

Day 164 — Deuteronomy 11: An Eyewitness Account

> "But it was your own eyes that saw all these great things the LORD has done." Deuteronomy 11:7 (NIV)

Observation
In continuing to challenge the Israelites about the road of conquest before them, Moses calls them to remember the mighty deeds of God in their midst. He challenges them to teach all things carefully to their children who were not yet born at the time of the deliverance from Egypt. It would be their testimony, what they had seen with their own eyes, that would speak powerfully to the next generation.

Application
Go back over three decades to a sunny Saturday morning in Louisville, Kentucky. Along with three close friends, I was about to tee off for a round of golf. Nearby, several hot air balloons were beginning their slow ascent into the sky. A sudden shift in the wind direction forced the balloons into the direct path of a tall television antenna. The first balloon gained enough altitude and narrowly escaped hitting the tower. The second balloon hit the very top of the tower. In a split second the balloon shredded and the gondola hung precariously some 1400 feet above the ground. The single occupant grabbed the tower, pulled himself onto the structure and began to climb downward until he reached a safe spot. Crazy, right? I would not have believed it had I not seen it with my own eyes.

There is no testimony more powerful, more moving, more engaging, and more transforming than that of first-hand experience. It is one thing to read history in a book, or a story in the paper, or hear a report from the evening news. It is quite another to actually live through a powerful experience and to speak of it as an eyewitness. Our words carry truth, our emotions carry power. We are story-formed creatures. We love a good story. We remember a powerful tale. One of the most enjoyable aspects of our days are when we come home to our spouse and say, "Let me tell you what happened at work today!" We love both the telling and the hearing. So, listen to the teaching of Moses offered in our focus verse. It is important for us to tell the story of what we have seen and felt in our own experience with God. Our eyewitness accounts of what God has done will speak powerfully and will be long-remembered by future generations. My challenge for you today is to tell the stories of God to your children and grandchildren and even to your friends. Speak of what you have seen, what you have felt, and how salvation, grace, and freedom came to your life. Your stories will help to transform future generations for the cause of Christ.

Prayer
Father, teach us the value of remembering your work in our lives in ways that we might share our testimony with those who come behind us. Amen.

Day 165 — Deuteronomy 12: Half-Hearted Discipleship

> "See that you do all I command you; do not add to it or take away from it."
> Deuteronomy 12:32 (NIV)

Observation
This chapter is devoted to very specific instructions about where and when to make sacrifices before God, how to cook the meat, what to do with the blood, etc. Through Moses, God gives the Israelites very specific details about how to dedicate themselves to the things of worship. There are also very strict warnings not to adopt the practices of those who worship false gods. God demands complete obedience. God's instructions are to be followed completely... nothing added, nor nothing taken away.

Application
An undergraduate student came to me recently to vent a little about his professor. Apparently, the student-teacher relationship was not going well and the student just needed to "unload" a little. He used these words, "Dr. Jones (*obviously a pseudo name*) is just terrible! You can tell he's taught this class way too many times. He's just going through the motions. Everyone in class agrees that he's just phoning it in." Well certainly it's not my place to judge the professor nor affirm the student's sentiments, but I understand the frustration. Most of us have encountered a situation in which the person leading us or our organization seems to be less than fully engaged... just phoning it in. Maybe you have given in to that temptation at some point. Maybe there was a moment when you didn't offer your best work, or your undivided attention, or your full energy to a project. Let's face it. We get tired. We get frustrated. We get a little lazy. It even happens in our pursuit of faith.

It's called half-hearted discipleship and many of us have learned to practice it well. God declares that we are to be "all in." The call to the Christian faith is not a part-time occupation. We do not have the option of acting Christ-like "most" days. Being his representative must become the essence of who we are. We cannot separate ourselves from that calling. What I do today matters... The words I choose to speak, the attitudes that I harbor, the places I go, the involvements I select, must all be done with the acknowledgment that I bear the name of Christ. I cannot live a life of compromise. I cannot accept a life of mediocrity. It is for God's kingdom and for God's glory that I was placed on the planet. None of us were created so that we could craft false idols and worship pagan deities. Our focus is clear, our allegiance is to be forthright. We are to live, move, and speak at God's bidding. To do so requires constant surrendering of self. So, are you "all in?" Have you committed your life to a courageous faith and not one of compromise? How you live the Christian faith matters. Live it well.

Prayer
Father, forgive us when we fail to offer our spiritual growth our best efforts. Amen.

Day 166 — Deuteronomy 13: Serious Business

> "That prophet or dreamer must be put to death for inciting rebellion against the LORD your God, who brought you out of Egypt and redeemed you from the land of slavery. That prophet or dreamer tried to turn you from the way the LORD your God commanded you to follow. You must purge the evil from among you." Deuteronomy 13:5 (NIV)

Observation
Moses offers a very strict warning to those who would seek after and worship false gods. In fact, Moses declares that those who attempt to mislead anyone into the worship of a false deity or pagan god must be stoned to death! He goes so far as to say that even if a family member encourages such disobedience that they too should be slain for their acts of rebellion against God. The idea is to purge the evil from among the people.

Application
I read a stark statistic the other day... The average American adult checks his/her cell phone 160 times a day, or once about every six minutes of waking hours. Sometimes it's a quick glance. At other moments, we take several minutes to check our mail, read a story, or send a text. What if the average amount of time spent per cell phone "glance" is 30 seconds? That means we are spending 80 minutes a day with our phones. Is that excessive? And do you see that relationship going away anytime soon?

In case you haven't noticed... God is extremely intolerant of false gods. Not only are we not to worship them, we are challenged to remove them from our midst. Anything that pulls our focus away from God is to be eliminated from our lives. My fear is that most of us have grown a little indifferent to those things that detract us from God. We flirt with the false gods and insist that we can overpower an addiction to them at any time. In fact, a lot of very useful and important tools used each day can become "the thing that we just can't live without" if we are not careful. We devote so much time and energy to such things that we push aside any time for growing our relationship with God. For example, in addition to the amount of time you spend on your phone, how many hours each day are you in front of your computer? How many hours are spent in front of the TV? How much time do you fritter away at the coffee shop? Please understand that our cell phones, computers, TVs, or habits are not inherently evil. What is evil is the way we allow such things to take precedence over the time that should be devoted to God. It's about balance. It's about priority. It's about keeping such things at arm's length and refusing to let them dominate our lives. Here's a simple test... Could you give up those things for a day? What about for a week? Claiming to have a heart for God and really having a heart for God can be two very different things.

Prayer
Father, forgive us when we serve the false gods we have created. Amen.

Day 167 — Deuteronomy 14: Generosity

> "At the end of every three years, bring all the tithes of that year's produce and store it in your towns, so that the Levites (who have no allotment or inheritance of their own) and the foreigners, the fatherless and the widows who live in your towns may come and eat and be satisfied, and so that the LORD your God may bless you in all the work of your hands."
> Deuteronomy 14:28-29 (NIV)

Observation

The second portion this chapter is devoted to Moses' teaching about offering a tithe to the Lord. In addition to honoring the Lord, the tithe is intended to help those who have needs. Notice from our focus verse that the Levites (priestly tribe that was not given an inheritance of land after the conquest), foreigners, the fatherless, and widows were to be blessed by the tithes given to God. Moses was calling the Israelites into a stewardship of hospitality in which the underprivileged were considered as a part of the community and their needs were addressed.

Application

Recently, I heard a discussion among some theologians about the use of the words "community" and "neighborhood." Often, we talk about meeting the needs of the community. I use that word frequently myself. But what if we substituted the word "neighborhood" in place of the word "community?" Does the meaning change? For me it does. Community has a sense of vagueness about it. Community seems to be both faceless and nameless. It's a group of folks, but not individuals. Neighborhood, on the other hand, seems more personal. When I think of neighbors, I think of names, faces, property, and children playing on the sidewalks. I think of people that I know by name or others to whom I offer a wave when they pass by. The needs become more specific because the people become more real. So, in the context of Moses' instruction, I begin to feel a stronger sense of responsibility to give my tithes, so that my neighbors can be blessed. So often we view our gifts to the church as merely a way of paying for bills, budgets, and bricks. But what if we began to see our giving as a real means of helping with real needs? What if we remembered that some of what we give to God finds its way in feeding our neighbors and in meeting their needs? This past weekend, I spent a little time helping a neighbor in his yard. I was blessed by being able to serve. Maybe the next time you begrudgingly write a check to your church, it will help you to think about meeting the needs of your neighbors and not just some vague sense of benevolence. Maybe the reason God loves a cheerful giver is because God loves how our gifts can help others. May God bless the tithes we offer.

Prayer

Father, thank you for my blessings. My I learn the joy of serving others through giving.

Day 168 — Deuteronomy 15: Canceling Debts

> "At the end of every seven years you must cancel debts."
> Deuteronomy 15:1 (NIV)

Observation

Moses gave the people a very clear command in terms of debts owed by fellow Israelites. At the end of every seven years, all debts were to be canceled and the loans forgiven. This law of canceling debts also applied to servants who worked in various households. The servants were also to be set free. Servants could stay with their masters if they chose to do so, but the offer of freedom had to be extended. The idea was that God's people were to set free those who were oppressed by debt or indenture because they too had once been oppressed in Egypt and set free by God.

Application

I once heard the story of a couple in the midst of a counseling session. The husband said, "Every time we get into an argument, my wife gets historical." The counselor tried to correct the husband by suggesting, "You probably mean she gets hysterical." "No," replied the husband, "Every time we argue she brings up everything that I have ever done wrong!"

What if we took this Old Testament principle seriously? What if we determined that all debts owed to us by anyone would automatically be canceled every seven years? It obviously would reflect a very generous heart, especially if the debt were a financial one. It would also reflect the heart of Christ if the debt was one of transgression. Think about it... What if we had to completely forgive any sin against us at the end of a seven-year period? What if we could only hold to a grudge or desire revenge for a limited period of time? What if the day came when we could no longer hate, enact revenge, or even bring up an old transgression? In other words, how freeing would it be if we truly learned to let go, and to let go forever? Most of us carry around a lot of non-forgiving attitudes towards certain people. There's that guy in high school that insulted us. There's the co-worker who once wounded us with his words. There's the family member that always belittled us. There's that spouse who betrayed us. There's that former friend who stabbed us in the back. If the truth be told, most of us carry around a large load of resentment, anger, and bitterness. To be Christ-like would imply that we let it go... that we forgive... that we extend grace. Think about how much of your life you have spent with a heart darkened by hurt, hatred, and anger. Carry it a while longer if you like, but you are only destroying your own soul. Is there someone you finally need to forgive? Is there a moment of grace you need to offer? Even seven years is too long to live a lesser life. Let go of the debt you think that is owed to you. Discover the freedom you will claim when you offer the freedom of forgiveness to someone else.

Prayer

Father, teach us to forgive, forget, and find healing. Amen.

Day 169 — Deuteronomy 16: Empty Handed

> "Three times a year all your men must appear before the LORD your God at the place he will choose: at the Festival of Unleavened Bread, the Festival of Weeks and the Festival of Tabernacles. No one should appear before the LORD empty-handed: Each of you must bring a gift in proportion to the way the LORD your God has blessed you." Deuteronomy 16:16-17 (NIV)

Observation

In our focus passage, Moses is reminding the Israelites to carefully observe three important feast celebrations each year, the Feast of Unleavened Bread, the Festival of Weeks, and the Festival of Tabernacles. The Feast of Unleavened Bread is a part of the Passover celebration recognizing God's delivering them from Egypt. The Festival of Weeks celebrated the gleaning of the first fruits of one's crop and was used to commemorate the giving of the Law on Mount Sinai. The Festival of Tabernacles was a harvest festival in which the people celebrated God's bounty and remembered the wilderness experience of 40 years when they once dwelled in "tents" or tabernacles. All three were to be carefully kept by the Jews, with the added detail that "no one should appear before the Lord empty-handed."

Application

Just as the ancient Hebrews were commanded to never appear before the Lord empty-handed, meaning that everyone was to contribute to the festivals with both sacrifice and offerings, we too are challenged not to appear before the Lord empty-handed. A life lived in sincere faith will always produce fruit. When we live out our Christianity authentically, consistently, and sacrificially, we will produce kingdom-fruit in the lives of others. Our faith should have rippling effects. Family, friends, co-workers—everyone—should be impacted by our walk of faith. The day will come when we will bring the Lord the results of our lives. It is on that day that we don't want to appear "empty-handed." We should be able to tell the stories of things we have done, of lives we have touched, of ministries we have performed. James suggests that "faith if it has not works, is dead..." (James 2:17 NASB). Understand clearly, we don't "do" good things to earn salvation... But if we actively live out our faith, then good works should be the natural result of our discipleship. We should come before God with the names of those with whom we shared our faith, a list of social ills we attempted to address, the number of people whom we forgave, the great causes in which we invested our time, the ministries to which we committed our resources. We are commanded to present our gifts, not our empty hands. So where are you investing your life? Where are you making a difference? Glorify God by the ways in which you spend your days. Don't show up at the banquet of the Lamb empty-handed.

Prayer

Remind us, O God, that the goal of our lives is not to be successful, but to be significant.

Day 170 — Deuteronomy 17: Staying Focused

> "It is to be with him, and he is to read it all the days of his life so that he may learn to revere the LORD his God and follow carefully all the words of this law and these decrees." Deuteronomy 17:19 (NIV)

Observation
Our focus verse refers to any future king that the Israelites would put in a position over the nation. The king is to be instructed to keep a scroll of God's laws and commandments close at hand. He is to keep it with him and read it all the days of his life. By giving careful attention to the Law of God, the king would learn to respect and fear the Lord and keep his heart from turning to other gods.

Application
Most of us keep the owner's manual to our cars carefully tucked away in the glove compartment. It really is a very important and useful guide to understanding and maintaining our vehicles. But to be honest, not many of us ever do a whole lot with it. We like having it close, but it doesn't really affect the day-to-day relationship that we have with our cars.

My fear is that many of us treat the Bible in much the same way. We keep it close, but is it a lamp unto our feet and light unto our path? Let's be honest... There are a lot of distractions. There are so many competing voices, so many involvements, so many time-consuming activities, that if we are not careful, we can neglect our careful pursuit of God. The kings of Israel were warned to the keep the Law close and to read it each day, lest they drift away. Why is it any less important for each of us to carefully guard our time with God's word? In the midst of all that bombards our lives each day, we must hold fast to the disciplines of spending moments in the presence of God and in taking the time to read and reread God's word. I wonder if we really keep the word of God close each day. Specifically, is it physically close? Is there a copy of God's word within reach at any moment of the day? What if we really began to think of the Bible as the road map for all our decisions and actions? What if we constantly asked, "What does God's word have to say about this?" I don't mean to sound flippant. It is not that we need to consult the word of God each time we start the car or buy groceries or take the kids to school. But we do need to develop a Biblical consciousness that governs our actions and penetrates our minds. In other words, we need to let God speak each day. Rather than allowing the Bible to become just a story book that we occasionally dust off to read, we need to allow it to become the map that guides us each day. How important is God's word for your life? Do you keep it close? Do you consult its wisdom or are you willing to simply "wing it" on your own?

Prayer
Father, teach us to love your word so much that we will hold it close each day.

Day 171   Deuteronomy 18: Living in Community

> "This is the share due the priests from the people who sacrifice a bull or a sheep: the shoulder, the internal organs and the meat from the head." You are to give them the firstfruits of your grain, new wine and olive oil, and the first wool from the shearing of your sheep, for the LORD your God has chosen them and their descendants out of all your tribes to stand and minister in the LORD's name always." Deuteronomy 18:3-5 (NIV)

Observation
In this chapter, Moses speaks of the provisions that are to be made for the priestly tribe of Levi. Because the Levites were to live differently than the rest of Israel, serving the spiritual needs of the nation, they were not to be given any allotment of land when the land was conquered. Instead, the members of every community were to support them by bringing them various gifts, like meat, grain, and wine. Because they were not to possess any land of their own, they would become dependent on the generosity of the community to provide for their needs.

Application
These verses always frightened me a little when I was pastoring churches. I was apprehensive to preach this passage in the fear that church members might take it literally. I was grateful to get a paycheck from the community of faith that I served as a pastor… and equally grateful that no one brought me any "internal organs or the meat from the head" of some bull that was slaughtered! I also don't know what I would have done with the raw wool from someone's sheep. (Although a nice wool suit would always make a lovely Christmas gift.) There is a bigger message here than just showering the preacher with gifts. It's a message about community. It's a message about living faithfully among the people of God, attempting to share when there are times of abundance and receiving help in times of need. There is a "give and take" to living in community. Communities share. They offer understanding and compassion. They sacrifice. They love. They come to the rescue of those in need. The truth is, we will make it together, or we will not make it at all. We desperately need each other, not only for the simple provisions of life, but for the greater gifts like love, hope, encouragement, and grace. I want to challenge you this morning to become fully invested in a community of faith. Go. Serve. Share. Invest. Receive. Heal. Forgive. Be patient. Rescue. You need the community called "church" and it needs you. There will be moments when you will be on the receiving end of generosity in your time of need and there will be times when you will be on the giving end of generosity when those around you are suffering. It's what joins us together and connects us to each other. May God bless you and your church this day.

Prayer
Father, thank you for the community of a church family. Amen.

Day 172 — Deuteronomy 19: A Place of Refuge

> "Determine the distances involved and divide into three parts the land the Lord your God is giving you as an inheritance, so that a person who kills someone may flee for refuge to one of these cities."
> Deuteronomy 19:3 (NIV)

Observation
In this passage, Moses is establishing three cities of refuge. These three cities were to be scattered strategically across the land of Israel. The purpose of these cities was to provide a safe haven for those who committed accidental murder against a neighbor. The example given by Moses in this passage involved an axe head that could fly off an axe-handle and accidentally strike a neighbor, killing him in the process. The one swinging the axe could flee to a city of refuge and avoid retribution of the neighbor's family. The purpose of the city was to provide shelter and protection while allowing for anger to subside.

Application
Decades ago, a tornado ripped through Tuscaloosa, Alabama, narrowly missing the home where my grandparents were living at the time. My grandfather heard the terrible sound of the swirling winds and knew that he needed to get my grandmother and himself to a safe spot. They rushed to the garage and hunkered down in the backseat of their Chevy Impala. Granddaddy thought the steel frame of the car would provide safety and it did.

The concept of refuge is important. We all need a "safe place" in which we can find comfort, rest, protection, and encouragement. We need that special place where we gain acceptance and find grace. Where can we find such a place? For me, the modern day "city of refuge" must become the local church. Understand that I am not speaking in terms of harboring innocent murderers as much as I am speaking about harboring the wounded soul. All of us need a place where we are loved unconditionally, accepted warmly, and needed vitally. We need a place where our spirits are given rest, our souls find comfort, and our lives gain encouragement. What an image for the church. Admittedly, there are many churches that are far from that image. Some churches develop an exclusive nature, a mean-spirit, or a judgmental attitude. But others seem to find the heart of Christ and become a place where sinners are accepted and where grace abounds. It doesn't happen by accident. Churches are only as good as the members who comprise them. So, if you want to be a part of a community of refuge, be a person of refuge. Be the kind of person in that community who role-models the spirit and heart of Christ. Be kind. Be inclusive. Extend grace. Offer acceptance. Listen. Pray. Heal. Forgive. Judge less and love more. I challenge you to build a place of refuge in your church by becoming a person of refuge.

Prayer
Father, thank you for giving us places of refuge and shelter. Amen.

Day 173 — Deuteronomy 20: Courage

> "When you go to war against your enemies and see horses and chariots and an army greater than yours, do not be afraid of them, because the LORD your God, who brought you up out of Egypt, will be with you."
> Deuteronomy 20:1 (NIV)

Observation

In this chapter, Moses challenges the people about their resolve as they head into battle. Moses knows that within a few weeks after his farewell speech to the nation, Israel will cross the Jordan and begin the conquest of the promised land. Moses knows that they will face great and mighty armies. When they see the strength of the foe, they will be tempted to cower in fear. And so, he reminds them that they will not face the enemy alone, that God will be with them, and that God will bring victory.

Application

Let's admit that sometimes the battles we face seem a little overwhelming. When we look at global complexities such as poverty, hunger, violence, and war… When we consider the extent to which hatred, greed, and selfishness manifest themselves in the hearts of all men… When we think of the lack of respect for human life and the lack of care for our environment, it all seems too great, too strong, too widespread. We try to live a Christian life, but we often wonder what "our" one little light of the Gospel will mean. We look to the great battle between darkness and light and we fear that the light might soon be extinguished. We fear that the battle will swallow us and that we will be swept away. But is that what the word of God declares? No. Read our focus verse again, and then read it another time or two… "When you go to war against your enemies and see horses and chariots and an army greater than yours, do not be afraid of them, because the Lord your God, who brought you up out of Egypt, will be with you." When we live out our faith and allow the Spirit of God to penetrate every facet of our lives, the battles in which we are compelled to engage are those of the kingdom, because the King has called us into the fray. We march forward at God's bidding. I am reminded that, yes, we face overwhelming struggles. But I am also reminded that we face those struggles with the power and promise of Almighty God. I don't know what battles you face this day. I don't know what great and noble causes fill both your heart and mind. I don't know the enemies that will come to your door. But I do know that God will be with you. And If God is for us, who is against us?" (Romans 8:31 NASB). Take hope and live with courage. You're stronger than you think.

Prayer

Father, we thank you for your indwelling Spirit that comforts, strengthens, and gives courage for the battles we face. Teach us this day to rely on the power that comes to us because you dwell within us. Amen.

Day 174 — Deuteronomy 21: No Compromise

> "If someone has a stubborn and rebellious son who does not obey his father and mother and will not listen to them when they discipline him, his father and mother shall take hold of him and bring him to the elders at the gate of his town. They shall say to the elders, 'This son of ours is stubborn and rebellious. He will not obey us. He is a glutton and a drunkard.' Then all the men of his town are to stone him to death. You must purge the evil from among you. All Israel will hear of it and be afraid."
> Deuteronomy 21:18-21 (NIV)

Observation
There are a few passages in Deuteronomy that seem a bit extreme, and this is one of them. Moses is declaring appropriate punishment for a rebellious son. If a husband and wife have a son who is both stubborn and rebellious, they are to take him to the elders of the town who in turn will instruct the men of the city of stone him to death. This is how such evil is to be treated. Pretty harsh, right? Stone to death a rebellious child? Take the car keys, yes. Cut off the cell phone, maybe. But stone him to death? Read the last phrase... "All Israel will hear of it and be afraid." God is very concerned about evil among the people. Such a strong purging of evil would surely become a detriment to others prone to such behavior.

Application
We need to draw from this passage a little lesson in maintaining holiness and purity before God. Read the entire Book of Deuteronomy carefully and you will notice that God cares a great deal about creating a nation that is pure and holy, whose heart is focused solely on doing the Will of God. In fact, God instructs the people to go to great lengths to ensure that holiness is maintained by God's children. I wonder how seriously we take the call to be pure and holy before God? Are we serious about purging evil from our midst? I'm not suggesting we should stone our sons when disobedient. I am questioning our tolerance for the profane and unholy. It is easier to look the other way when something immoral unfolds around us. It is easier to turn a deaf hear to some evil voice that calls those around us to sinful living. It is easier to adopt a "live and let live mentality" when we do not want to cause a stir in our work environments, neighborhoods, or family dynamics. In other words, we lean into compromise. Do we stand up enough? Are we forceful enough? Are we courageous enough to make a difference? Or have we become okay with living a life of compromise and allowing others to do the same around us? Purity will not come to our culture, until it comes to us. Let us resolve to live the kind of lives that honor God daily and that defend the teachings of God's word.

Prayer
Father, give us the courage to live out our convictions and give us discernment to know that our convictions are based solely on the teaching of your word. Amen.

Day 175 — Deuteronomy 22: A Responsible Community

> "If you see your fellow Israelite's ox or sheep straying, do not ignore it but be sure to take it back to its owner. If they do not live near you or if you do not know who owns it, take it home with you and keep it until they come looking for it. Then give it back. Do the same if you find their donkey or cloak or anything else they have lost. Do not ignore it."
> Deuteronomy 22:1-3 (NIV)

Observation

Moses offers an important principle about being a responsible member of a community. The idea behind his words is to take both initiative and responsibility for helping a neighbor recover that which is lost. Notice the last phrase... "Do not ignore it." As a member of a community, we are not to overlook or ignore our discovery of someone else's property. We are to treat the lost item in the same way we would hope someone would treat our lost possession. Knowing that it belongs to another and that it is important to that person, we safeguard it until it can be returned.

Application

Sometimes things get lost. They become misplaced. In our neighborhood, on occasion a neighbor's dog slips past the invisible fence. When I see the dog, I know what to do. I call to him and then collect him in my arms. I walk to my neighbor's door and ring the bell. It's what we do because we are neighbors and friends. We help the lost find their way.

This principle has implications that reach far beyond a lost dog or donkey or a misplaced cloak. Though we are certainly charged with trying to help lost items connect with their rightful owner, I think there is more for a community member to consider in these words. What if the lost item is not a *thing*, but a *person*? And what if the community is not a local *town*, but a local *church*? Does that add another layer of responsibility? It should. Because we are joined together in Christ, as a body of believers we share the responsibility of helping all those within the body. If a husband is losing his wife because of his neglect or abuse of her, aren't we bound to intervene and attempt to heal that situation? If a family is losing their teenager to the wrong crowd or to the temptations of drug abuse, don't we have some responsibility to help? If a widow begins to pull away because of the loneliness of her grief, are we not responsible for offering care and compassion? Here's the point... We are joined together as brothers and sisters in the family of faith. We are linked. We are connected. We are bound. And so, let us take the responsibility to offer our help, speak our encouragement, and care with our hearts. We cannot ignore the needs of those whom we claim as being our brothers and sisters.

Prayer

Father, give us an overwhelming sense of community that is proven through action. Amen.

Day 176 — Deuteronomy 23: Keeping the Promises

> "Whatever your lips utter you must be sure to do, because you made your vow freely to the LORD your God with your own mouth."
> Deuteronomy 23:23 (NIV)

Observation
In this chapter, Moses presents several rules and regulations that are to govern life among the Israelites. Some may seem bizarre to the casual reader, but remember that God was trying to create a holy people who would live in a holy land. Our focus verse speaks to the idea of integrity. Moses demanded that whatever a person promises to do, he must keep his word and fulfill his vow. Our reliability and integrity are tested with each promise we make.

Application
Do you remember the famous scene from the television show *Seinfeld*, when Jerry and Elaine are at the counter of a rental car company? Jerry discovers that the company does not have a car for him to rent, even though he has made a reservation. He says, "Anyone can take a reservation… it's the holding of the reservation…." It's easy to make promises. It's harder to keep them.

Are you a promise keeper? Do you keep your word? Do you do the things that you say you will do? Each commitment we make, great or small, testifies to our authenticity and trustworthiness. If people cannot trust the promises we make, they will get to the point where they refuse to trust who we are, or what we claim to be. If we claim to be God-followers, people who bear God's image before the nations, and we turn out to be filled with falsehood, doesn't that reflect on the God whom we claim to represent? Our lack of integrity not only brings shame to us, but also brings dishonor to God. Simply put, we have to be people of integrity, whose word matters. We have to be trustworthy in both the small and great promises we make. For most of us, it's the small promises we break. We make simple vows that we easily forsake. For example, ever promise a child to spend a few minutes playing with them, only to break that promise? Ever tell your spouse you will be home early and then you get home late? Ever promise when borrowing a dollar that you will pay it back the next day, only you don't? Do you see what we do and how we act? We make small promises that we become flippant about keeping. And so, when we make the really big vows, no one trusts our word. To be faithful in the big things implies that we are also faithful in the small. So, pay attention to the promises you make, this day and every day. Do what you say you will do. Keep your vows. Honor your commitments. Your reputation is on the line.

Prayer
Father, may we become men and women of integrity. Teach us to carefully guard both the great and small commitments of our lives. Amen.

Day 177 — Deuteronomy 24: Learning to Give

> "When you are harvesting in your field and you overlook a sheaf, do not go back to get it. Leave it for the foreigner, the fatherless and the widow, so that the Lord your God may bless you in all the work of your hands."
> Deuteronomy 24:19 (NIV)

Observation
Moses is teaching the nation a lesson in hospitality and generosity. He instructs the farmer not to "clean pick" the wheat field but to leave a little for the foreigner, the fatherless, and the widow. He offers the same instruction about harvesting grapes and olives. Again, the farmer is to leave a little from the abundance of his crop so that the poor among the population will have something to eat. In a very real sense, Moses is asking each prosperous farmer to share in the responsibility of providing for those whose circumstances have put them in positions of need. Generosity is to be offered to all who are in need, even to the immigrant who inhabits the land.

Application
I often wonder about the ways the word of God could affect American life if we were to read it carefully and take it seriously. The scriptures really do call us to a higher ethic in terms of our treatment of the poor and needy. Rather than ignoring their needs or turning a deaf ear to their plight, or even throwing out an attitude that says, "Why don't those lazy people just get a job," shouldn't we consider the call of scripture to do more? We often fail to remember that there is no such thing as a self-made millionaire. Those who have done well, have gained success by God-given talents, abilities, and opportunities. Do the prosperous among us really think that they have no responsibility to use their wealth in ways that honor God? But let's allow the teaching to get even more personal. Though most of us are not millionaires, we certainly have what we need to survive and much of what we want. To live in America, to have a home, to drive a car, to have food in the pantry, sets us in the top 10% of the world's population. We are clearly blessed and clearly commanded in passages like this one to share with those in need. Here's a challenge for you… What if you did not allow yourself to buy anything you already have without giving away what you intend to replace? For example, if you are buying a new coat, give away the old one. If you are buying a new watch, give away the old one. If you are buying a new dress, give away an old one. Do you get it? Rather than hoard more stuff, bless another life by sharing what you can live without. What if you did the same when you head to grocery store? If I am going to buy a ham, I need to buy one to give away. If I am buying a can of green beans, I need to donate one to a food pantry. You will enjoy your prosperity more when you learn the value of generosity.

Prayer
Father, make us grateful recipients and cheerful givers. Amen.

Day 178   Deuteronomy 25: A Call to Honesty

> "Do not have two differing weights in your bag—one heavy, one light."
> Deuteronomy 25:13 (NIV)

Observation
As he has been doing over the past few chapters, Moses continues to offer words of counsel and warning to the Israelites. Contained in the focus verse is a call to fairness in dealings with others. Merchants were to treat everyone with honesty and equality. There were some who would unscrupulously use two different standards of measurement when weighing items to sell. By having two different weights, the merchant could cheat someone attempting to pay a fair price for a certain amount of grain. The buyer could be deceived into thinking that he was buying more than he actually was. So, the driving principle that Moses was attempting to teach was that of honesty.

Application
Recently, my wife and I replaced our washer and dryer. We went to a local store, picked out a nice set, and made the purchase at a fair price. Then we got down to the nitty-gritty of the deal. There was a delivery charge. A disposal fee for the old units. New hoses and dryer vent costs. What seemed like a good deal turned out to be rather expensive. I'm not saying anything about the deal was dishonest, but it sure seemed like we were being fleeced. It will make me think twice the next time it comes to buying an appliance from those folks.

There is a lesson contained in this passage in terms of business ethics. The message is to practice honesty and transparency in every business transaction. The wise merchant, the one who longs to honor God in all actions, is the one who treats all people with fairness and every transaction as a means to demonstrate integrity. Here's the point... Our integrity is always on the line with every decision and transaction we undertake. Those who go to great lengths to always do the right thing and to always treat others with fairness build a reputation of honesty while bringing glory to God. When we are dishonest in our dealings, our poor conduct not only reflects on ourselves, but also reflects on the lordship of Christ in our lives. Right or wrong, people connect our reputation with that of Christ's. We represent him before the world and so when our hearts are impure and our dealings have no credibility, it reflects negatively on the reputation of our Lord. We need to understand that we never act in solitude. Christ is always joined to our actions. It is important therefore, to be honest and noble in both the great and small things of life. We will forge our reputation on the consistency of our actions.

Prayer
Father, may we always strive to be people of great integrity, knowing that what we do, reflects on you. Amen.

Day 179 — Deuteronomy 26: Gentle Reminders

> "The LORD your God commands you this day to follow these decrees and laws; carefully observe them with all your heart and with all your soul."
> Deuteronomy 26:16 (NIV)

Observation
Moses once again challenges the nation to carefully observe all that God has set forth. The decrees and laws that God has passed down to the nation through the work of Moses are to be regarded with priority. With all their heart and soul, the people are to give attention to following the commandments of God. It will be their obedience that will bring success.

Application
I still remember the words of my middle school football coach. His name was Coach Doss and his favorite coaching remark was, "Do your duty!" If he said it once, he said it a thousand times. It was his way of reminding us to stay focused on the key responsibilities of our position.

Ever wonder why Moses has to remind the people so often to do the right thing... to follow carefully the commandments of God? Could it be that he reminds them so often because they *need* to be reminded so often? From the time we were children, our parents reminded us repeatedly about certain things... "Don't run with scissors in your hand, wash your hands before you eat, brush your teeth, stop, look, and listen..." Remember all those childhood reminders? They were necessary in order to train our way of thinking. When reminded enough, the message will sink in. The same thing happens in the life of a church. Rick Warren, author of *The Purpose Driven Church*, insists that every church needs to be reminded at least once a month why it exists. He's right. We do need constant reminders of our purpose and place. Again, the more often we are reminded, the more likely we are to remember.

The same thing holds true for every believer. The reason Moses teaches us to carefully observe all that God has set forth is because we are good at forgetting those things. The more we remind ourselves, the more our hearts and minds will be trained to do the right thing. Repeated instruction leads to correct behavior. I challenge you to get to that spot where you gather with other believers in order to be reminded of all that God intends for you to be doing. Worship is always great, and we desperately need the community it provides each week, but beyond those moments of corporate learning that come through proclamation, each of us also needs the dynamic of a small Bible study group where we can listen, ask questions and explore our faith. Participating week after week will allow us to grow in our faith. So, pay attention to your interaction with the word. Be careful to observe all that it commands.

Prayer
Father, remind us again and again, to observe all that you have taught us. Amen.

Day 180 — Deuteronomy 27: Biblical Billboards

> "Build there an altar to the LORD your God, an altar of stones. Do not use any iron tool on them." Deuteronomy 27:5 (NIV)

Observation

As the Israelites crossed into the promised land, they were to collect large stones with which to build an altar to the Lord on Mount Ebal. Once set in place, these large stones were to be covered with plaster and the commands of God were to be written upon them. Notice the careful instruction of our focus verse... "Do not use any iron tool on them." Here's is why that is significant. Iron tools were tools that had been forged by the hands of men. To use them in building the altar would be to defile the altar. God desired a pure altar on which sacrifices could be made, one not made from the product of human craftsmanship, but one made of the things created by God.

Application

Part of the instruction given about building the altar on Mount Ebal was that it needed to be covered in plaster and the words of God written carefully upon it. Mount Ebal was a tall barren mountain. Placing an altar on its peak with words written in bold letters would certainly be visible to all who gaze upon the mountain. The altar would serve as a sort of ancient billboard, reminding people about the commandments of God.

Drive in and around Nashville where I work and you will notice a lot of billboards. Some are electronic with changeable messages and images. The billboards along the way advertise everything from fancy cars to Grand Ole Opry tickets. The idea is to plant an idea in the minds of all those who go racing past them each morning on the commute into the city. And it works... The constant, visible reminders plant seeds in the mind of every driver. Those signs affect lunch choices, car purchases, and even educational opportunities.

When God commanded that the word be written in bold letters on a white background, surely the people could read it from even a great distance. It would become a constant reminder of how God intended for them to live. We would do well to have such a reminder. We need to have contact with the word of God each day. I wonder what visible reminders we could establish before our eyes each day. Billboards might be a little extreme to pull off. But what about a verse taped to your mirror? Maybe a verse stuck on the refrigerator with a magnet? What about a paperweight on your desk, or a small sign above the doorway of your office? A little reminder of God's expectations for your life can't be a bad thing. Post the word in places you will encounter it each day.

Prayer

Father, teach us of the importance of your word. May it be a constant, consistent reminder to us each day of your expectations for our lives. Amen.

Day 181 — Deuteronomy 28: Risky Business

> "Just as it pleased the LORD to make you prosper and increase in number, so it will please him to ruin and destroy you. You will be uprooted from the land you are entering to possess." Deuteronomy 28:63 (NIV)

Observation
Chapter 28 is a unique and lengthy chapter. In this chapter, Moses describes the blessings that will come to the nation as they obey the Lord in all things. But then, after the good news, comes the bad news. Just as God will bless the obedient, God will punish the disobedient. Much of the chapter, in fact, is dedicated to a long list of curses that will come to Israel if she forsakes the Living God.

Application
I grew up in a time when corporal punishment was still used in my middle school. Mr. Muschamp was the headmaster of the school and role of disciplinarian fell to him. He kept a thick, wooden paddle in his office and occasionally, a lesson was taught with a good swift smack. We all understood the concept of crime and punishment. If you practiced obedience and compliance to the school rules, you never had to experience the paddle. But if you broke the rules, a visit to the headmaster's office was ordered.

I have to confess that this verse makes me a little uncomfortable. I like the fact that God is pleased to make us prosper when follow God's ways and offer the obedience of our hearts. But I do not like that "it will please him to ruin and destroy us," for our disobedience. Something about the way the text describes God as "being pleased to destroy us" is a little unnerving. How can a God who loves us so strongly, be pleased to ruin us so severely? I'm sure there are some who would chalk up this verse to an "Old Testament vs. New Testament" view of God. It's not that simple. This verse means what it says... God will bless and God will destroy based on our loyalty. There is a sense of justice found in the kingdom of God. Though we are quick to speak of mercy and grace, we cannot dismiss judgement as though it doesn't exist. It does. And the bad news is that all of us are deserving of judgement. But not all of us will fall under such wrath. There is a way of escape, a way of salvation. The love of Jesus Christ transforms our punishment into reward. We are saved from ruin through our faith in Christ. It is not that we become sufficiently obedient enough to escape punishment, but that we become sufficiently claimed by Christ to find grace and forgiveness. Don't underestimate the threat of punishment. Don't under appreciate the sacrifice of Christ.

Prayer
Father, teach us to fear the wrath that will surely come to those who practice disobedience. Teach us to embrace the love that Christ offers. Amen.

Day 182 — Deuteronomy 29: All In

> "When such a person hears the words of this oath and they invoke a blessing on themselves, thinking, 'I will be safe, even though I persist in going my own way,' they will bring disaster on the watered land as well as the dry." Deuteronomy 29:19 (NIV)

Observation
As the book of Deuteronomy draws towards a close, Moses has once again gathered the nation unto himself so that he might give them final reminders and challenge them to renew their covenant with God. In our focus verse, Moses cautions the people about being too cavalier with the Covenant of God. The temptation for some would be that of entering a covenant with God and then acting as though it doesn't matter. To think that God would bless them because of the covenant made, while they continue to act in disobedience would bring the wrath of God.

Application
I want you to understand the perverted logic that Moses was trying to address with his people. There were some who reasoned, "If I make a covenant with God, God will have to protect me and prosper me, regardless of how I act." They felt that their lives would be protected and blessed even though they insisted on "going their own way." What they failed to understand about the covenant was its two-way nature. God promised to bless the nation and the nation promised to live as God's covenant people. To act in disobedience and to express a lack of loyalty to God would surely disrupt the agreement.

Here's the parallel to our practice of faith. Many of us have chosen to enter a relationship with God through our faith in Christ. We placed our trust in God, confessed Jesus as Lord, prayed a sinner's prayer, and walked the aisle of a church. The next part of the journey is what gets a little sketchy for some of us. There are many who believe that having taken those steps will provide all the "fire insurance" needed. In other words, "Because I have become a Christian, I have taken all the action needed. I can now live my life anyway I choose." Not so fast. Faith is a journey with multiple steps. Whenever we join our lives to Christ, we surrender to his lordship. We begin a life of discipleship. That commitment demands much of us. The call of the Gospel is a call to transformation and change. It is not that we have enough of Jesus to simply escape hell, we should know enough of Jesus to want to follow him. We are called to mature, to grow, and to become obedient. We are called to become disciples, right? Such a calling disallows a lazy, insipid faith. It demands our heart, our souls, our all. Do more with your faith. Commit to a life of asking, seeking, knocking, and serving. See where the journey will lead you.

Prayer
Father, may our commitment to Christ be life-changing and destiny altering. Amen.

Day 183 — Deuteronomy 30: The Wisdom of the Word

> "Now what I am commanding you today is not too difficult for you or beyond your reach... No, the word is very near you; it is in your mouth and in your heart so you may obey it." Deuteronomy 30:11, 14 (NIV)

Observation

All that God was commanding the Israelites to do—all that God desired for them to obey—was certainly within their hearing and comprehension. It was not beyond their reach. The ways of God were understandable and the message was clear... "Choose obedience." Moses reminded them that the word was near them. It was "in their mouths and in their hearts," meaning that it had been discussed, proclaimed, and understood. They would have no excuse for not doing all that God demanded.

Application

A couple of weeks ago I upgraded the software on my computer. The process was advertised as being quite simple. Just download the upgrade and the process would all but take care of itself. Yeah, right. The process was anything but simple. There were no printed instructions to read, and I found it very difficult to get through to technical support. Apparently, thousands of others were having similar problems. A lot of things can be that way. When the directions are unclear or the instructions seem confusing, it is hard to sometimes know what choices to make. Not so with the Will of God. All that God expects of us—all that God demands—is clearly contained within God's written word. The greater our devotion and investment of time in the word, the greater our understanding and wisdom. God longs to be revealed to us. God has not hidden expectations away in some hard-to-reach spot. Just the opposite. It's written in black and white. The only question concerns our willingness to be students of the word. So, let me ask... "How seriously do you take the word of God? Does it claim authority over your life? Are you careful to read it and apply it?" There really is no excuse to be offered saying, "I just didn't know right from wrong, obedience from disobedience." It's all right there, waiting for you to discover. Take the word seriously. Let it matter in your life.

Maybe it's a question of how often you allow yourself access to the word. Is it a daily discipline, or is your time with the Bible "hit or miss?" I read recently that the average adult in the U.S. will look at his or her smart phone 160 times a day. It begs the question... "What has more control over your actions and thoughts?" God's word or your phone? Let me challenge you this day to invest in the word with a little greater intentionality.

Prayer

Father, thank you for revealing yourself to us through your written word. May our desire to follow you, force us into moments of daily devotion with your word. Amen.

Day 184 — Deuteronomy 31: Parenting 101

> "Their children, who do not know this law, must hear it and learn to fear the Lord your God as long as you live in the land you are crossing the Jordan to possess." Deuteronomy 31:13 (NIV)

Observation

God told Moses to write down all the law that God had proclaimed. And so, Moses wrote all that God had said and the writings were kept with the Ark of the Covenant. God wanted the word written so that future generations who had not heard God speak would listen to the word and would know to fear God. God's concern was not just for the current generation. God desired that each new generation would hear the commandments.

Application

In my role as the director of a leadership program here at Belmont, I encounter a lot of data that relates to the status of congregational life here in the U.S. By now, most of you are aware that the millennial generation has become the most "unchurched" generation in the history of our nation. Of the 70 million who make up this group, fewer than 17% will find their way into church life. Equally frightening is the statistic that reveals that 59% of the children of the current generation will leave the church as adults. There is work to do.

Read our focus verse again, slowly and carefully. "Their children, who do not know this law, must hear it and learn..." The ancient Israelites were burdened with the responsibility of teaching the ways of God to their children. It was important for them to *hear* in order to *learn*. It begs the question, "Who will pass along the instruction of God to future generations if not us? Who will teach our children if not us?" It is reasonable to expect that as children grow into adulthood, that they will learn a few things on their own. They will learn new concepts and new ideas. Education will expose them to new ways of thinking and various philosophies. What they may or may not learn on their own are the ways of God. The most important link between children and the teachings of God is parents. Parents cannot assume that a church nor a Christian school can replace their crucial role in the religious education of their children. As parents, both teaching Biblical principles and role-modeling Christian behavior clearly rest on our shoulders. It ought not surprise us when our children grow up to leave the church and abandon the faith if we have failed to make church a priority and the teachings of scripture as essential learning. Simply put, we cannot neglect such a vitally important responsibility. Children need to know the love of God, the salvation of Christ, and the grace of the Gospel. How will they know if we, as parents, fail to teach them?

Prayer

Father, we thank you for the privilege and responsibility of parenthood. Amen.

Day 185 — Deuteronomy 32: Missed It by that Much...

> "This is because both of you broke faith with me in the presence of the Israelites at the waters of Meribah Kadesh in the Desert of Zin and because you did not uphold my holiness among the Israelites. Therefore, you will see the land only from a distance; you will not enter the land I am giving to the people of Israel." (Deuteronomy 32:51, 52 (NIV)

Observation
Chapter 32 contains a very long "song" in which Moses once again declares the possible destruction that will come to Israel if the people fail to honor God as they take possession of the promised land. They have the real ability to choose blessing or cursing based on their level of obedience. The song itself is very poetic in style, carefully crafted. (The reader may be reminded of the style of the Book of Psalms. In fact, Moses did write Psalm 90.) The end of the chapter takes a very different turn. After the recitation of the song, Moses is told that he is to go to the top of Mount Nebo where his life will end. God will first allow him to see the promised land from a distance, but he will not be allowed to enter it.

Application
It all seems bittersweet, doesn't it? It seems a bit harsh on the part of God not to allow Moses the opportunity to enter the promised land. He got so close that he could look over and see what the nation would inherit, but he would not be allowed to go. So, the key question is, "Why not?" After hearing the call of God, after going toe-to-toe with Pharaoh, after leading the rebellious nation for 40 years in the desert, you would think that Moses would have earned his way into the promised land. Here are two reasons why he didn't. First, it wasn't his role. God called him for a very specific purpose: Leading the nation out of captivity and through the wilderness. That was his part to play and he played it well. Like Moses, God calls us to very specific roles of leadership, to very specific moments in which we are to do God's work. Our role is not to question where or when or for even how long we are called to a task, but to simply be radically obedient when that task is set before us. Second, Moses had made a mistake years earlier by not "upholding God's holiness before the people." Though a bit vague to us, Moses certainly remembered. (Apparently on the day that Moses struck the rock and made drinking water flow for the Israelites, he did so without giving honor to God in ways that he should have.) There is a faith lesson here reminding all of us that there is always a humility demanded before God. Even when called to great positions of leadership, we must always maintain a humble heart and an obedient spirit. Go serve in the places God calls and bring God honor as you do.

Prayer
Father, thank you for entrusting portions of your kingdom's work into the hands of each of us. May we be found faithful in our servitude and loyal in our praise for you. Amen.

Day 186 — Deuteronomy 33: Safe Place

> "The eternal God is your refuge, and underneath are the everlasting arms.
> He will drive out your enemies before you, saying, 'Destroy them!'"
> Deuteronomy 33:27 (NIV)

Observation
Chapter 33 represents Moses' final words to the people. In this chapter, he offers a blessing to each of the 12 tribes of Israel. Read it carefully and you will notice how each tribe receives a special word from the Lord. Our focus passage is a portion of the blessing given to the tribe of Asher. Moses reminds his hearers that God is their refuge and underneath God's strong arms their enemies will be driven out of the land.

Application
Let's talk about refuge for a moment. We all seek places of refuge at times. A student seeks a safe place from the peer pressure and teasing of high school life. A businessman seeks refuge from the day-to-day stress of his job. A single mother of two seeks a place of tranquility and sanity in the midst of her hectic world. A cancer patient seeks a place of shelter from the onslaught of a deadly disease. A poor worker seeks refuge from the never-ending bills that show up in his mailbox. A widow seeks relief from the unrelenting grief that invades her soul. A homeless man seeks a place of warmth in winter's cold. You get the point... All of us need a place of rest, a place of peace, a place of sanity. We need a strong shelter from the world that swirls around us. So, where do we find such a place? Some run to the local bar and try to find relief in a bottle. Some run to infidelity. Others pursue peace by never slowing down, fearful that life will pass them by if they do. Still others hope to find respite in a good book or an expensive vacation. There has to be a better option. Remember our focus verse... "God is our refuge and underneath are the everlasting arms." Only God, the one who controls our destinies, sets the course of our lives, and arranges the people and places of our existence can offer us the kind of peace we long to know. Jesus found great refuge in the practice of prayer. When he spoke about a "private prayer closet," some suggest that he was making a reference to the rabbinical practice of completely covering one's head and face with a prayer shawl to remove the distractions of the world. Wherever and however you find it, I invite you to spend more time in God's presence and less time with your stress. Even now, God's waiting to hear from you. Run to that safe place and find the grace, the peace, and the joy you need.

Prayer
O God, our help in ages past, our hope for years to come, be thou our guide while life shall last and our eternal home. Amen.

Day 187 — Deuteronomy 34: Fighting the Beast Called Grief

> "The Israelites grieved for Moses in the plains of Moab thirty days, until the time of weeping and mourning was over." Deuteronomy 34:8 (NIV)

Observation
This final chapter of the book of Deuteronomy tells of the death of Moses. Having looked over into the land of promise atop Mount Nebo, Moses dies at the age 120. Appropriately so, the nation mourns the loss of her great leader for a full month. For 30 days they gathered in the plains of Moab and wept over the man who had led them out of bondage and through the wilderness. At the end of those days, Joshua takes the mantle of leadership and begins to lead the nation during the time of the conquest.

Application
Over the course of a lifetime, each of us will deal with grief. We grieve over a thousand different things. Sometimes we grieve over bad decisions we made that affect us for years. We grieve over a loss of innocence in the lives of our children. We grieve over a loss of mobility and strength. We grieve over old school buildings when torn down in the name of progress or over an old family home that has been razed. We grieve over an old tree that is blown down in a storm or over a favorite garment that is no longer wearable. And most importantly, we grieve over the loss of those we love who have died. There are many facets to our grief and many levels of sadness and remorse. Most of us tend to bump up against some form of grief on nearly every day that we live. Here's the question I want to raise… "Is there an appropriate length of time through which we should grieve?" I do know some folks who are so lost in their grief that they now fail to live life in the present with any sense of joy, purpose, or hope. Their sense of loss remains so strong that days become tedious and troublesome. Is there a moment when we declare an end to grief and move on with the business of life? Is 30 days enough? Is 300 days enough? Who's to say? Grief has its own timetable in every life. If you know of someone paralyzed by grief, pray for that person right this second. Ask God to lift their spirits and to restore a sense of hope. If you are one of those persons who is struggling just to keep on living, declare in the name of the Lord that some small piece of your grief is over. Decide that you will take your grief-energy and use it more productively. Decide that you will express your grief in new ways… Rather than pull inwardly, begin to think outwardly. Honor your loved one by taking on a new challenge to help others. Rather than grieve yourself to death, push yourself into a new place of serving others. That's not an easy step to take, but it does offer a better way to live.

Prayer
Father God, comfort us in our sorrow and give us a lasting hope. Amen.

Day 188   Joshua 1: Leadership 101

> "Study this Book of Instruction continually. Meditate on it day and night so you will be sure to obey everything written in it. Only then will you prosper and succeed in all you do." Joshua 1:8 (NLT)

Observation

The story of the conquest of the promised land begins with this opening chapter to the book of Joshua. God speaks directly to Joshua and transfers to him the promise once made to Moses: "I will be with you; I will never leave you nor forsake you" (Joshua 1:5 NIV). God tells Joshua to be strong and courageous. Joshua then relays the words of God to the people. He gathers the nation together and tells them to prepare. In just three days they will cross the Jordan and begin the conquest. Surely these are words of great joy and perhaps great anxiety as the people listen. The forty-year journey is done. It's time to move forward. Yet they also know that once they cross the Jordan, they will engage the enemy… there is no turning back.

I want you to notice the words of God spoken to Joshua in our focus verse. The Book of Instruction (Law) is to be studied by Joshua continually. He is to know it through and through. The key to his future success as a leader is to carefully obey it. Only then will he prosper.

Application

Here at Belmont University, I direct a leadership program designed to help faith-leaders lead effectively and efficiently. Obviously, I find myself in many leadership-related conversations. In fact, yesterday a student organization approached me to speak to an upcoming conference on how to develop as a leader while still a college student. It has been my experience that leadership is often a combination of nature and nurture. Some of the qualities needed to be an effective leader seem to be wired into a person's DNA. Some are just "born leaders." Others are carefully crafted into becoming leaders. Mentors, education, and experience all contribute to the learning process. But notice the formula for success offered in this opening chapter of Joshua. Sure, Joshua had experience. And yes, Joshua was physically strong. And yes, Joshua was recognized by Moses to be his successor. But according to God, none of that would guarantee his success as a leader. His success would come as a result of a fidelity and passion for the word of God.

Let's talk about your role as a leader. Perhaps you are a leader in your office, your neighborhood, your family, or your occupation. Maybe you lead in your church. There are many places to lead. But if you long for success in any endeavor, pay attention to what God says to Joshua. Study the Bible. It is as we make a constant, careful, and deliberate investment in God's word that we will gain the insight, wisdom, and patience to lead well.

Prayer

Father, teach us to invest in your word. Amen.

Day 189 — Joshua 2: Whose Side Are You On?

> "No wonder our hearts have melted in fear! No one has the courage to fight after hearing such things. For the Lord your God is the supreme God of the heavens above and the earth below." Joshua 2:11 (NLT)

Observation
As Joshua prepares the nation for battle, he sends two spies across the Jordan to spy out the land, especially the city of Jericho. To gain intelligence about the area the spies go to what may seem as a very unlikely source. They visit Rahab, a prostitute in Jericho. Their plan is strategic in several ways. First, it is likely that they could avoid detection. Surely it was not uncommon for men to visit her abode. Second, because of her interaction with the community, she would have a knowledge of the city, its workings, and its leaders. Who better to advise these spies about the strengths and vulnerabilities of the city? Notice from the narrative how quickly she offers her allegiance to these men. She has heard the stories of God's provision and protection of the Israelites. In our focus verse, she affirms that the God of the Israelites is the supreme God of the heavens and the earth.

Application
Most of us are loyal to the things we value. I'm a Bama fan, always have been, always will be. My wife is an Auburn grad and so she cheers for Auburn, always will. We are a little crazy about team loyalty, but hey, it is football, and it is the SEC. We are also loyal about other things like support for our nation, our political parties, our hometowns, etc. We defend our families, our neighbors, our institutions. It's just how loyalty works… especially when we are convinced that our cause is just and that our beliefs are rock solid. But consider the story of Rahab. She was a resident of Jericho. She gained her livelihood from the citizens of Jericho. She and her family had a home that was built into the wall of the city. If the Jericho Panthers played the Jerusalem Bears in football, she would have worn the team jersey and face-painted all the kids. But notice when it came down to survival, she knew beyond the shadow of a doubt where her loyalties needed to be placed. She said in essence, "I choose the God of Israel, not the leadership of Jericho." Ultimate loyalty needs to be settled in our hearts as well. We need to decide in whom or what we will place our trust. And there are options. "Some boast in chariots and horses" (Psalm 20:7 NASB), others trust in their own intellect and savvy, still others trust in riches and gold "where thieves break in and steal" (Matthew 6:19 NASB). And then there are those who trust in the Lord God Almighty whose power is great, whose wisdom is beyond comprehension, whose presence is constant, and whose grace is unlimited. So, who gets the loyalty of your heart today? It needs to be settled.

Prayer
Father, may our trust be always and only in you. Amen.

Day 190 — Joshua 3: Walking on New Ground

> "Meanwhile, the priests who were carrying the Ark of the LORD's Covenant stood on dry ground in the middle of the riverbed as the people passed by. They waited there until the whole nation of Israel had crossed the Jordan on dry ground." Joshua 3:17 (NLT)

Observation

The events recorded in this chapter point to a most significant moment in the history of the Israelites. This chapter tells the story of the crossing of the Jordan River, which signifies the beginning of the conquest. There is no turning back. As God had done 40 years earlier at the beginning of their journey when parting the waters of the Red Sea, God will once again part the waters, this time of the Jordan River. In very dramatic fashion, the Levitical Priests step into the river while carrying the Ark of the Covenant. As soon as their feet touch the water, the river ceases to flow. The water piles up "like a wall." The Priests will continue to stand on the suddenly-dry riverbed while the entire nation passes before them.

Application

When I was a kid growing up in North Georgia, we spent a lot of time during the summer months skiing and swimming in Lake Allatoona, just north of Atlanta. Some friends owned a cabin at the lake that they generously shared with us. We kept a boat at the dock and spent many summer days on the water. During the winter months, the Army Corps of Engineers would significantly drop the level of the lake. From time to time we had to visit the cabin and reposition the dock. It was always interesting to see the lake during those winter months when the low levels exposed all the things covered by water in the summer months. There were stones and stumps that we could never notice in the warmer months. I think about the nation of Israel walking across the dry riverbed of the Jordan. The ground under their feet was always covered by water, except for this single day. In fact, as the story continues, the priests are asked to take up 12 stones from the riverbed to build an altar on the other side.

Sometimes our journey of faith is like that... our pursuit of God takes us to places we have never been, to those places we cannot even imagine... places where we see and experience things of which we can only dream. There is mystery, excitement, and joy as we dare to step where God is leading. But don't miss this fact... we can only walk on the sacred, exciting, and holy ground of God's pathway as we are willing to risk all in pursuit of God's purpose. To be honest, the rushing river of life keeps most of us on the riverbank, frozen in apprehension, wondering what's on the other side. But as we willfully choose to take a step in the direction of God's call for our lives, suddenly the waters part and we find ourselves stepping on the ground where faith and providence intersect our lives. It's a good place to stand.

Prayer

Father, may we know the exhilaration of risk and the rewards it can bring. Amen.

Day 191 — Joshua 4: A Lasting Testimony

> "Joshua also set up another pile of twelve stones in the middle of the Jordan, at the place where the priests who carried the Ark of the Covenant were standing. And they are there to this day." Joshua 4:9 (NLT)

Observation
As the Israelites crossed over the Jordan, God instructed Joshua to get 12 men, one from each of the tribes of Israel, to gather 12 large stones from the riverbed where the Priests were standing. They were to pile up the stones in Gilgal as a lasting memorial to the miracle of God that took place on this occasion so that when future generations asked, "What do these stones mean?" they were to respond by telling the story of God's provision. Notice that Joshua also sets up another pile of stones in the middle of the Jordan as a memorial to God's miracle. And then notice the phrase, "And they are there to this day." That phrase was obviously added by the final editor of the Book of Joshua. There is no exact answer as to who wrote the book. Certainly, parts of the book contain personal pronouns that indicate that Joshua himself added some of the material. It is believed that the final edits of the book were completed about the time of the early monarchy during the reign of David or Solomon. It is apparent therefore, that these stones in the middle of the Jordan were still standing many generations after Joshua had placed them there.

Application
I wonder what we will leave behind that will still be standing generations later? We all seek a sense of permanence. We want our lives to matter and certainly would be gratified if something we did spanned the distance of multiple generations after we are long gone. A few bits and pieces of my early life are still standing strong. All the houses I have ever lived in are still standing. Every school that I attended are still in existence. Every church that I have served is still opening the doors each Sunday. But I know those things will eventually be gone. The winds of time will sweep them all away and that's fine. I'm more concerned about the legacy that I will leave, a legacy not defined by brick and mortar, but by influence, shared faith, and family characteristics. Will it matter that I existed? Will it be important to anyone that I once lived on the planet?

The stones that we should strive to stack on the riverbanks of our legacies, must be carefully selected and carefully attended. If we desire to be remembered as faithful believers, honest citizens, and compassionate human beings, then we must work with all our might to live out those qualities each day that walk the planet. We will craft our legacy with deliberate choices, important stands, and "agape-love" relationships. Choose your stones well.

Prayer
Father, create in us a legacy of faith. Amen.

Day 192 — Joshua 5: Full Compliance

> "When Joshua was near the town of Jericho, he looked up and saw a man standing in front of him with sword in hand. Joshua went up to him and demanded, 'Are you friend or foe?' 'Neither one,' he replied. 'I am the commander of the Lord's army.'" Joshua 5:13-14 (NLT)

Observation

Several significant events occur in this chapter. First, there is an indication that as the nations that inhabit the land hear about the miraculous crossing of the Jordan, they are all but paralyzed in fear. Second, while encamped at Gilgal, God requires that all the men of Israel be circumcised as a sign of the renewal of God's covenant with Israel. Third, the nation celebrates the Passover observance, feasting on the produce from the land of Canaan. Because God is now feeding them with the fresh produce of the promised land, the provision of manna forever ceases. Fourth, as Joshua nears the town of Jericho, he is met by "The commander of the Lord's Army." He falls on his face in reverence and promises obedience to whatever the Lord will require of him. And like the earlier experience of Moses who stood before the presence of God, Joshua is asked to remove his sandals because he stands on holy ground.

Application

Recently, the road crews in the town of Franklin, Tennessee, where I live were resurfacing one of the major roadways. The work was being done at night to lessen traffic delays. To accomplish the work, several lanes had to be closed. And just to make sure that motorists like me understood the importance of compliance, a police officer was posted at the appropriate spot, complete with his squad car and flashing lights. Message delivered. When someone in authority gives us instructions, we would do well to heed them. As Joshua encountered the commander of the Lord's Army, he was reminded of two things. First, he was reminded that God was leading the conquest. God's Spirit and presence would be with Joshua as he led the people. Second, he was reminded that his role was that of full compliance to the instructions of God. Maybe we need to hear those reminders as well. We should never doubt for a moment that God is leading our journey, continuing to position the people, places, and moments in our lives in a way that will bring God glory. God goes before us into each new day. No experience we face is a surprise to God. Keep the faith… God knows what God is doing. Our role, like that of Joshua, is to practice Godly obedience as a way of life. It is as we align ourselves with God's purposes, desires, and plan that we will find success. You don't need to remove your shoes this morning, but you do need to realize that you stand on holy ground. This is God's world, and we are privileged to be included in God's work.

Prayer

Father, remind us today that you are the authority and that our role is obedience. Amen.

Day 193   Joshua 6: What Can Cause the Strongest Walls to Fall?

> "When you hear the priests give one long blast on the rams' horns, have all the people shout as loud as they can. Then the walls of the town will collapse, and the people can charge straight into the town."
> Joshua 6:5 (NLT)

Observation
This chapter is among the most dramatic chapters recorded anywhere in scripture. Chapter 6 tells the story of the defeat of Jericho when the walls came tumbling down. God had promised to deliver the city and its king into the hands of Joshua. Very detailed instructions were to be followed to ensure the victory. For six days in a row, the priests of Israel were to carry the Ark of the Covenant around the exterior of Jericho. Seven priests were to march in front of the others, each carrying a ram's horn. The fighting men of Israel were to follow the Ark of the Covenant in the procession. (There is some debate as to how many fighting men were a part of the procession. Some estimate that as many as 40,000 soldiers marched in the procession. Others argue for more of a representative group of 4000 to 5000.) On the seventh day, the procession marched around the city in silence seven times. On the seventh trip, the priests blew their horns, the people shouted in unison, and the walls crumbled. The victory was swift and complete.

Application
There are many walls in our culture that need to fall. There are many strongholds that need to crumble to dust. I am not talking about walls made of mortar and stone, but rather those that originate in the hearts and minds of men and women. They are strong, secure, and hard to breech. There are walls of racism that need to be scaled by the power of Christian love and understanding. There are walls of poverty that must be defeated by the conviction to share with those in need. There are walls of ignorance that can only be torn down by the strength of education. There are walls of bitterness that can only crumble in the light of forgiveness. There are walls of anger that must be broken by the power of grace. There are walls of misunderstanding, resentment, intolerance, and hatred that must shatter before the presence of God.

So please notice what it takes to tear down the walls. There are two factors. The first is the power of the living God. It is only by God's direct and willful intervention that enemies are defeated and walls are broken. The second is the unity of God's people. It was only when the children of Israel marched and then shouted together that the wall of Jericho crumbled. It is as people of faith unite under the banner of God's love, God's strength, God's wisdom, and God's grace that the powerful strongholds will lose their strength. Let's work together to tear down the walls.

Prayer
Father, teach us today that we are better when we united. Amen.

Day 194 — Joshua 7: The Great Purge

> "Get up! Command the people to purify themselves in preparation for tomorrow. For this is what the LORD, the God of Israel, says: Hidden among you, O Israel, are things set apart for the LORD. You will never defeat your enemies until you remove these things from among you."
> Joshua 7:13 (NLT)

Observation
In the opening of this chapter, we read that a man named Achan had seized some forbidden items when the city of Jericho fell. He had taken some treasure for himself and had hidden it beneath his tent. As a result, when the Israelites go into the next battle against a small town named Ai, they are soundly defeated. They cannot believe nor understand why God would allow their enemies to triumph. God reveals that there is sin in the camp… that someone has practiced disobedience. Eventually, the guilty party is discovered. Achan reveals that he has taken a robe, some silver coins, and a gold bar. He and his family are stoned to death and their bodies burned to rid the nation of the result of his sin. God was seeking to establish both a sense of purity and obedience among God's people.

Application
Read that focus verse closely again. God told the nation that they would never defeat their enemies until they removed the "forbidden" items from their midst. This verse is a powerful reminder that there are victories that we will never claim in our lives until we purge from our hearts and minds those things that are disobedience before God. To state it another way… we can never move forward in our spiritual and emotional development until we resolve issues in our past. We have to remove those "forbidden items" that limit us from becoming the people God longs for us to become. Obviously, we have to remove the sins that "so easily entangle us" (Hebrews 12:1 NASB). God is faithful to remove our sins as far as the east is from the west. God will remember our sins no longer through the redemptive work of Christ, but before that happens, we must confess our sins and repent of our actions. We must agree with God that what we have done, the transgression we have committed, is detestable. We have to own up to our mistakes and not white wash them into acceptability. Then we must repent. To repent means to "change directions." The call to walk in newness will force us to abandon poor choices so that we can pursue God without encumbrance. As we admit our sins and cry out for redemption, we will find grace, healing, and the ability to move forward. So, jettison the hidden sins and unconfessed transgressions. It's time to move ahead.

Prayer
Father, thank you for the healing that comes through confession. Amen.

Day 195 — Joshua 8: The Tip of the Spear

> "Then the LORD said to Joshua, 'Point the spear in your hand toward Ai, for I will hand the town over to you.' Joshua did as he was commanded."
> Joshua 8:18 (NLT)

Observation
This chapter the story of the second battle of Ai. This time, the Israelites claim total and complete victory. Using 30,000 troops and an ambush strategy the city completely falls to the hands of Joshua and his men. The 12,000 residents are completely obliterated according to God's instruction, as God purifies the nation for God's purpose. At the end of the chapter, an altar is built and sacrifices are made before God as an act of grateful worship. As the chapter closes, Joshua gathers the entire nation together and reads every word of the Book of Instruction to them, both young and old, so that they will be careful to remember and put into practice all that God has decreed.

Our focus verse reminds me of the earlier instruction given to Moses when the Israelites were fighting against the Amalakites. Moses was instructed to hold up the rod in his hand over the battlefield and as he did, the Israelites gained momentum. When he could no longer hold the rod, Aaron and Hur held up his arms so that the rod would be lifted high and the battle would be won (Exodus 17). In this story, Joshua is commanded to point the spear in his hand toward Ai. He will continue to do so until the full and complete victory is claimed (8:26). Why did he point the spear? Simple. Because God told him to do that. How long did he hold the spear? Until God's purpose was completed.

Application
Consider for a moment what you and I are called to point at the enemy. Chances are that God is not going to call upon you this morning to hold up a wooden rod or a sharp-tipped spear. But God is going to call upon you to hold up God's word in the face of your enemies. Please don't misunderstand… I am not challenging you to find the biggest leather-bound King James Bible you can hold and wave it all day long at every person you meet. That is not an effective strategy for doing kingdom work. What I am challenging you to do today is to take that word, deeply implanted within you as the result of constant study, prayerful meditation, and Holy Spirit leadership, and apply it to every conversation, every attitude, and every relationship you encounter. It is the word of Truth. It is the power of God unto salvation for all those who will believe. When you hold the word tightly and offer it with grace and wise discernment, the enemies of God will flee from your presence. When you fail to hold it, evil will triumph. Why not select a single Bible truth this morning and write it on a card to carry in your pocket and on your heart as guide? Hold it against the enemies you face and watch God work.

Prayer
Father, let us acknowledge the power of your word and share its truth. Amen.

Day 196 — Joshua 9: Leaving Out One Important Step

> "But when the people of Gibeon heard what Joshua had done to Jericho and Ai, they resorted to deception to save themselves." Joshua 9:3-4a (NLT)

Observation
The nations west of the Jordan are gearing up for battle against the Israelites. The people of Gibeon have heard about the military power of Israel and the providence of God in their midst. Knowing they too will be defeated, their cities decimated, and their families destroyed, they resort to trickery to save their lives. They saddled their donkeys with weathered saddle bags, carried their wine in old, patched wineskins, put on worn-out sandals and ragged clothing, and carried moldy bread. They wanted to create the appearance of having come from a very distant land. The begged for a peace treaty and the deception worked. Joshua made a binding commitment of peace. When the deception was discovered, the binding oath had to be honored. The Gibeonites were not destroyed but became enslaved as woodcutters and water carriers for the Israelites for many generations.

Application
You have to admire the Gibeonites for their resourcefulness in the face of certain defeat. Their plan worked and their people were spared destruction. You also have to admire Joshua's integrity for keeping the oath that he had made. Though it was a foolish vow, the result of deception, he still displayed the character of honesty. What you must wonder about, however, is Joshua's ability to be deceived and taken in by these strangers. Here's the problem according to verse 14: "So the Israelites examined their food, but they did not consult the Lord"(NLT). They made their plans and said their vows without having sought the wisdom of God.

It's the same mistake we tend to make repeatedly. We plan our days, dream our dreams, create our agendas, and make our decisions all according to what we think is best. We buy into a self-sufficiency that claims our wisdom is flawless and our judgements are sound. What a foolish posture to take. James writes, "Look here, you who say, 'Today or tomorrow we are going to a certain town and will stay there a year. We will do business there and make a profit.' How do you know what your life will be like tomorrow? Your life is like the morning fog—it's here a little while, then it's gone. What you ought to say is, 'If the Lord wants us to, we will live and do this or that.' Otherwise you are boasting about your own plans, and all such boasting is evil" (James 4:13-16 NLT). It's a hard lesson to learn and most of us tend to learn it through uncomfortable experiences. Simply stated, "We have to keep God in the loop." As the source of all wisdom and understanding, shouldn't a prayer to God be our first step? As you plan your day and make your decisions, you would do well to "consult the Lord."

Prayer
Father, forgive our foolish self-sufficiency. Teach us a Godly reliance. Amen.

Day 197 — Joshua 10: The Great Day

> "So the sun stood still and the moon stayed in place until the nation of Israel had defeated its enemies. Is this event not recorded in The Book of Jashar? The sun stayed in the middle of the sky, and it did not set as on a normal day. There has never been a day like this one before or since, when the Lord answered such a prayer. Surely the Lord fought for Israel that day!"
> Joshua 10:13-14 (NLT)

Observation
Adoni-zedek, King of Jerusalem, has heard about the defeat of Jericho and Ai and how the Gibeonites have now established a treaty with Israel. He forms an alliance with four other kings in southern Canaan to fight against Gibeon. The Lord tells Joshua to go to battle against this coalition saying that "not a single one of them will be able to stand up against you" (10:20). The battle goes well and the Canaanite kings along with their armies flee in retreat. Joshua prays that the sun will stand still so that the day will be extended, giving the Israelite warriors the opportunity to fully defeat their enemies. God answers his prayer with a supernatural stilling of the sun in the sky.

Application
What would you consider to be the longest day of your life? Most of us would equate the longest day with being the most troubling day we ever experienced. We would point to a day of tragedy when a catastrophic event occurred or when grief came crashing into our lives. We might speak of the day when some life-changing heartache came our way. Rarely do we refer to the longest day as being the best day we've ever lived. We tend to think that painful tedious days seemingly have no end, while days of joy and gladness seem to race by. What seems to creep along, a week at work or a week of vacation?

But for Joshua, the longest day ever was in fact one of his best days. On his "long" day, he defeated five kings, destroyed their armies, and claimed a resounding victory. The truth is that we will have a lot of good days and bad days when time will seem to speed up or slow down. But let's talk for a moment about our best day. The best day you will ever experience is the day when you put your trust and faith in Jesus Christ as your Lord and Savior. That day may have occurred when you were a child or maybe as a teenager at a summer camp. Maybe it happened in college or even later. The point is not *when* it happens, but that it *does* happen. That moment in time, really is a moment when our world stands still. It is the moment when our hope is secured and our destinies are set. You may live 30,000 or even 40,000 days before you are done… but you will never live a greater one. As you remember your great day, praise the God who made it all possible.

Prayer
Of all the days we will ever know, thank you for the one that matters most. Amen.

Day 198 — Joshua 11: Cessation from War

> "So Joshua took control of the entire land, just as the LORD had instructed Moses. He gave it to the people of Israel as their special possession, dividing the land among the tribes. So the land finally had rest from war."
> Joshua 11:23 (NLT)

Observation

As quickly as the kings in the southern Canaanite alliance had been defeated, pressure from the north began to catch the attention of the Israelites. King Jabin of Hazor heard about the defeat in the south and so he began to amass a huge army against Israel that included many kings in the northern region of Canaan. In fact, the Bible describes this huge, combined fighting force as a "vast horde." The Lord instructed Joshua not to be afraid to go to battle against them. By God's strong hand the army of Israel prevailed. In time, the entire region was conquered by Joshua and his army. The land was given to Israel as their "special possession" as described by God. The final verse of the chapter is the one that caught my attention: "the land finally had rest from war."

Application

Recently, I experienced one of those pesky dental problems that took multiple office visits to resolve. First, it was recurrent pain that had no real rhyme or reason. The dentist said to keep watch over time, which I did. Almost six months later the problem resurfaced. To make a long story short, there was an abscess, root canal work, tooth repair, and new crown… a total of five visits to finally have the situation resolved. I still remember the relief I felt when the dentist finally said, "It's all done, and you should be good to go." Whether it's a tooth problem, a relationship that is unsettled, or a financial disruption, most of us have known the anxiety of a slow-to-resolve situation. What a relief when such matters are finally settled. It's good to have some portion of our lives that we can claim to be "at rest." But have you noticed that rarely can we claim perfect peace and rest in our lives for very long? Each day brings challenges and needs. No sooner do we "fix" one problem before a second one tends to surface. So, is there a way, amid daily struggles, to find a lasting peace and contentment? Jesus says "yes." "Then Jesus said, 'Come to me, all of you who are weary and carry heavy burdens, and I will give you rest. Take my yoke upon you. Let me teach you, because I am humble and gentle at heart, and you will find rest for your souls'" (Matthew 11:28-29 NLT). Christ offers us the path to peace. His instruction for us is that we will find the rest we desire as we deepen our relationship with him. Knowing Christ and trusting him more fully each day provides assurance, hope, grace, gladness, forgiveness, and providence. We really can find "rest from war" as we learn the value of trusting him through the experiences of each day.

Prayer

Father, remind us today of the lasting peace and joy of knowing Jesus. Amen.

Day 199 — Joshua 12: Filling the Void

> "In all, thirty-one kings were defeated." Joshua 12:24 (NLT)

Observation
Chapter 12 offers a list of the defeated kings that Israel overthrew during the time of the conquest. The list begins with a brief overview of the two kings conquered by Moses east of the Jordan River prior to the conquest led by Joshua. (Remember that this land was given to the tribes of Rueben, Gad, and the half-tribe of Manasseh.) The remainder of the chapter lists the names of 31 additional kings that were defeated by the Israelite army under the leadership of Joshua. The territory of these 31 kings lay west of the Jordan. It is interesting to consider that most of these kingdoms came into being during the time the Israelites lived for 400 years in bondage in Egypt. God gave victory to the army of Israel because of God's desire to create a nation wholly dedicated to Godself.

Application
Here's what I want you to see as you read the story of the conquest. There were 31 kings and kingdoms residing in the land of Israel at the time of the conquest. Obviously, when the 12 sons of Israel departed the land of Canaan to live in Egypt, a tremendous void was left in the land. In time, the country was overrun, and various clans and tribes began to establish residence in the land. Soon many small nations and city-states were established. So as the void was created, forces moved in to fill that void. Jesus tells a parable that illustrates the same message. "When an evil spirit leaves a person, it goes into the desert, searching for rest. But when it finds none, it says, 'I will return to the person I came from.' So it returns and finds that its former home is all swept and in order. Then the spirit finds seven other spirits more evil than itself, and they all enter the person and live there. And so that person is worse off than before" (Luke 11:24-26 NLT). Here's the point... any void created in our lives will soon be filled by something else. A lot of things compete for our time, energy, and attention. And not all those competing entities are worthy of dwelling in our hearts and minds. As soon as we allow ourselves to be distracted, confused, or despondent, a lot of temptations long to slip through the cracks. If we are not careful to guard our hearts and minds, evil will overtake us, filling the void created when our focus is lost. So how do we keep from allowing a void to be created. It all comes down to spiritual discipline. We have to give constant and careful attention to the things of our faith. We have to read the word. We have to fill our minds with scripture. We have to pray. We have to worship. If we keep filling our lives with the building blocks of faith, we will keep a void from being created. So, guard you heart this morning. Make sure that you haven't left room for something unwanted to slip in.

Prayer
Father, fill our lives to overflowing with your Spirit alone. Amen.

Day 200 — Joshua 13: No Time to Rest

> "When Joshua was an old man, the LORD said to him, 'You are growing old, and much land remains to be conquered.'" Joshua 13:1 (NLT)

Observation
The previous chapter outlined all the territories claimed and all of the kings defeated under the leadership of Joshua. At this point in his life, surely he looks to slow down a bit. The body is tired, the will to fight is diminished, the constant warfare has taken its toll. Joshua has the scars of a long life of harsh conditions and fierce battles. But just as Joshua leans back to savor the successful and victorious life he has lived, suddenly the call of God reverberates in his mind again. God says in essence, "There is still much to be done." God speaks specifically about territory yet unclaimed in the deep south and in the far north. And as always, God promises to "drive the people out of the land ahead of the Israelites" (Joshua 13:6 NLT). (The remainder of the chapter is devoted to a recap of the allotment of land to the 2½ tribes that will settle east of the Jordan.)

Application
As you read this devotional thought you are probably anticipating my thoughts. You probably think, "He's going to hit the theme of senior adults staying active in ministry and in the life of the church." That is certainly an important theme, one that can surely be drawn from this passage, but let me go in a slightly different direction. I think the idea of "resting along the way" has probably found all of us, not just those collecting Social Security. It's human nature. Whenever we accomplish a major victory in our lives, we tend to rest on our laurels and think that maybe we have done enough, at least for now. We take our "foot off the gas" and coast for a while. That's a dangerous posture to take and here's why… the forces of evil are relentless. They never rest. They wait for an opportune time to attack us. And it is when we take our ease, stopping long enough to pat ourselves on the back to congratulate ourselves on all the good that we have done, that we allow the enemy to gain on us. The journey of faith contains no resting places. We must continually move forward in our pursuit of God. That pursuit continues as long as we live. And surely it must continue even today.

Years ago, while a college student, I ran a 5K race on behalf of my fraternity as a part of a field day competition. I jumped out to an early lead. I was leading the field for much of the race. A friend from the cross-country team was helping to pace my steps. But somewhere past the halfway mark I got a little tired. My legs slowed and my mind wanted to rest. I didn't run with the intensity that the race demanded. I was passed and could never reclaim the lead. I finished second. Why? I didn't pay attention to my steps. Run with endurance.

Prayer
Father, give us renewed energy today to run with perseverance and strength. Amen.

Day 201   Joshua 14: Claiming What Is Yours

> "So give me the hill country that the LORD promised me. You will remember that as scouts we found the descendants of Anak living there in great, walled towns. But if the LORD is with me, I will drive them out of the land, just as the LORD said." Joshua 14:12 (NLT)

Observation

This chapter reveals a special request made by Joshua for the portion of land that he and his tribe are to inherit. As the land west of the Jordan is being divided, Caleb reminds Joshua of the promise he once received from Moses. As you may well recall, when Moses sent 12 spies into the promised land to bring back an assessment of strength, military might, and the fertility of the land, only Caleb was quick to say that if the Lord would lead the battle, the Israelites could take the land. It was the report of the other 10 spies who convinced the nation not to attack which resulted in a 40-year waiting period. Now at the age of 85, Caleb reminds Joshua of the promise once made to him. Joshua honors the promise and grants the land.

Application

At some point in our lives, each of us has been promised to receive something from someone else. Maybe you were promised a reward for making good grades in school. Maybe your boss promised you a raise. Maybe you were promised a car on your sixteenth birthday. Perhaps someone has promised to take you on a wonderful vacation. We count on the promises made to us being kept. And when the promises are fulfilled, there is such excitement and joy. So, go back and read the focus verse for today and notice who once gave a promise to Caleb… "So give me the hill country that the Lord promised me." God made the promise, and because God is absolutely trustworthy, the promise was kept and the land was given to Caleb. Do I need to remind you this morning that the same God has made promises to you… a lot of them? And knowing that God is trustworthy, we revel in the joy of knowing every promise made to us will be kept. Every promise. Let's name a few. God has promised eternal life to those who trust in Christ as Savior and Lord. God has promised to forgive us of our sins, completely erasing the sins from God's mind if we will confess our sins. God has promised continual presence of the indwelling Holy Spirit. God has promised to hear our prayers. God has promised to supply all our needs according to God's riches. God has promised the power to overcome temptation. God has promised wisdom. The list goes on and on. It should encourage you this morning to know that the God who makes those promises has the power and will to bring every one of them to fruition. God is absolutely trustworthy. You will receive all that God has promised.

Prayer

Father, we are blessed by your promises and grateful for each one. Amen.

Day 202 — Joshua 15: Claiming the Prize

> "Caleb said, 'I will give my daughter Acsah in marriage to the one who attacks and captures Kiriath-sepher.'" Joshua 15:16 (NLT)

Observation
The narrative of this chapter is specific to the allotment of land given to the tribe of Judah. All the boundaries are well defined along with the many cities included in each territory. The city of Jerusalem is specifically mentioned as one of these key cities. Contained within the narrative is a side story about the land given to Caleb, which falls within this territory. Caleb promises his daughter Acsah in marriage to the one who will attack and capture the city of Kiriath-sepher. Othniel wins the battle and claims the prize.

Application
If we are honest, most of us like to be rewarded for the things we have accomplished. A little recognition goes a long way and so when deserved, we enjoy having a new plaque on the wall or a trophy on the shelf and maybe a little bonus in our pay. Sometimes, it is the incentive of receiving an award that gives us the energy and initiative to do really good work.

In this story, the reward for winning the battle was the gift of a bride. Though it is not told in the narrative, Othniel may have fought a little harder and planned a bit more carefully, knowing that such a wonderful prize awaited him. Having Acsah as his wife was the incentive needed to push forward into victory.

Maybe it helps each of us to know that a reward awaits all of us who labor long and hard at our faith. Paul talked about it… "I press on toward the goal to win the prize for which God has called me heavenward in Christ Jesus" (Philippians 3:14 NIV). For all of us, there is an incentive to guard our hearts, to protect our minds, and to safeguard our lives. The reward is to know Christ and to enjoy life with him forever. We labor for the kingdom that is to come. We practice our faith and power through our battles with evil so that we will win the prize. There is no greater reward than to claim the eternal life that God, through Christ, wills for us to enjoy.

Sometimes there is a tedium to our walk of faith. Admittedly, we all hit those dry spots. We grow weary of worship and tired of the daily disciplines of prayer and meditation. Sometimes the words of scripture just don't seem to fit our situation for the day. And yet we are to press on. It's the promise of the reward that keeps our feet moving and our journey on track. So be encouraged today, even if your walk of faith seems a bit stalled. Keep chasing the dream of knowing Christ and the reward most assuredly will come.

Prayer
Father, we thank you today for the prize we will one day claim as the result of our faith. Amen.

Day 203 — Joshua 16: Flirting with Danger

> "They did not drive the Canaanites out of Gezer, however, so the people of Gezer live as slaves among the people of Ephraim to this day."
> Joshua 16:10 (NLT)

Observation
Chapter 16 describes the allotment of land given to the tribes of Manasseh and Ephraim. As in the previous chapter, exacting details are given concerning the boundary lines for each territory. (I encourage you to turn to the map in the back of your Bible or go online and get a visual frame of reference as to how all the tribes were positioned after the time of the conquest.) Our focus verse references the town of Gezer. Gezer was a large and important Canaanite town at the juncture of the coastal plain and the hill country. It apparently will not become Israel's possession until the time of King Solomon. As you will recall, God had instructed the Israelites to completely overthrow the nations and people groups that inhabited the land. Why then did they fail to fully conqueror this city? Some suggest that it was a matter of battle fatigue. Others suggest that it could be a lack of faith that prevented an overthrow. Here's why it matters… Even though the population became the slaves of Israel, their presence in and around the people of God opened the door to the strong influence of pagan culture and worship practices.

Application
There's an old proverb that goes something like this… "If you let a camel stick his head under the flap of your tent, pretty soon you will have a camel in your tent." I like the image of that proverb. There is a lot of wisdom in that expression. It speaks of the power of temptation in our lives. If we dare begin flirting with temptation… even if we just allow ourselves to start playing with the possibilities in our minds… soon we will be numbered as a victim of temptation's unrelenting draw. That's why Jesus once counseled his followers with these words, "But I tell you that anyone who looks at a woman lustfully has already committed adultery with her in his heart" (Matthew 5:28 NIV). Jesus knew that the journey from thought to action was a very short path. He understood that poor behavior begins with the first wayward thought. When the ancient Israelites failed to remove the Canaanites completely from their midst, they opened themselves up to a dangerous pagan mindset. It begs the question for us… "What temptations are we currently allowing to hang around in our minds and hearts?" Are there thoughts, situations, flirtations, or temptations that you are still allowing to have access to your psyche? As hard as it is to say no to temptation, it is much harder to clean-up the debris that such devastation leaves in its wake. Be strong. Just say no.

Prayer
Heavenly Father, keep us strong and faithful amid the temptations that bombard our lives each day. Amen.

Day 204 — Joshua 17: Own a Piece of the Rock

> "These women came to Eleazar the priest, Joshua son of Nun, and the Israelite leaders and said, 'The LORD commanded Moses to give us a grant of land along with the men of our tribe.' So Joshua gave them a grant of land along with their uncles, as the LORD had commanded."
> Joshua 17:4 (NLT)

Observation

This chapter continues the allotment of land to the various tribes. The narrative begins with the allotment given to the half-tribe of Manasseh. (Remember that half of the tribe had previously received a portion of land on the east side of the Jordan.) Within the extended tribe was a family headed by a man named Zelophehad, who had no sons. His daughters came before Joshua to remind him that the Lord, through Moses, had promised that they would receive an allotment of land. Joshua heard their petition and granted them an appropriate allotment. (The remainder of the chapter continues the details of land distribution among the various tribes.)

Application

I must admit that my heart and mind resonate a little with the daughters of Zelophehad. I understand their desire to own a little land, to have a portion of ground that they can call their own. Maybe it's a security thing… but I feel the same longing. Some little voice deep down inside tells me that I should own some land… that I should have a plot of ground to call my own. To be clear, I do own the ¼ acre that my house rests upon. But I really want to have a little more… maybe a field somewhere, a small pasture, a wooded parcel or maybe even some mountain acreage or a beach front strip of land. My desire is not to develop the real estate into some commercial concern, but to just have a few acres to call my own. I can't really explain that longing, but I'd love to have a few acres.

The truth of the matter is that I probably won't ever do that. There are still too many student loans, mortgage payments, and day-to-day needs to absorb my paycheck. Please don't get me wrong… I am extremely grateful for all that I own and feel blessed to experience the life that I do. Maybe it's a matter of perspective about which I need to be reminded. Jesus said, "Watch out! Be on your guard against all kinds of greed; life does not consist in an abundance of possessions" (Luke 12:15 NIV). Sometimes I need the reminder, and maybe you do as well, that the value and worth of my life is not found in things I possess or property that I own. My value and worth are found in my relationship with Jesus Christ. Because I have been claimed by him, I have been adopted into God's family. Why worry about a few acres when I'm a joint heir to all the riches of God's glory?

Prayer

Father God, thank you for our blessings, both those we now hold and those we will hold. Amen.

Day 205 — Joshua 18: More than a Coin Toss

> "And when you record the seven divisions of the land and bring them to me, I will cast sacred lots in the presence of the LORD our God to assign land to each tribe." Joshua 18:6 (NLT)

Observation

Chapters 18 and 19 of the Book of Joshua describe the allotment of land for the remaining seven tribes. In order to give equity and ownership to those involved, Joshua sends out 21 men, three from each tribe, to map out the land and to divide it into seven equal parcels. Joshua indicates that once the land is surveyed, that he will assign the various portions by casting sacred lots. As the will of the Lord is determined through this process, the land will be distributed accordingly.

A word about the casting of lots… most of you are somewhat familiar with the process. It is mentioned 70 times in the Old Testament. Although precise details are not offered, the process most likely involved a small container with two stones, perhaps one white and the other black. The stones would be placed in the container, shaken, and then poured out on the ground. Based on how the stones fell, the direction of God's plan was determined. I often tell Old Testament classes that I teach that the process was sort of a "holy rolling of the dice." But certainly, it was more than that. It was recognition of the limits of human wisdom. When a decision had to be made, and those making the decision lacked discernment, they would pray and ask God for God's will to be made evident through the casting of the lots. It was a total reliance upon God's perceived will. It was as though they acknowledged, "God, we cannot discern the choice to be made. We will accept whatever direction you determine."

Application

Have you ever been faced with a tough decision and you can't decide what to do? How do you resolve such a dilemma, especially when it's a choice of two really good options? Sometimes we ask for someone's opinion, or we make a list of pros and cons, or maybe we just flip a coin. Decision making can be difficult. Is there a better way? Jesus says, "But when he, the Spirit of truth, comes, he will guide you into all the truth" (John 16:13 NIV). Jesus promised that when the Holy Spirit came to indwell human flesh, that he would guide each of us in all truth. Christians believe that at the moment of our conversion we receive the Holy Spirit. That means the source of all wisdom and knowledge is already inside each of us. So, when dilemmas come and hard decisions are unclear, we are to pray with intentionality, asking the Spirit to reveal in both quiet and vivid ways, the direction we are to take. So, if you are facing a huge decision today, don't reach for the dice… call out to the Spirit.

Prayer

Father God, thank you for the gift of the Holy Spirit and the wisdom he provides. Amen.

Day 206 — Joshua 19: The Mighty Oak

> "Its boundary ran from Heleph, from the oak at Zaanannim, and extended across to Adami-nekeb, Jabneel, and as far as Lakkum, ending at the Jordan River." Joshua 19:33 (NLT)

Observation
Joshua 19 describes the final allotment of land given to the remaining six tribes: Simeon, Zebulon, Issachar, Asher, Naphtali, and Dan. Both territory and towns were described in each allotment. At the end of the chapter, a special allotment is set aside for Joshua as the Lord had promised. He selects the city Timnatha-serah in the hill country and rebuilds it. Typically, when the land tracts are described they are defined by rivers, brooks, seas, mountains, cities, etc. There is usually some very specific geographic marker to define the border. But notice in our focus verse, that part of the border of Naphtali's portion is defined by an oak tree. It's like Joshua said, "Go to that big oak tree and take a left." My guess is that it must have been a very prominent feature on the landscape, known to all who traveled that way.

Application
Got a favorite tree? That may sound like a weird question, but most of us have a tree or two that we like to see in the fall or in whose shade we like to rest in the summer. Maybe you have tree in the back of your memory that you climbed as a child. I remember visiting my maternal grandparents as kid. They lived in Orlando, Florida. One of the local city parks had a huge Osage Orange tree that we used to visit. Once, while on a trip out west, my family visited the huge redwood trees of California. A bit closer to home, there are some trees in my neighborhood that have such rich color in the fall and beautiful blossoms in the spring. I always notice them. Until recently we had Bradford pear tree in our front yard. It split one night with several large branches landing on my car. The rest had to be cut down and the stump removed. It is surprising to me how differently the landscape looks with the yard now missing one of its residents. Sometimes I think about the great men and women of faith who were once a part of my family. I think about their influence, direction, and counsel. They stood among us like strong and sturdy oaks. I miss them now that they are gone. I think of men and woman like my grandparents who lived such strong lives of faith that their influence is still felt in my life today. I don't know about you, but I want to be that kind of person in the life of my children and grandchildren. I want to be the strong oak for my generation. It won't happen by accident. Influencing the faith of others requires a consistent living of the faith in my life. And so, I practice the disciplines of faith each day. I want to continue to grow strong in the Lord so that others might do the same.

Prayer
Father God, make us like a strong and mighty oak of faith. Amen.

Day 207 — Joshua 20: Run for Your Life

> "Anyone who kills another person accidentally and unintentionally can run to one of these cities; they will be places of refuge from relatives seeking revenge for the person who was killed." Joshua 20:3 (NLT)

Observation

Back in the book of Numbers, Chapter 35, God had instructed Moses concerning cities of refuge that were to be established within Israel. The purpose is explained in the final verse of our focus chapter. "These cities were set apart for all the Israelites as well as the foreigners living among them. Anyone who accidentally killed another person could take refuge in one of these cities. In this way, they could escape being killed in revenge prior to standing trial before the local assembly" (20:9 NLT). There were six cities designated as cities of refuge, located strategically throughout the land. Offenders could find refuge and protection in these cities until they could be properly judged. If the crime was indeed an accident, they could live in these cities without threat of revenge until the High Priest serving at the time passed away. At his death, they could return to their hometown having been proven innocent.

Application

The law indicated that a person caught in the predicament of having taken a life accidentally and unintentionally, could run to one of these cities. I tend to think that is a very literal statement. In my mind's eye, I can envision a person, upon discovering what he has done, literally dropping everything and running for his life to one of these cities. There would be no time to pack, say goodbyes, or make provision for the journey. Just run! As soon as a blood relative of the deceased heard the news, surely, he would come running to enact revenge. There may have been incidences where the person fleeing for their lives made it to the city just a few strides ahead of his pursuer.

I hope I never have to experience something like that in my lifetime. I pray there is never a moment when I have to literally outrun someone who wants to take my life. What a frightening prospect that would be. But equally as frightening is this verse from the writings of Peter. "Stay alert! Watch out for your great enemy, the devil. He prowls around like a roaring lion, looking for someone to devour" (1 Peter 5:8 NLT). As believers, we need to be awakened to the dangers around us. We need to remember that Satan longs to disrupt our relationship with God. He longs to "devour" us. The good news is that we have a city of refuge towards which we can run. His name is Jesus. Though the enemy pursues us, his protection is sufficient. "Greater is he who is in you than he who is in the world" (1 John 4:4 NASB). Christ alone is our true refuge and our strength. Run to him this day and every day.

Prayer

Father God, thank you for your watch care and protection over us. Amen.

Day 208   Joshua 21: The Joy of a Promise Kept

> "Not a single one of all the good promises the LORD had given to the family of Israel was left unfulfilled; everything he had spoken came true."
> Joshua 21:45 (NLT)

Observation
All 12 tribes of Israel were allotted portions of land after the conquest was complete except for the tribe of Levi. The Levites had been set aside by God as the Priestly tribe. God had commanded Moses that towns and pasturelands be given to them from within the various territories inhabited by the other 11 tribes. This chapter names the towns given to the Levites as their possession. Joshua cast lots to determine which towns were included. According to the record, a total of 48 towns and surrounding pasturelands were transferred to the Levites. The chapter ends with our focus verse which is somewhat of a summation of the Joshua narrative. The land had been conquered and the people had taken possession of towns and cities. All that God had promised had come to fulfillment.

Application
Anyone can make a promise. It is in the keeping of a promise where both the giver and the recipient find joy. For the past 32 years, I have known the joy of preaching each Sunday. Over the course of those years, I pastored five different congregations. But to each congregation I made a promise. The promise was to always be prepared every time I stepped into the pulpit. I promised that I would always take the time needed to spend moments in God's word so that when I stood to preach the following Sunday, I would always have a fresh message from God to share. It has brought me such a sense of joy and fulfillment to have faithfully kept that promise. I hope that it blessed the people to whom I preached each week. There is great joy in a promise kept.

Consider for a moment the really big promises that you have made to others and to yourself. Promises to be true to your convictions, to be consistent in your faith disciplines, to be loyal in your friendships, or to be faithful in your marriage vows. How well we keep our promises displays much about our character. We should be careful about the promises we make and dedicated to fulfilling each one. Our goal should be that of imitating our Heavenly Father, about whom it was said, "Not a single one of all the good promises the Lord had given to the family of Israel was left unfulfilled; everything He had spoken came true." Pray today that God would give you the strength and courage to keep all your promises, both great and small.

Prayer
Dear Father, we are grateful that you are always trustworthy and that every promise you make is kept. Help us to live with the same resolve. Amen.

Day 209 — Joshua 22: Crisis Averted

> "Far be it from us to rebel against the LORD or turn away from him by building our own altar for burnt offerings, grain offerings, or sacrifices. Only the altar of the LORD our God that stands in front of the Tabernacle may be used for that purpose." Joshua 22:29 (NLT)

Observation
With the conquest finally complete, the eastern tribes of Reuben, Gad, and Manasseh, are blessed by Joshua and sent home. He praises their efforts and loyalty and tells them to share the plunder they have accumulated with their relatives once they return home. These soldiers stop on the way back to build an altar at a place called Geliloth. The rest of Israel is greatly offended by their actions. They cannot imagine that fellow Israelites would build any altar other than the one in front of the tabernacle. In fact, they are ready to go to war with these three tribes fearful that God would impose wrath on all of Israel because of their sinful actions. These three tribes answer critics by informing them that the altar is not for sacrificial purposes but is simply a memorial… a reminder and witness that the tribes on the eastern side of the Jordan will continue to have full access to worship privileges at the tabernacle. Once the explanation is given, all the tribes depart in peace.

Application
This story is a powerful reminder of what happens when there is a lack of communication. This crisis began with misinformation, false assumptions, and wrong perceptions. The nation of Israel nearly broke out in civil war because of the misunderstanding. Once cooler heads prevailed, anger and thoughts of battle began to dissipate. Many areas of conflict continue to arise when there is a lack of communication. When messages and motives are not clearly announced, it is easy for others to form opinions or have thoughts that may or may not be accurate. The solution, long before problems begin to escalate, is in learning how to communicate effectively. All of us have either been misunderstood or we have misunderstood others. Are there ways to improve the lines of communication within a marriage, family, or organization so that problems are minimized? Yes. Here are a few tips. #1—Always communicate face-to-face whenever possible. Words posted on social media or sent in a text can be misread or misunderstood. Therefore, talk directly to someone whenever possible. #2—Communicate with clear language and easy-to-understand facts. Always try to state your message as clearly as you possibly can. #3—If you are a listener, don't be afraid to use a feedback loop. "This is what I hear you saying… is that correct?" #4—If the level of conflict is already making the dialogue difficult, don't be afraid to ask a third-party to help. The third-party is not present to take sides, but to offer clearer communication.

Prayer
Dear God, help us to learn the art of clear communication with you and with others.

Day 210 — Joshua 23: Got Any Enemies?

> "Each one of you will put to flight a thousand of the enemy, for the LORD your God fights for you, just as he has promised." Joshua 23:10 (NLT)

Observation

The final two chapters of Joshua consist of Joshua's farewell speech to the nation. He is described in verse 2 as being "very old." It is clear that his days are numbered, so he longs to offer final words of instruction and advice. He calls together all the elders, leaders, judges, and officers of Israel. He reminds them to be careful to follow everything in the Book of Instruction that Moses had given them. He also warns against intermarriage with the survivors of the nations now conquered that still live among the Israelites. Their worship practices and false gods could be a "snare and a trap" for Israel. Notice the promise made in our focus verse. Joshua reminds the people that God will continue to lead them and fight for them in battle as always.

Application

What a great promise is offered to the people of God in this verse. With God's Spirit deeply embedded within us, and with our allegiance firmly declared in God's sovereignty, God will go before us in the battles that we face. Each of us will put to flight "a thousand of the enemy." Got any enemies hanging around your life these days? For most of us the enemies are not flesh and blood men and women draped in battle attire. I don't leave my house each day worried about the Canaanites, Hittites, or even the Philistines. The enemies I face are different. I face the enemies of greed, guilt, and temptation. I battle the enemies of jealousy, envy, and anger. I take on the enemies of shame, remorse, and hopelessness. There are many others out there as well. Surely you can name several. But look again at the promise… with God's intervention in our lives, each of us can put to flight a thousand of the enemy. As long as there are enemies that seek to destroy the people of God, there will always be God's empowerment to defeat every single one. Even when the odds seem overwhelming and our resources seem depleted, still the enemies will fall. So how do we win the day-to-day battles? First, we awaken to acknowledge each morning that God's Spirit indwells our lives. We have power. Second, we arm ourselves with truth. We "load-up" with God's word and let it speak to every situation. Third, we pray for discernment to both see the enemy and engage the battle. We give attention to that which seeks to destroy us. And fourth, we claim the promise that with each battle, the way of escape is provided (1 Corinthians 10:13). Enemies can only have the power over us that we allow them to have. God's Spirit will grant victory if we seek God's strength and yield our lives to God's authority. Get ready… there are battles to face… and win today.

Prayer

Dear Father, thank you for the ability we have to defeat our enemies today. Amen.

Day 211 — Joshua 24: A Stone of Testimony

> "Joshua said to all the people, 'This stone has heard everything the LORD said to us. It will be a witness to testify against you if you go back on your word to God.'" Joshua 24:27 (NLT)

Observation
As the chapter opens, Joshua gathers all the nation together at Shechem to offer his final words of instruction and challenge. He recounts all the history of Israel from the days of Abraham to the present day. He reminds them to fear and serve the Lord. Embedded in his words is that very familiar challenge… "Choose today whom you will serve. …as for me and my family, we will serve the LORD" (24:15) The people swear their allegiance to God and promise to follow all of God's ways. Joshua takes a huge stone and rolls it beneath the terebinth tree just beside the tabernacle of the Lord. He reminds the Israelites that this stone has heard their words of commitment before the Lord and will testify against them if they break their vow. Joshua dies at the age of 110 and is buried.

Application
You've heard the old expression… "If these walls could talk…" But let me change it up a bit. "What if this stone could talk?" Joshua placed a stone, a permanent and lasting reminder, in a place where the people would be forced to remember their promise before God. Joshua said it would testify, or bear witness, if they failed to honor God.

I have a stone in my front yard. It's a small, rounded chunk of Georgia granite. It was in my father's yard for a number of years and now he has passed it on to me. (It's a long story…) I did a little research on the rock and discovered that it is more than 4 million years old. At some point it surely rested in a riverbed. It has been worn smooth by the water's flow. Every day it sits undisturbed in my front yard, close to the door of our home. Each time I exit or enter, it sees my steps and knows of my journey. If God gave it voice, what would it say about my life and the journeys I have taken? Would it testify that I have been faithful and loyal to Christ? Would it declare that I have been trustworthy and kind? Would it speak of compassion for my neighbors and service to my community? Would I want it to speak, or would I prefer it to keep silent?

Most of us would not fare well under the constant scrutiny of an ever-present, watchful eye. If indeed, someone watched all our days, there would be moments about which we would be proud and then there would be those days that we would long to forget. God sees it all, and really does know each step, hear each word, and see each action. But through it all, God loves us still. God forgives. God redeems. God claims us. Let us today find comfort in God's continual presence in our lives, and joy in God's continual grace.

Prayer
Dear Father, thank you for your watch care and your healing grace. Amen.

Day 212   Judges 1: The Strong Power of a Little Compromise

> "It came about, when Israel became strong, that they put the Canaanites to forced labor; but they did not drive them out completely."
> Judges 1:28 (NASB)

Observation
When the Israelites entered the promised land under the leadership of Joshua, God told them to drive out their enemies completely from the land. They were to leave no trace of the people who once lived in the land. They were to tear down their cities, destroy the altars to pagan deities, and completely remove the people from the land. It was God's intention that the Israelites would create for themselves a land that was solely dedicated to God... one that had no trace of the former inhabitants who worshipped false idols. Our focus verse encapsulates a problem that would plague Israel for much of the next 400 years. Because of their unwillingness and inability to completely drive away the pagan nations, they would know little peace as these people continued to produce conflict in the land.

Application
God had given the Israelites a formula for success. They were to rid the land of all the evil influences. Altars to pagan deities, places of worship to false idols, and even those who gave allegiance to such things were to be removed. God desired the sole focus of the people and their nation. Their lack of attention to God's directive would lead to years of trouble and warfare.

The story of the ancient Israelites should speak strongly to each of us. God desires our hearts and minds completely. God desires pure worship and fidelity. And so, we must carefully guard the influences that shape our daily lives. We live with the false notion that a little compromise won't hurt a thing. We relax our values and water down our ethics. We give God most of our lives and most of our allegiances, but not all. We retain small pockets of selfishness and a few areas of self-rule that we refuse to surrender. In not giving ourselves fully to God, we allow room for the enemy to quietly gain a foothold. We fail to understand that even a little compromise produces a great weakness in each of us. The challenge is to live fully for God without even a hint of compromise. Take a moment this morning and check for the weak places in your armor of faith. Are there places where you will confess your vulnerability? Do you have areas of your life that are not under the Spirit's control? God is Lord of all or not Lord at all. Devote the entirety of your life to God and leave no space for compromise.

Prayer
Father, may your will be done in us completely this day. May we forever rid ourselves of the compromise that can destroy our faith. Amen.

Day 213 — Judges 2: Stubborn Grace for Stubborn People

> "But it came about when the judge died, that they would turn back and act more corruptly than their fathers, in following other gods to serve them and bow down to them; they did not abandon their practices or their stubborn ways." Judges 2:19 (NASB)

Observation
During the time of the Judges, the people of Israel surely tested God's patience. Because of their disobedience and worship of false gods, God allowed the Israelites to fall under various oppressive nations or groups of people. The Israelites would then cry out to God, and God would raise up a "judge" or "deliverer" to free them once again. But not many days later, they would fall into the same pattern of disobedient behavior. In fact, the book of Judges displays a cyclical pattern of 13 various judges, called to deliver Israel each time the nation faltered. We read the story of the Israelites and wonder how they could behave in the way that they did. They had known the blessings of God. They had seen God's miraculous work with their own eyes. They knew that pursuing God with all their might would bring blessing and success. And yet, time and again, they wandered away and then in desperation, they called out to God for help once again.

Application
I'd like to think that modern-day God-followers have long since left such ridiculous behavior behind. But the truth is, we are not much better than the ancient Israelites. How many times do we find ourselves in jeopardy because we have chosen to live outside of God's guidelines? How often have we become so obstinate that we choose self-sufficiency over God-dependency? And then, when life gets way out of balance, how many times do we call on God to "pull us out of our troubles" once again? I have a friend who struggles with alcohol abuse. It's an addiction that has plagued his life for years. He lost his job, his home, and almost his marriage because of that powerful influence in his life. I don't mention him to judge him in any way, but to use his story as an example. Each time his behavior brings his life to a crisis point, he resolves to do better and to get the help he needs. He wants to be rescued. And then the addictive demons take hold of him once again. Family and friends are wearied by his renewed promises and repetitive actions. In like fashion, surely it must frustrate the heart of God when we abuse grace by seeking forgiveness without really seeking to change our ways. Yes, God loves us intensely and forgives us abundantly, and longs to set us free from our sins. But maybe it's time for us to seek ways to stop the cycle of temptation in our lives that seems to always pull us in the wrong direction. May we be as relentless in our fight against sin as God is relentless in offering grace.

Prayer
Father God, convict us. Forgive us. Heal us. Amen.

Day 214

Judges 3: A Failure to Act

> "So the people of Israel lived among the Canaanites, Hittites, Amorites, Perizzites, Hivites, and Jebusites, and they intermarried with them. Israelite sons married their daughters, and Israelite daughters were given in marriage to their sons. And the Israelites served their gods." Judges 3:5-6 (NLT)

Observation

Chapter 3 opens with these words, "These are the nations that the Lord left in the land to test those Israelites who had not experienced the wars of Canaan. He did this to teach warfare to generations of Israelites who had no experience in battle" (3:1-2). It is clear that there are still nations within the land that need to be defeated by the people of God. In particular, the Philistines, Canaanites, Sidonians, and the Hivites remain. The problem with not ridding the land of these people is told in our focus verses. Sons and daughters began to intermarry with the people of these various tribes and in so doing, they began to adopt pagan influences, including the worship of their false gods. Soon, the Israelites will find themselves oppressed. The remainder of the chapter tells the stories of the first two judges of Israel, Othniel and Ehud.

Application

Once a year I visit the dermatologist. He takes a few moments to scan my skin for potential problem areas. I am fair-skinned and blonde-haired and throughout life spent many days in the sun. So, skin cancers are a very real concern. From time to time he finds a spot and removes it. On a few occasions, when the report comes back a little suspect, he goes in a little deeper to make sure that all the potentially dangerous cells are removed. I appreciate his thorough treatment. It's the same way with sin in our lives. Until we become serious about changing the patterns, influences, and situations in our lives that lead us into temptation, the battle will continue. Here's the problem… we go to the Lord with a repentant heart. We are grieved by the sin in our lives. We recognize that we have made poor choices and we beg for a second chance. And then it happens… we quickly drift right back into the same patterns of poor choices. That scenario will continue over and over again until we finally learn the lesson of completely removing the factors that cause our sinful condition. When Jesus spoke on this same topic, he said to take radical steps like these… "And if your eye causes you to sin, gouge it out. It's better to enter the Kingdom of God with only one eye than to have two eyes and be thrown into hell" (Mark 9:47 NLT). Jesus was not instructing us to purposefully maim our bodies, but he did want us to understand the serious nature of repetitive sin and how we must take deliberate steps to win the battle. Examine your life this morning. What are the areas you need to address? Maybe you need to take some drastic steps.

Prayer

Father God, help us to see those things that lead us to sin so that we can change. Amen.

Day 215 — Judges 4: Busting the Stereotypes

> "Now Deborah, a prophetess, the wife of Lappidoth, was judging Israel at that time. She used to sit under the palm tree of Deborah between Ramah and Bethel in the hill country of Ephraim; and the sons of Israel came up to her for judgment." Judges 4:4-5 (NASB)

Observation
In the listing of the judges of Israel who brought deliverance from oppression, the third whose story is told is named Deborah. There are a few noteworthy things to consider. First, she is a woman. In a culture dominated by men, God raised up a woman to be the key leader of Israel and through whom God would bring deliverance. Second, she is also a prophetess. God's Spirit is in her in a unique way among the people of the land so that she could function in the role of a prophet. She should foretell the truth of God and foretell the events that God was going to bring to pass. Third, she had the respect of the people. Everyone came to her for judgement. They received counsel from her wisdom and knowledge.

Application
Here again is the great lesson that God can call whomever God chooses to accomplish whatever God wills to accomplish. We tend to get a little bogged down in gender roles and function, especially in the life and work of the church. There are roles that we tend to limit only to men, or certain functions that we will only assign to women. Even our mission boards get a little gender biased when it comes to the people they will send and those they will not. Maybe the role of the church is to affirm and not to judge. Maybe our role as the people of faith is to acknowledge the unique gifts and talents that God has placed in each person and then to give those individuals the avenues to serve where their gifts can best be used. My father, who has long mentored me in the faith, used to say, "The shape of one's anatomy should not determine the extent of God's calling in one's life."

My goal this morning is not to advocate nor judge who should serve in what capacity in the life of any one local church. I very much believe in the autonomy of the local church, meaning that with guidance of the Spirit, each church should choose its own leadership. What I am suggesting is an exciting, open-mindedness to see in every person both God's giftedness and God's calling. So, don't label me as a liberal... just as a person who takes the message of scripture seriously. With all that needs to be done for the world-wide cause of Christ, I can't imagine that we would want to exclude half of all potential harvest workers.

Prayer
Father, thank you for calling and equipping all of us to places of kingdom service. Amen.

Day 216 — Judges 5: Sunrise, Sunset

> "'Thus let all Your enemies perish, O LORD;
> But let those who love Him be like the rising of the sun in its might.'
> And the land was undisturbed for forty years." Judges 5:31 (NASB)

Observation
In case you didn't read the entire fifth chapter of Judges, you need to know that it is an extended song of praise. In the song, Deborah, the Judge of Israel, and her General, Barak, recount the heroic deeds of Jael, who killed the Canaanite king whose name was Sisera. Jael, who was not Jewish, used a tent-peg to kill the Canaanite general as he lay sleeping in her tent. Thus, the song is an offering of praise to God for deliverance that came at the hands of Jael. The image that drew my attention as I read this chapter is this closing line from the song itself, "Let those who love Him (God) be like the rising of the sun in its might."

Application
Let's chase that image for a moment. How are the people of God similar to the rising of the sun? First, there is great power as the sun climbs its way above the horizon. The sun peaks and the morning sky comes to life. Invested in the people of God is the power of the Lord. As God's people arise and awaken to their tasks, the power of God is displayed through every life, changing hearts, attitudes, and nations. As the sun rises, there is also this shattering of darkness as the light appears. Again, as the people of God live fully the life God has invested in their hearts, the darkness of this world begins to shatter. The light of Christ dispels the night and quickly chases away evil from every crevice and cranny. Third, the sun rises with amazing consistency. Each day it is the same... The sun rises and sets as it remains steadfast in its course. Would that we, as the people of God, should display such consistency. It is as we live out our faith day to day, through such consistent behavior and role-modeling, that our world is forever impacted.

There is also embedded within the imagery of the rising sun, a call to unity. Our power and strength come as we labor together and celebrate the common cause of living our Christian faith before the world. I am reminded that none of us are called to change the world alone. We join forces with all the saints of God scattered around the globe... ALL those who love God are like the rising sun.

A new day has begun. The sun has once again arisen as I look out my window. It is another day for God's people to change the world... for you to change your world.

Prayer
Father, thank you for investing in us, your power and might. May we live boldly and consistently the life you ordain for each of us. Amen.

Day 217 — Judges 6: The Quest for Proof

> "Behold, I will put a fleece of wool on the threshing floor. If there is dew on the fleece only, and it is dry on all the ground, then I will know that You will deliver Israel through me, as You have spoken." Judges 6:37 (NASB)

Observation
The next judge of Israel whom God raised to free the Israelites from the oppression of the Midianites was named Gideon. The angel of God told Gideon that he would lead the people in battle. To truly convince himself that God was with him, Gideon asked God for a sign. Gideon told God that he would place a wool fleece on the threshing floor. If, on the next morning, the fleece was wet with dew while all the surrounding ground was dry, then Gideon would know that God was indeed with him. The next morning, the dry was ground, but Gideon squeezed a bowl full of water from the fleece.

Application
Let's be honest, sometimes we too need a little convincing. There are those moments when we want to cry out to God and ask for a tangible, visible sign. We say things like this, "Just show me a sign that you are real and I will follow. Just give me a sign and I will do your work. Just perform a miracle and I will do whatever you ask." Sound familiar? Most of us have had such a conversation with God. We want to condition our faith on what we can see and touch and experience. It's the old "If, then" scenario that we offer to God. "If you will show me a sign, then I will do what you ask. If you give me a sign, then I will know the answer." Is that really the way we should respond to God's leadership? Are we really in a position to put God to the test? Should we really threaten disobedience if God doesn't act on our whim for a sign?

The truth is that God will give us a sign if needed. If God needs to work through a miracle, God will display it. But it is not our place to demand anything of God. Who are we that we should paint God into some tiny corner and demand a "dog and pony" show? If we can only believe in what we can see, then where is the element of faith? Paul reminds us that we "walk by faith and not by sight." So maybe, instead of pleading for a sign before we will become compliant, we should become compliant in order to discover where and how God is already at work in our world. What we really need is not a sign from God, but rather a bold and mature faith that reveals God to us even in the absence of some miraculous deed.

Prayer
Father, thank you for making yourself known to each of us as we are careful to trust you with each step of our journey. Amen.

Day 218   Judges 7: More Than You Think

> "He divided the 300 men into three companies, and he put trumpets and empty pitchers into the hands of all of them, with torches inside the pitchers." Judges 7:16 (NASB)

Observation
Chapter 7 relates the battle scene when Gideon leads the Israelites in victory over the Midiannites. Rather than say that Gideon led the battle, it is certainly more correct to say that God led the battle. The battle is truly a miraculous moment. I want you to notice what the 300 men of Israel took with them into battle. Trumpets and empty pitchers. No swords. No battle axes. No chariots. Just trumpets and empty pitchers. In the middle of the night, when Gideon gave the signal, all the men blew their trumpets, shouted a war cry, and broke the pitchers they had in their hands. The loud sound brought such confusion in the middle of the night that the Midiannites actually grabbed their own swords and ran wildly in the night, killing each other.

Application
Amazing, isn't it, what God places in our hands to do God's will. Imagine how something as simple as a trumpet and a water pitcher could be used of God to defeat a mighty army. God used 300 courageous men to do something great. So often we look at our small resources and cower in fear declaring that our materials are too limited and our power too small. We question what God can do. Have we not read the story of Gideon? Have we not read the story of the feeding of the 5000? Do we not yet realize that God can take the small and simple things and do great and powerful acts with them? I wonder what you hold in your hand this morning... What resources are at your disposal. Chances are you probably have more than a trumpet and a water pitcher. You probably have things like a wallet, a car, a cell phone, a few friends, the ability to read and write, maybe a Bible, a job skill, or a pair of good work gloves. Can you image what God could do with your life if you were just willing to commit all that you have into God's hands? What if you offered the simple things in your hands to the glory of God? What armies could be defeated? What darkness shattered? Let's stop talking about our limited resources and start talking about the power of God.

    Do a little asset mapping this morning. Name three resources you have at your disposal today. And then ask, "How can I use them in a way to further the work of the kingdom?" It is one thing to remind yourself of the tools you hold in your hand... it is another to apply them to the work that needs to be done. So, get busy today. Make a donation. Call a friend and encourage them. Pray about a ministry need. Visit the hospital. Figure it out. Take what God has placed in your life today and use it for God's glory.

Prayer
Father, thank you for equipping us so well to do your work. May we offer all that we have as tools with which your kingdom can be built. Amen.

Day 219 — Judges 8: Forgetting to Be Faithful

> "Then it came about, as soon as Gideon was dead, that the sons of Israel again played the harlot with the Baals, and made Baal-berith their god. Thus the sons of Israel did not remember the LORD their God, who had delivered them from the hands of all their enemies on every side."
> Judges 8:33-34 (NASB)

Observation

Most of chapter 8 contains the story of how Gideon led his army of 300 to defeat the Midianites. God blessed Gideon with wisdom and strength and soon the oppression of the Midianites was erased. But as is the pattern of the book of Judges, notice how the people soon fell away from their respect and fear of God and began to chase after false gods. Even though God had been careful to deliver them, they quickly abandoned God, forgetting the blessings God had brought their way.

Application

My wife makes delicious pumpkin bread each fall, especially around the holidays. It's a favorite in our household. Just the scent of it baking fills the house with a holiday atmosphere. Over the years, she has made hundreds of loaves. But even now, each time she bakes, she takes out the well-worn recipe card and carefully follows each step. Why? Consistency. She wants every loaf to be exactly like the one before it. Consistency is a good thing.

I hate to admit it, but we are a little like the ancient Israelites. It seems our memory of God's blessings is so faint, that we quickly abandon our love for God to chase after other pursuits. It is amazing to me how quickly we seem to forget the abundant blessings that God has brought our way. Rather than remember all that we have, we tend to focus on what we don't have. Our desire for other things seems never to be satiated. Though we may show God a little respect and gratitude on Sunday, by Monday, our thoughts of God seem to dim as we run after the gods of success, power, and pleasure. We fall into the same trap as ancient Israel. We cry out to God for help and when provided we quickly praise God. But give us a few days and our discipleship begins to falter. We soon find ourselves making many poor choices and decisions because of our lack of fidelity to the ways of God. Suddenly our lives are in shambles again and so we cry out to God to "pull us once again out of our mess!" Such inconsistency... Surely God is worthy of greater respect. Surely our faith is capable of greater consistency. Surely the thought of God's blessings in the past can teach us to obey and follow God in the present. May we commit ourselves this day to faithful and consistent obedience to the God who continually delivers us.

Prayer

Father, this morning we confess our inconsistency. Give us pure hearts, dedicated lives, and loyal discipleship. Amen.

Day 220 — Judges 9: Taking Matters into Our Own Hands

> "When the men of Israel saw that Abimelech was dead, each departed to his home. Thus God repaid the wickedness of Abimelech, which he had done to his father in killing his seventy brothers." Judges 9:55-56 (NASB)

Observation

Abimelech was the wicked son of Gideon who wanted to seize control of Israel after the death of his father. In order to gain support among the people, he used deceitful lies and even talked wicked men in helping him to kill his seventy brothers whom he viewed as a threat to his leadership. After three years of turmoil and warfare, his reign of terror came to an end when, as he attempted to besiege the city of Thebez, a woman dropped a millstone on his head! Unable to recover, Abimelech instructed a servant to end his life. As our focus verse indicates, God repaid the wickedness of his actions.

Application

There are moments when we attempt to force the will of God for our lives. We, in our own minds, determine the who, what, when, and where of our days. Thinking we know what is best, and driven by a desire to impose self-will above God's will, we begin to take matters into our own hands. We overrule Godly instruction, and common sense, and we begin living our lives purely according to our own agendas. The result? We fail. The crash will always come. We discover the foolishness of our behavior and we plead with God to make things right. We want God to clean-up the messes that we have made. Look at the example of Abimelech. Not content to wait and see the will of God for the nation, he set out on a murderous reign of killing his brothers, a deed repaid by God himself.

There is a better way. It's the path of seeking the will of God before we make the key decisions rather than asking God to clean up the mistakes we lay at God's feet after we have chosen the path of disobedience. It's like the old adage we learned as children when we arrived at a railroad crossing, "Stop, look, and listen." God's word reminds us of God's promise of wisdom if we will seek God. Let's slow down and pray through our thoughts, long before they ever become actions. Before you charge forward to address the concerns of the day that stretches out before you, take a few moments for reflective thought. Will my actions glorify God? Will they align with God's will and purpose? Will they heal, help, and encourage others? In order to build the kingdom through our actions, we have to put the king in the place of prominence. And in order to give God both rule and reign, we have to step away from the throne.

Prayer

Father, give us both enough grace and common sense to learn how to seek your counsel long before we make our plans. Amen.

Day 221   Judges 10: Cause and Result

> "Go and cry out to the gods which you have chosen; let them deliver you in the time of your distress." Judges 10:14 (NASB)

Observation
In case you didn't take the time to read the tenth chapter of Judges this morning, you would want to know that these words that serve as our focus verse are spoken by God to the Israelites. After years of serving the Baals and other false deities, and after years of oppression, Israel once again turned to God in the hope that God would once again ease their pain. It's the same pattern... Israel keeps making poor choices, and they keep calling on God to get them out of trouble. You can tell that God's patience is being stretched to the limit. How long is God willing to bail them out of yet another huge mess?

Application
You know the old expression... "You made your own bed, now you have to lie in it." One of life's toughest lessons is learning that there are consequences to our actions. Not all our mistakes can be easily erased. Not all our poor choices can be resolved in a moment of time. Some mistakes take years to correct. Some wounds take a lifetime to heal. How foolish we are to think that we can live the "high life" and never pay the bill that such living brings our way? The good news is that God is patient... really patient. God forgives and forgives and forgives. But do not make the mistake of thinking that your sins don't matter. Don't conflate God's patience with acceptance of your poor behavior. Sins separate us from Holy God. Apart from the grace offered to us in Jesus Christ, we have no hope. Let us never get soft on sin. Let us never think for a moment that God casually dismisses our sins with ease. God covers them with the blood of Jesus. So how can we respond so flippantly at times to our mistakes?

Let's admit that there is a fine line to walk. On the one hand, it is wrong for us to wallow for years with the regret and shame of our sinfulness. God did not create us to live in bondage. As we seek and gain God's forgiveness, we must learn to forgive and free ourselves from those mistakes. But on the other hand, it is wrong for us to quickly discount our sins reasoning that the grace of God will quickly forgive and so they are no big deal. They are a big deal. We need to remember our sins long enough so that we resolve never to repeat them. The pain of disappointing God should linger long enough that we let our brokenness push us into great God pleasing action. Everyone will make mistakes. It's our nature. The key is to learn from our poor choices so that we don't abuse God's grace with continual poor choices.

Prayer
Father, forgive us when we chase after foolish things. May our hearts become pure and our resolve become strong. Amen.

Day 222 — Judges 11: Promises Made… Promises Broken

> "Jephthah made a vow to the LORD and said, 'If You will indeed give the sons of Ammon into my hand, then it shall be that whatever comes out of the doors of my house to meet me when I return in peace from the sons of Ammon, it shall be the LORD's, and I will offer it up as a burnt offering.'"
> Judges 11:30-31 (NASB)

Observation
This passage of scripture is sometimes referred to as "Jephthah's tragic vow." Here's the story in a nutshell… Jephthah was led by God to go and battle against the sons of Ammon. Though God asked for no promise or vow, Jephthah promised that if he returned in victory, he would make a sacrifice to God as tribute for God's help. Never thinking for a moment that his only child, a daughter, would come bounding out of the house, he foolishly promised a burnt offering. When the day of victory came, she comes running out to greet her victorious father. He must be faithful to his vow and two months later she is slain.

Application
We make a lot of foolish promises that we never intend to keep… especially the ones we make to God. "God if you will just help me this one last time… If you will forgive me again… If you will get me out of this situation… If you will help me pass this test… If you will help me close this deal… Then I will come to church every Sunday, tithe every week, read my Bible every day, help the poor, volunteer at the mission…" Sound familiar? It should. Most of us have made those kinds of empty promises to God. We offer God those "if-then" types of promises. We try to bargain with God to gain God's favor. And so, we make promises that we may intend to keep, but do not.

Here's the deal… We are already the objects of God's good grace. God already longs to bless us and help us in our times of need. What God desires from us is not another empty promise, but a deepening relationship. How foolish to make a deal with God. What if God really made us keep our promise? What if we had to be honorable and truthful? If so, most of us would think a lot more carefully about the vows we make. Let's remember that God already loves us… always will. Let's forget about the foolish vows. Let's concentrate on building a relationship with God that will change our hearts and give direction to our days. Don't get me wrong, I'm not suggesting that you refuse to make a vow to the Lord about something important. I'm just suggesting that when you do, make sure that you are willing to keep your promise. Maybe it's a simple as learning to love God more and making fewer of those foolish and empty bargains.

Prayer
Father, we thank you that we are already loved by you. Teach us that you desire obedience more than a thousand empty promises. Amen.

Day 223 — Judges 12:5-6: Christians with World Views...

> "The Gileadites captured the fords of the Jordan opposite Ephraim. And it happened when any of the fugitives of Ephraim said, 'Let me cross over,' the men of Gilead would say to him, 'Are you an Ephraimite?' If he said, 'No,' then they would say to him, 'Say now, "Shibboleth."' But he said, "Sibboleth," for he could not pronounce it correctly. Then they seized him and slew him at the fords of the Jordan. Thus there fell at that time 42,000 of Ephraim." Judges 12:5-6 (NASB)

Observation
Relationships between the various tribes of Israel were not always positive during the time of the Judges. In fact, two tribes, the Gileadites and the Ephraimites engaged in outright civil war with each other. In our focus verses this morning, a simple variance in the dialect between the two tribes became a distinguishing mark. When the men of Gilead asked any stranger coming from Ephraim to pronounce a certain word and they pronounced it incorrectly, the stranger would be killed because the Gileadites would know they were from the rival tribe. So intense was the civil war that 42,000 men of Ephraim died, and the influence of that tribe was all but erased from history.

Application
It is always tragic when conflict and disagreement arise between any people, but especially tragic when families begin to divide. All these soldiers who fought against each other were distant cousins. Each could trace his lineage back to the 12 sons of Jacob; they all had the same ancestral father. How tragic that they learned to hate each other when in most cases they didn't even know each other. Isn't that the case with much of our hatred? So often we are conditioned by prejudice and experience to hate others based on things like race, nationality, gender, religion, and even language. (I actually witnessed a Pakistani family get verbally assaulted this week by a white family at an amusement park of all places!) My fear is that racial hatred and bigotry is once again on the rise here in the U.S. With the rising number of ethnic groups and the shrinking of the majority race, many feel threatened and even angered. Surely the people of faith can do better. Surely we can rise above hatred and begin to see others through the eyes of Christ. I challenge you to become intentional about building a relationship with a family that is not like yours. I encourage you to reach beyond skin tone, or language, religion, or place of origin and discover new relationships that will help you to grow as a Christian with a world view. After all, don't we all share the same Father?

Prayer
Father, teach us that hatred is always wrong. May we learn to rise above our fear and our anxious worry in order to model the love of Christ each day. Amen.

Day 224 — Judges 13: Is Your Difference Showing?

> "But he said to me, 'Behold, you shall conceive and give birth to a son, and now you shall not drink wine or strong drink nor eat any unclean thing, for the boy shall be a Nazirite to God from the womb to the day of his death.'"
>
> Judges 13:7 (NASB)

Observation

Chapter 13 of the Book of Judges begins the story of Samson. A man from the tribe of Dan whose name is Manoah, has a wife who is barren. She is visited by the angel of God and told that she will have a son and that he is to be a Nazirite. Our focus verse describes the conversation as the wife relates to her husband all that the angel has said to her.

A word about being a Nazirite. A Nazirite vow is a special vow which sets apart a person before God for a special task. A Nazirite vow could be sworn out for a very limited time, or as is the case for Samson, for a lifetime. There were three conditions that made up the vow... 1. No wine or strong drink. 2. No cutting of the hair. 3. No contact with dead bodies. The idea was to show to observers that a person under such a vow had been dedicated to God for a specific task or duty. Someone under a Nazirite vow would have certainly stood out among his peers. Not to drink wine in a culture that drank wine almost exclusively would have been noticed. The length of hair which had never been cut would also be immediately noticeable. And, according to Levitical law, contact with the dead would render a person ceremonially unclean. To remain pure before God, no contact with the dead was allowed. So... from birth on, a clear message was being sent that God would use Samson in a special way to free the Israelites from the oppression of the Philistines.

Application

Most of us don't live under the constraints of a Nazirite vow, but certainly our lives should bear some testimony to the fact that we serve the Living God. As believers in Christ, our lives should possess some distinctive attributes. Something about who we are, how we live, and how we respond to others, should be evident before the culture in which we live. In other words, our distinctiveness should show. People should look to our lives, our lifestyles, our words, and our involvements, and know that something about us is different. The world should know that we have been claimed by Christ. My question this morning is simply this... "Are we living lives that in some way distinguish us from the lives of non-believers?" Is there more hope? More grace? More love? More compassion? More sensitivity to human need? There really should be. We are called to be different in order to make a difference. Let's let our distinctive character and calling show.

Prayer

Father, thank you for claiming us through the blood of Jesus Christ. May we live as a distinctive people whose deliberate living of faith will draw others to you. Amen.

Day 225

Judges 14: Cracked Pots

> "However, his father and mother did not know that it was of the LORD, for He was seeking an occasion against the Philistines. Now at that time the Philistines were ruling over Israel." Judges 14:4 (NASB)

Observation
As Samson grew into manhood, he saw a Philistine woman whom he longed to take for his wife. His parents were very much against such a wedding because the Philistines were oppressing Israel at the time. They both agreed that he should marry one of the Israelites. But Samson insisted and soon the arrangements for both the wedding feast and the marriage were arranged. What Samson's parents failed to realize was that God was directing the unfolding action. The potential marriage would provide an opportunity for God to begin the process of freeing Israel. In the providence of God's timing, what often seems to be a mistake can be transformed into a moment for God to be glorified.

Application
Isn't it nice to know that God is greater than our mistakes? Sometimes, when we have made the worst of decisions, delighted in poor choices, and betrayed our best intentions, that even then God can do great and mighty things. Sometimes, some of our worst moments become the opportunities for God's power to be displayed. Paul reminds us of this truth as he writes to the church in Rome, "And we know that God causes all things to work together for good to those who love God, to those who are called according to His purpose" (Romans 8:28 NASB). God moves in spite our mistakes. God uses us in spite of our short comings. God does incredible things in spite of our failures. The key is to entrust the days of our lives to God, who has a way of taking the broken pieces of our lives and transforming them into a beautiful mosaic. We read in Proverbs, "Trust in the Lord with all your heart, and do not lean on your own understanding. In all your ways acknowledge Him, and He will make your paths straight." (Proverbs 3:5-6 NASB). Let us never rejoice in our mistakes but let us acknowledge that our mistakes do not have to define who we are. Even a broken vessel can carry the hope of the Gospel. God can take the worst moments of our lives and transform them into the first sentence of our testimonies. It's good to know that we serve a God who continues to transform our mistakes into opportunities to build God's kingdom and glorify God's name.

Prayer
Father, we thank you that even our worst days can be moments when your grace is displayed and your purposes are accomplished. Amen.

Day 226   Judges 15: Choosing Grace

> "Samson said to them, 'Since you act like this, I will surely take revenge on you, but after that I will quit.'" Judges 15:7 (NASB)

Observation
This chapter tells the story of escalating revenge. It begins with Samson's anger at the fact that his father-in-law had given away his bride to his companion. To strike back, Samson captures 300 foxes, ties their tails together, lights them on fire, and sends them through the wheat fields. The entire Philistine wheat crop is destroyed. In response, the Philistines grab his wife and her father and burn them to death! In response to that action, Samson then kills 3000 Philistines while in a state of rage.

Application
If you are any kind of a baseball fan at all, you will know the unwritten rule of revenge. It goes like this... a pitcher intentionally throws a pitch at batter. In the next half inning, the opposing pitcher is expected by his team, to throw at one of the other team's batters. And when that happens, typically both benches empty and a huge brawl ensues on the field. You have seen that happen in baseball, right? You have probably seen it happen in your own dealings with others as well.

Do you see the pattern that develops within this story? One violent act leads to retaliation, which leads to further violence, which leads to more retaliation. It's the cycle of escalating revenge and unfortunately many of us are often caught in it. Someone wrongs us and we become angry. Driven by our anger, we strike back. Our enemy then retaliates and harms us further, so we in turn, strike back with even greater harm. It's easy to understand, right? One bad action leads to another. In fact, the problem of escalating revenge is so much a part of human nature that Levitical law required a "tooth for a tooth." The idea behind the law was to limit revenge. The law required that a person could only do to an enemy what that enemy had first done to them. The Law attempted to limit the escalating revenge. Jesus, of course, offered a radical new way of dealing with conflict. His solution? "If someone strikes you on your right cheek, offer the other cheek also" (Matthew 5:39 NLT). The Jesus ethic demands that we move toward peace and away from revenge. It demands an immediate cessation from revenge. Turning the other cheek can be a very difficult stance to take. It defies human nature and logic. It also ends conflict. Let me challenge you this morning to examine how you are dealing with those who have offended you. Are you plotting revenge or are you seeking to forgive? Which is the way of our Lord?

Prayer
Father, teach us that revenge is not ours to offer. Remind us that as Christians, our path is always that of forgiveness and grace which leads to peace. Amen.

Day 227 — Judges 16: "Where Is Your Heart?"

> "Then she said to him, 'How can you say, "I love you," when your heart is not with me? You have deceived me these three times and have not told me where your great strength is.'" Judges 16:15 (NASB)

Observation
This verse is lifted from the great saga of Samson and Delilah. Samson has fallen in love with Delilah, but she has been paid to find the source of his great strength. As the story unfolds, she attempts several times to discover the source of his strength, but he deceives her. He continues to make up one tale after another. After three deceptions, she finally plays the "love card." She basically says, "If you really loved me, you would tell me." It was not so much about love, but manipulation. He yields to the pressure and actually tells her the source of his strength. His hair is cut and he is captured by the Philistines.

Application
I was talking recently to an "alleged" college football fan who supports an orange-wearing team here in Tennessee. I asked her who the next opponent was on the schedule. She didn't know. I asked her about the season record. She didn't know. I asked her that name of the head coach. She didn't know. I began to get the impression that she claimed an allegiance but in reality, she wasn't much of a fan. Maybe a lot of us "alleged" believers in Christ are the same way. We claim we really love the Lord, but when it comes down to the proof in our lives, there is not much to show.

This morning, I want to use Delilah's words in a slightly different way. Rather than hear these words spoken by Delilah to get to the heart of Samson, let us hear these words as though Christ were speaking them to us. "How can you say, 'I love you,' when your heart is not with me?" It is one thing to claim a love for Christ... It is quite another to express that love daily. How can we indeed claim a love for Jesus when are hearts are far from serving him?

Love is always demonstrated through action. The devotion of our hearts is not measured with mere words, but with tangible expression. How does Christ know that you really love him? How is the profession of your faith made evident in practical deed? A few thoughts... We love when we serve. We love when we give. We love when we sacrifice. We love when we practice obedience. We love when our hearts are given fully to him and to the work of his kingdom. Let me encourage you to move beyond a "lip-service" expression of faith this week. Go and do something! Let your actions speak louder than words.

Prayer
Father, we are grateful that we can praise you with our lips. Teach us to also praise you with the work of our hands and the obedience of our hearts. Amen.

Day 228 — Judges 17: Who Is King?

> "In those days there was no king in Israel; every man did what was right in his own eyes." Judges 17:6 (NASB)

Observation
This single verse really begins to define the theme of the rest of the book of Judges. By this point in her history, Israel began clamoring for a king. All the nations around them had kings and because of such leadership, most of those nations knew some sense of prosperity. Not the Israelites. Their lack of prosperity was not tied to the lack of a king, but instead to a lack of fidelity to God. God had always promised to lead the nation. There was no need for a king because God was to be the authority throughout the land. However, the rising sense of wanting a king represented a rising sentiment that God alone was not enough to lead the nation. To desire a king was to reject God. Because of the moral decay within Israel, everyone lived according to their own standard of judgment.

Application
Sometimes I rely solely on my own thoughts and opinions. And when I do, I usually get it wrong. I have discovered that it always helps to involve others in key decisions. Collective wisdom outranks personal opinion almost every time. Be even beyond the wisdom that is gained through shared decision-making processes, the greater wisdom needed comes from a careful petitioning of God. Whenever I ask people to join me in both thought and prayer, it seems that better choices are made.

One of the great sins of our nation is our sense of self-sufficiency and personal hubris. Because of our fierce independence, most of us tend to reject any real sense of authority. We like calling the shots. We enjoy being the rulers of our domain, the masters of our souls. We raise the standard of personal intelligence as though we have a clue about the best choice to make in any situation. The problem is that we lose sight of God along the way. We forget that our allegiance is not to ourselves, but to our God. Have we not become like ancient Israel in that each of us does "what is right in our own eyes?" Using mere human intellect and judgment is a slippery slope of moral decay. The ultimate authority of our lives can never be public opinion nor cultural ethic. We must always remain a people of the book... people whose judgment and morality are not based on a sliding scale of cultural whim nor situational ethics. The word of God must remain the standard that we raise... the moral compass that gives direction to our days. It is never about what we "think is right;" it is always about what God's word demands from us.

Prayer
Father, may we never become so proud, so arrogant, or so self-sufficient that we forget for a moment that you alone are the guardian of our days and the judge of our thoughts. Amen.

Day 229 — Judges 18: Who Influences Your Life?

> "Then the five men who went to spy out the country of Laish said to their kinsmen, 'Do you know that there are in these houses an ephod and household idols and a graven image and a molten image? Now therefore, consider what you should do.'" Judges 18:14 (NASB)

Observation
The story that is told in Judges 18 speaks of the moral decline of the nation. Not only was civil war between the various tribes becoming more common, but the rise of idol worship also was prevalent as well. In this particular story, the tribe of Dan was searching for new land to settle. As a part of their conquest, they took from a man named Micah (not the prophet who bears that name) an idol that was in his home along with a priest who was leading the worship of that idol. As the people of God, they should have detested the idol and destroyed it. Instead, they embraced the false god and took it along with them in order to worship it as well.

Application
We are influenced by everyone that we encounter… positively or negatively. With each conversation and each interaction, something of that person "rubs off" on each of us. If the new acquaintance is a person of faith, with moral integrity and Godly wisdom, then the encounter will challenge us to be stronger in our faith and to walk more closely in cadence with God. However, if the new acquaintance has a disregard for spiritual things and lives by selfish motivation and priority, then we can be pulled in a very negative direction. In other words, people either lift us up, or they drag us down. The point is to be discerning. Though we certainly want to influence the world around us with a positive message of salvation in Christ, we must be careful that "the world" does not influence us in a way that our witness deteriorates and our faith-values are compromised. So, guard the circle of your closest friends. Ask the honest questions of influence. Are these friends pushing me to be my best? Are they challenging me to be strong in my faith? Are they helping me to walk more closely with God? Be careful of those whose hearts are not pure and whose ways are not righteous. Be a world changer, not one who is easily changed by the world. Paul echoes the same thought in his word to the Christians in Rome, "And do not be conformed to this world, but be transformed by the renewal of your mind, that you may prove what the will of God is, that which is good and acceptable and perfect" (Romans 12:2 NASB). Be careful out there. Be strong. Be the person of influence.

Prayer
Father, teach us to guard very carefully, the key influencing people in our lives. May we strive to seek relationships with those who will help us to draw closer to you and not those who distract our Christian walk. Amen.

Day 230 — Judges 19: Purging the Evil

> "All who saw it said, 'Nothing like this has ever happened or been seen from the day when the sons of Israel came up from the land of Egypt to this day. Consider it, take counsel and speak up!'" Judges 19:30 (NASB)

Observation

Today's lesson is a little shocking and gruesome to say the least. It begins with a Levite taking a concubine from the city of Bethlehem. (A concubine is a female servant usually brought into a home for the purpose of bearing children. She was considered a member of the family and was afforded a status above other servants and slaves.) This particular woman ran away from her owner, back to her home. The Levite goes to retrieve her with the intention of "speaking kindly" to her. He is welcomed into the home of her father for five days before she and the Levite begin the journey home. It is along the way that unspeakable evil occurs. While staying overnight in Jerusalem, the woman is taken away by the locals, raped all night, and left for dead on the doorstep. The Levite finds her dead body the next morning. He takes her body home, cuts it into 12 pieces, and sends a body part to each of the 12 tribes of Israel. It was shocking to all who saw it. The Israelites realize the extent of wickedness that has befallen their nation.

Application

There are a couple of lessons to draw from the story. First, there is a lesson for our nation. We have long enjoyed speaking of our nation as a "Christian" nation. We pride ourselves on living in the land of the free and the home of the brave. The truth is that America can only be a Christian nation when the Christians living within her borders actually live fully for Christ. When Christians refuse to live out the ethics of Jesus, when Christians refuse to demand justice, equality, fairness, and respect among all the inhabitants of our land, how can we dare to call ourselves a Christian nation? It is not about the beliefs of the founding fathers... It is about the sustaining beliefs of those now living in the land. Surely part of the lesson this day is a call for Christian citizens to live nobly, act bravely, and serve sacrificially.

The second lesson is one directed to each of us as believers. When we see evil within our own lives, are we quick to rid ourselves of its cause and influence, or do we simply attempt to manage some sense of compromise? In other words, how serious are we about being God-followers? Do we consciously and consistently pray to remove the sin in our lives? Do we separate ourselves from the things that draw us away from God? Maybe like the ancient Israelites we need a little wake-up call before it is too late. If we allow evil to quietly invade our souls, who will turn our hearts to righteousness once again? Be vigilant, courageous, and strong.

Prayer

Father teach us that any compromise with evil has the potential of destroying us. Amen.

Day 231 — Judges 20: Crime and Punishment

> "And we will take 10 men out of 100 throughout the tribes of Israel, and 100 out of 1,000, and 1,000 out of 10,000 to supply food for the people, that when they come to Gibeah of Benjamin, they may punish them for all the disgraceful acts that they have committed in Israel."
> Judges 20:10 (NASB)

Observation
This chapter continues the story of punishment against the men of Gibeah (city near Jerusalem which was a part of the land belonging to the tribe of Benjamin). For the first time in many years, the tribes of Israel united to punish that which had been done in Gibeah. The intent was to purge the evil from the city. The tribe of Benjamin refused to do battle against the men of Gibeah and so what followed was a very bloody civil war which would result in the obliteration of the tribe of Benjamin.

Application
"Just wait till your father gets home!" Ever hear those words as a child? I did… and more than once. And… it was never a happy moment when I heard them. Typically, my brother and I would get into some bad behavior that overwhelmed my mother's ability to deal with two unruly boys. And so, she would remind us that punishment would arrive when my father walked in the door. (Of course, it was always my brother's fault that we got into trouble. I was a perfect child.) Even at a young age I learned the lesson of crime and punishment.

The theme of crime and punishment threads its way throughout the pages of scripture. In this story, those who acted shamefully toward the Levite and his concubine (see yesterday's devotion) are punished for their evil deeds. The message is consistent throughout the Bible… Disobedience always carries a price. Those who commit acts of evil are always punished. God does not delight in evil, nor does God ignore the sin of those practice such deeds. There is always punishment for sin. Paul reminds us in his writings in the New Testament book of Romans, "For all have sinned and fall short of the glory of God" (3:23 NASB). "For the wages of sin is death" (6:23 NASB). Again, hear the clear message… There is always punishment for sin. God cannot ignore the disobedience in our lives. So, where is the hope for we are all sinners. The hope is where it has been for the past 2000 years… in the blood of Jesus Christ. The love of Christ compelled him to die in our place. His death paid the price of our disobedience. We stand forgiven in the presence of God, not because of anything we have done, but as a result of what Christ was willing to offer. This morning we have both the promise of forgiveness and the hope of new life. Let us rejoice that our disobedience is met with grace.

Prayer
Father, we thank you that our sins are forgiven and our punishment is retracted because of the sacrifice of Jesus. May we know the blessings of grace this day. Amen.

Day 232 — Judges 21: Fixing the Tear...

> "And they commanded the sons of Benjamin, saying, 'Go and lie in wait in the vineyards, and watch; and behold, if the daughters of Shiloh come out to take part in the dances, then you shall come out of the vineyards and each of you shall catch his wife from the daughters of Shiloh, and go to the land of Benjamin.'" Judges 21:20-21 (NASB)

Observation

Talk about speed dating... In this final chapter of the book of Judges, the tribes of Israel became saddened that the tribe of Benjamin would be eliminated from the land. And so, provision was made for the survival of the tribe. The Israelites had pledged that none of their daughters would marry anyone from the tribe of Benjamin. So, to furnish women for the surviving men of Benjamin, a plan was made to help the men literally 'grab' some women at Shiloh during a yearly festival. (These were non-Hebrews.) Any woman that went out from the celebration and danced among the vineyards could be taken by the men of Benjamin as they laid in wait among the vineyards.

Application

Though this is certainly a rather bizarre ending to the story of the Judges, I do find in the narrative a small lesson in grace. If you read the chapter carefully, you will discover that the sons of Israel felt a sense of remorse concerning the tribe of Benjamin and sought to discover ways to begin the process of restoration. There was a sense of brokenness that was met with a plan for healing.

I wonder about the broken relationships in our lives. Along the journey, we sometimes abandon relationships that were once important to us. Because of injury or insult or even poorly chosen words, we sometimes let broken relationships go unresolved. We cast aside friendships that were once vital and relationships that were once meaningful. Is it not a sad commentary on each of us when we become comfortable with the death of such relationships? I know that not every broken relationship can be mended, not every scar can be healed... but I do think the Spirit of Christ in us should move us toward reconciliation whenever possible. We should seek ways to restore that which is broken and heal that which is torn apart. The process begins with simply praying for those with whom we long to be reconciled. Your daily prayer for reconciliation will begin to change your heart and perspective towards that person with whom you need to reconcile. Forgiveness is a choice that has to be made daily. For whom do you need to pray this morning? What broken friendship needs a new start? Why not begin this day with a prayer for healing in the midst of one of your broken relationships?

Prayer

Father, may we be quick to forgive, steadfast in offering grace, and proactive in healing that which has been broken. Amen.

Day 233 — Ruth 1: Misplaced Blame

> "'Don't call me Naomi,' she responded. 'Instead, call me Mara, for the Almighty has made life very bitter for me.'" Ruth 1:20 (NLT)

Observation
The story of Ruth is set during the time when the Judges ruled over Israel. A severe famine occurs in the land, forcing a young family to leave Bethlehem and sojourn in the land of Moab. The writer gives a very brief account of what takes place in Moab. Elimelech, the father, passes away. The sons grow up and marry, but they too pass away. The remaining family consists of the grieving widow, Naomi, and her two daughters-in-law, Orpah and Ruth. When the famine ends and life returns to normal in Bethlehem, the decision is made to return. Naomi encourages her daughters-in-law to return to their families. Orpah decides to return to her family, but Ruth pledges to stay with Naomi. When they arrive in Bethlehem, the town is excited. But Naomi instructs the residents to call her by the name Mara, which means "bitter." She declares that God has made her life bitter.

Application
She's not the first, nor will she be the last, to blame God for the sorrow she experienced. She views the upheaval in her life as the direct result of God's will. "God has made this happen." She believes that she has become the object of God's displeasure. Her mind tells her that the bad things which have come her way, have happened because God wanted them to happen. Sound familiar? Over the years, I have counseled with a lot of people who fatalistically blame God for the difficulties of life.

Often, we find ourselves in difficult spots because of the poor choices we have made. We choose the wrong path and we suffer as a result. This story gets at something a little different from that scenario. This is a case of bad things happening in the life of a good person. That's a little harder to explain. It's true, sometimes it seems that there is no one left to blame other than God when difficulties unfold. Who can explain a flood, or a tornado's random destruction, or the senseless path of a wildfire? Who can answer the mystery of a young life taken too soon, or a cancer's rage in the life of a faithful person? I'd like to tell you that there are always rational explanations, but the truth is sometimes nothing will ever make sense. Who to blame then? Maybe it's not a question of whom to blame, but in whom we place our trust. Life on this earth is not perfect. It is flawed and fragile and all of us live with the uncomfortable inconsistencies of life. But we also live with the perfect love of the Father who holds us close in the midst of tragedy and who will one day welcome us to a perfect and lasting kingdom. We will suffer because we are human. We will live because we are God's.

Prayer
Father grant us grace and courage for the living of each hour. Amen.

Day 234 — Ruth 2: The Joy of Hospitality

> "While she was there, Boaz arrived from Bethlehem and greeted the harvesters. 'The LORD be with you!' he said. 'The LORD bless you!' the harvesters replied." Ruth 2:4 (NLT)

Observation
This chapter continues the story of Ruth and the beginning of her relationship with Boaz. Boaz is described as a wealthy and influential man. By happenstance, or more correctly, by the providence of God, Ruth finds herself gleaning leftover grain in the fields of Boaz. Boaz sees her and inquires about her. He meets her and grants her permission to gather grain along with his workers. He also offers her water from the well and when mealtime rolls around, she is invited to eat the food provided to the workers. By the end of the day she gathers an entire basketful of grain, more than enough to provide for the needs of both Ruth and Naomi. As you read the narrative, you begin to glimpse the spark of a relationship between Ruth and Boaz.

Application
As I read this passage, I was struck by the interaction between Boaz and his harvesters as he arrives on the scene. He greets them warmly and they respond with the same sense of welcome that only a carefully-forged relationship can offer. It is obvious that Boaz has treated them fairly and provided for them carefully. There is a mutual respect and sense of hospitality between the influential man and the workers of the field.

This passage has something to say about the way we treat all the people with whom we interact each day. It is human nature to treat some with great respect while disregarding those who are "beneath our station." Notice in most professional work settings, the people of position and power are treated with great respect and dignity while the more common employees tend to be ignored. But whenever we make judgment calls about someone's worth or value based on the coins in their pocket or the degrees on their wall, have we not lost sight of the value of every person? New Testament writer James speaks about the sin of partiality whenever we make such distinctions (James 2:1-9). Boaz, a rich landowner with a number of workers in his field, treats the common laborer with the dignity and kindness deserved and they offer him the same consideration.

Go back and carefully examine the ministry of Jesus. He made no distinctions between the rich and the poor, the strong and the weak. He ate with sinners and saints, touched the broken bodies of the powerful and the powerless, offered grace to rich tax collectors and poor prostitutes. So, when is it ever right for us to exclude anyone from the reach of our hospitality? Notice the people around you today. Speak words of kindness to all. Treat them with fairness.

Prayer
Father may we be gracious representatives of you this day. Amen.

Day 235 — Ruth 3: A Sadie Hawkins Dance

> "'I am your servant Ruth,' she replied. 'Spread the corner of your covering over me, for you are my family redeemer.'" Ruth 3:9 (NLT)

Observation
As this chapter opens, Naomi is concerned for her daughter-in-law Ruth, thinking that it is time to help Ruth move on with her life by finding a husband and establishing a home. Boaz, because of his acts of kindness and relative status, is the obvious choice to be sought out. Naomi instructs Ruth to bathe, put on her best dress, and spray on a little perfume. Ruth is directed to go to the threshing where Boaz has been at work. He falls asleep on the pile of grain he has collected in order to protect it until the next morning when it can be carried away. She uncovers his feet and lays down. At midnight, he discovers that a woman is sleeping at his feet. She identifies herself and asks for him to play the role of the family redeemer. He pledges to marry her if the closest relative will not do so. The next morning, he goes to town to get the process started.

Application
I have to admit that when I was in college, I was always a little scared when one of the sororities on campus sponsored a Sadie Hawkins dance when the girls got to ask the guys to the dance. I always preferred it to be the other way around. I liked being able to choose my date, not having my date choose me. To be sure, it was always fun if you had a girlfriend at the time and you knew that you were going to be asked by her. It was scary, however, when you weren't "spoken for" and so any girl could offer an invitation. That was long before the days of caller ID and it sometimes made me nervous to answer the phone. Oh, the golden days of college…

Notice in the narrative that Ruth is the one who initiates the marriage proposal. She says to Boaz, "Spread the corner of your covering over me…" That was a fancy way of saying, "Bring me into your family and into your household." He, of course, is more than willing to do so and makes provision to marry her.

It's nice to be chosen, especially by the right person. In John 15:16 Jesus says, "You did not choose Me but I chose you…" (NASB). What an amazing thought. Before we ever even realized our need of a Savior, Christ chose us. He died for us while we were yet sinners. When we were the unworthy, scarred-by-sin, rejects in the corner, Christ invited us out onto the dance floor and offered us this exciting dance we call life. I don't know how your high school and college days were spent… if you got a lot of invitations or spent a lot of time in your room because you were unwanted. But I do know how the rest of your life can be spent. Christ chooses you. He invites you to spend a glorious and exciting life with him. Just respond to the invitation.

Prayer
Father God, we thank you for the inclusion that we experience in Christ. Amen.

Day 236   Ruth 4: If the Shoe Fits

> "Now in those days it was the custom in Israel for anyone transferring a right of purchase to remove his sandal and hand it to the other party. This publicly validated the transaction." Ruth 4:7 (NLT)

Observation

This fourth and final chapter of Ruth tells the story of the public and official transaction undertaken by Boaz to claim Ruth as his wife. As the scene opens, Boaz travels to the city gate, which is a structure at the entrance to the city where business was conducted. He gathers 10 elders to witness the conversation and transaction. He speaks to the closest relative of Elimelech, Naomi's former husband, and asks if he wants to redeem the land and marry Ruth. He is unable to do so. He transfers the rights of purchasing property to Boaz with the symbolic handing off of his sandal. Boaz then purchases the land from Naomi, who still claimed rights to it, and marries Ruth. They have a son whose name is Obed. Obed will become the grandfather of King David. The Book of Ruth ends with a brief genealogy.

Application

A little explanation about this whole transferring the sandal thing. Sandals were the ordinary footwear in the ancient Near East, but they were also a symbolic item of clothing, especially in the relationship between the widow and her legal guardian. This is perhaps because land was purchased based on whatever size triangle of land the buyer could walk off in an hour, a day, a week or a month (1 Kings 21:16–17). Since they walked off the land in sandals, the sandals became the moveable title to that land. When the relative of Naomi removed his sandals, he in effect, was presenting the title to the land to Boaz. (I just refinanced my house a few weeks ago. My wife and I had to sign a lot of papers, including papers to transfer the title from one mortgage company to the next. At no point in the process were we asked to swap our sandals. Would have been weird, right?)

Instead, let's talk for a moment about the transfer of ownership that occurs when we place our faith in Christ. We don't offer him a shoe, but instead we offer him our hearts. We surrender ownership of all that we are to his lordship. We give him our loyalty, our time, our talents, our energies. We declare that he has the right to demand anything of us because we have given ourselves to him. As you walk through the journey of this day, consider every conversation, every decision, and every action. Ask yourself, "Have I transferred this area of my life to the lordship of Christ?" Giving away a sandal would be easy. The giving of your heart takes effort.

Prayer

Father God, may we offer to you this day, all that we all. Amen.